Master Builders of Steam

Master Builders of Steam

H.A.V. Bulleid

LONDON

IAN ALLAN LTD

First published 1963
Second impression 1965
Third impression (paperback) 1970
New edition 1983

ISBN 0 7110 0177 4

Published by Ian Allan Ltd, Shepperton, Surrey; and printed by Ian Allan Printing Ltd at their works at Coombelands in Runnymede, England

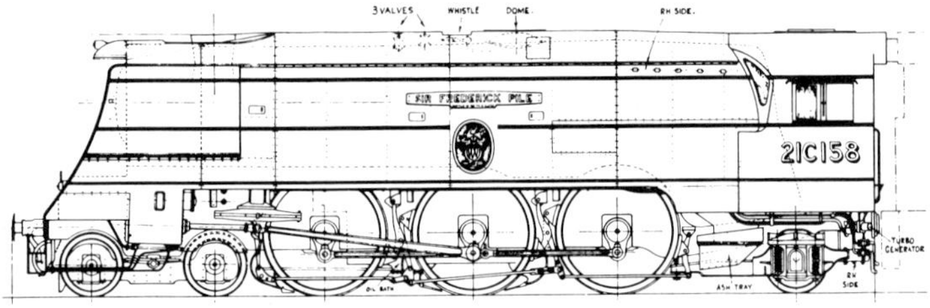

CONTENTS

Above: G.N.R. Atlantic No. 251 with original chimney. *British Rail*

PREFACE

The author of this book, given an advantageous view-point (and using it, as a practical engineer should), has told us that these data and anecdotes and reminiscences have at least some value in illuminating the humanistic art of engineering.

We agree.

In the course of our careers, we have all mulled things over with each other and learned therefrom. Problems shared are problems solved, etc.

O. V. S. Bulleid

H. G. Ivatt

W. A. Stanier

INTRODUCTION

The main design achievements of six famous Locomotive Engineers are herein described, with a measure of biographical detail to establish the background.

As in real life, so in this book, there are digressions. They are intended to illustrate the various ingredients of engineering design, and the factors that commonly affect it. To emphasize this slant, I got my father, my uncle, and the C.M.E. under whom I served my apprenticeship, to sign the preface.

I gratefully acknowledge the assistance I have received from many friends, acquaintances, librarians, authors—and relatives. Specifically, vital help in the form of data, drawings and photos was given by British Railways—Derby, Doncaster, Euston, London Bridge, Marylebone, Swindon, Waterloo, and the Archive—and C.I.E., Inchicore. Also by the Institutions of Civil, Mechanical, and Locomotive Engineers; and by *The Engineer* and *The Railway Gazette*. And of course I could not have managed without the detailed help of Sir William Stanier (Chapters 4 and 5), H. G. Ivatt (Chapters 1 and 6) and O. Bulleid (Chapters 1, 2 and 3).

Most of the photos were supplied by British Railways and the Ian Allan organization: the rest are individually credited.

Abergavenny, 1963 H. A. V. Bulleid.

Above: S.R. "Merchant Navy" class 4-6-2 No. 21C1 *Channel Packet.* *British Rail*

INTRODUCTION TO THIS EDITION

Here, twenty years later, are a few more "human touches" concerning these six Master Builders.

H. A. Ivatt's rapport with footplate staff was particularly good and when in 1883 he wrote an Inchicore catechism for them he did not mind pulling their legs, as in Question 66: "Is it a sign of a good driver when his tool boxes are dirty, and full of rusty spanners, and old nuts, and bits of iron, and other rubbish, and when he carries on the back of his tender enough fire tools, old point rods, etc, to stock a small railway?" No prize for the answer.

H. N. Gresley's interest in bird life showed when he described the tube incrustations in fireboxes as swallows' nests. He also liked topical jokes and laughed aloud at a title in a Russian spy comedy film I made in 1933 — *So dumb, he thought Metropolitan Vickers meant London clergy.* Later he asked me if there was an easy way of getting correct exposures, adding "I don't mean f/8 and all that stuff."

My father had a lifelong liking for weak tea, and this exasperated some of his tougher LNER colleagues when it was the only drink available at the occasional Kings Cross meetings. Voices were raised, led I think by R. A. Thom, comparing it very unfavourably with Gorton or Doncaster tea. So O. V. B. arranged for a strong brew to be made in a tea can at Doncaster and to be kept brewing by a guard during its journey to Kings Cross, where he had it served at that day's meeting. Allegedly it only just poured, and silenced the opposition, at least temporarily.

Of the six, Churchward alone spent his whole working life on the same railway, and his dedication to it often showed — as when in 1914 he bade farewell to Holcroft saying "Now remember this; wherever you may go or whatever you may do, always stick up for the Great Western."

W. A. Stanier had an unusual and time-saving technique for signing letters; if he liked the letter he initialled it *WAS* after which his clerk accurately applied a rubber stamp facsimile of *tanier*. He was in Calcutta on a Machine Tool Mission in 1944, not so long after he became Sir William, and having forgotten to pack a brief case he sent his bearer to buy him one and to "get my initials put on it". These duly appeared as S.I.R. Stanier was much amused and remarked "All right, South Indian Railways."

H. G. Ivatt had an exceptional rapport with machinery to which he sometimes attributed human feelings as in his comment "The engine didn't like it" when, on a "Precursor", the driver saw he was going to overshoot a signal, wound into reverse and opened the regulator. Sometimes the calm H. G. I. demeanour could prove exceptionally withering: C. S. Cocks told me he once tried to explain to him why his piston head lock-nuts still worked loose. Ivatt patiently heard him out and simply said "I am sorry for you."

All six had different foibles but all notably contributed to 20th Century steam engines, as the following pages testify.

Ifold, Sussex, 1982. H. A. V. BULLEID.

Above: Gresley's streamlined class "A.4" Pacific No. 60029 *Woodcock* approaching Peterborough on the up "Capitals Limited" non-stop express, 1952. *J. G. Click*

CHAPTER 1

H. A. Ivatt and G.N.R. developments

Mrs. Matilda Ivatt of Coveney, Isle of Ely, made this comment on her first-born in a letter dated 15th November 1853:

> Master Henry is tall and slender, he is a poor talker but picks up new words every day now, and will try short sentences soon I think.

This earliest report on Henry Alfred Ivatt, born 16th September 1851, neatly sums up his physique and his careful mental approach. He gathered quite a few prizes and displayed an engineering bent whilst at Liverpool College, and so at the age of 17 his father, Rector of Coveney, apprenticed him under Ramsbottom at Crewe Locomotive Works.

Young Ivatt worked hard during his apprenticeship, and so for that matter did young Aspinall; they shared digs for a time. They saw the appointment of F. W. Webb as C.M.E. in 1871 from an apprentice's viewpoint—probably rather disinterested. Engines under construction at Crewe included 2-4-0 express passenger engines, " Newton " class, and 0-4-0 and 0-6-0 saddle tanks.

As soon as his apprenticeship was over, Ivatt became an ordinary fireman, based on Crewe North shed which then, as now, covered the passenger workings. Whilst working a mid-morning fast passenger train to Euston one day, a young man came along at Stafford with a permit to ride on the footplate. He introduced himself as Lord Haddo, took a lively interest, and when he left them at Euston the driver's incredulity was evaporated by the appearance of a footman to meet him. When, a few days later, a present of game arrived at Crewe North shed addressed to the " Driver and Fireman ", Ivatt said " We'll share them like this: you take the birds, I'll write the thank-you letter ". This he duly did: and very many years later the young enthusiast, now Lord Aberdeen, met to talk further about engines with the young fireman, now Locomotive Superintendent of the G.N.R.

In August 1873 Fireman Ivatt was regularly booked to work the Limited Mail between Crewe and Carlisle. After the serious derailment to the night Scotch Tourist Express at Wigan on August 3rd 1873, he minutely inspected the track before proceeding. He therefore appeared as a witness at the inquiry and was handsomely complimented by Colonel Tyler on the way he presented his evidence.

After six months in the Traffic Department, Ivatt was appointed Assistant Foreman at Stafford: one night in 1874 he arrived at the Shed to find one of the older first-link drivers refusing to work his booked train, the up mail, because his regular fireman had reported sick at short notice and he would not agree to the alternative firemen offered. Ivatt, with some premonition, solved this impasse by arranging to be the fireman himself:

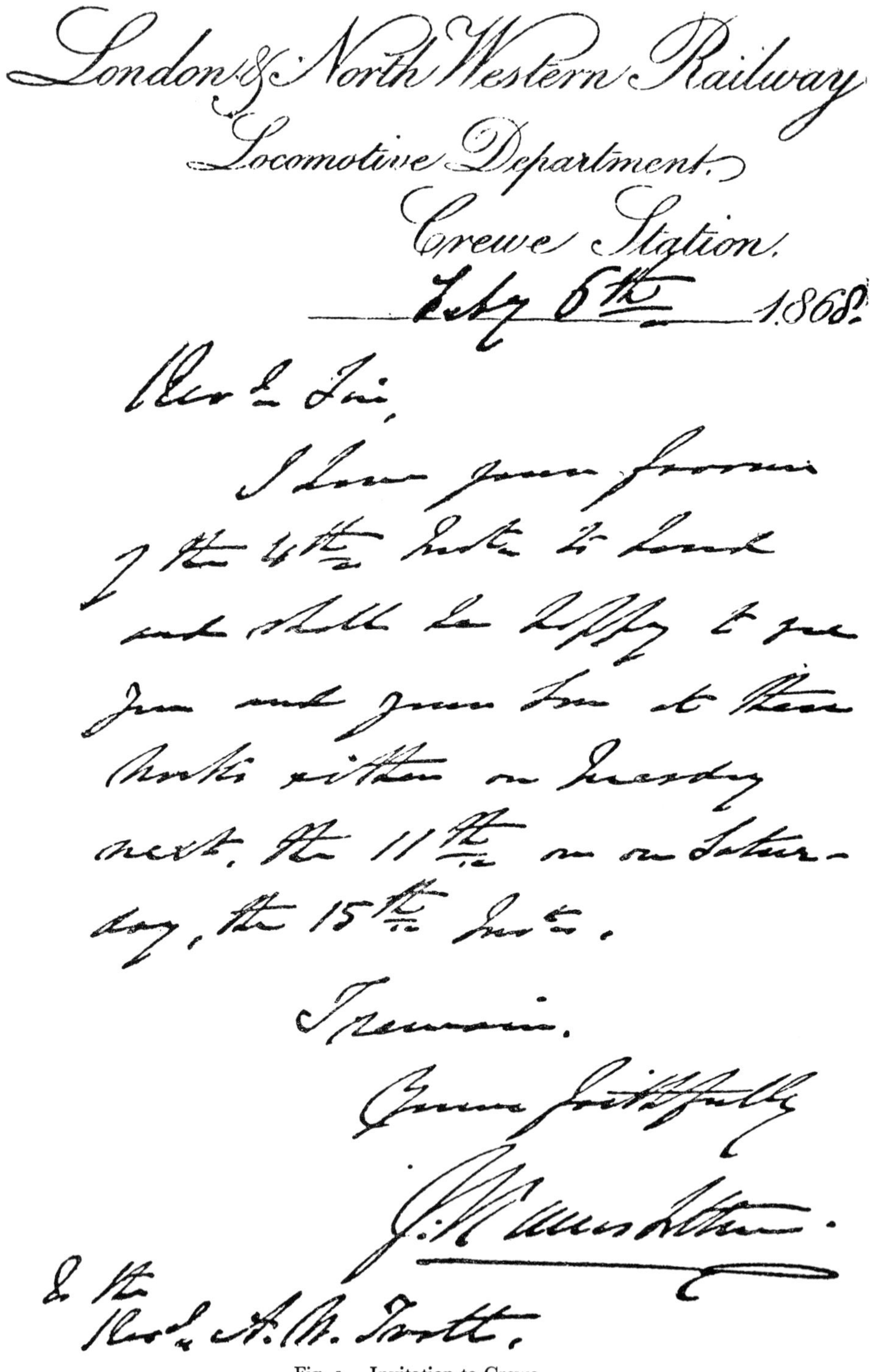

London & North Western Railway
Locomotive Department.
Crewe Station.
Feby 6th 1868.

Dear Sir,

I have your favour of the 4th inst. to hand and shall be happy to see you and your son at these works either on Tuesday next, the 11th or on Saturday, the 15th Inst.

I remain,

Yours faithfully
J. Ramsbottom.

To the
Revd. A. M. Scott.

Fig. 1. Invitation to Crewe.

and with the reluctantly obedient driver emphasizing the need for a good look-out for the junction signals, they duly set back on to their train and got away. Ivatt knew the road well from his past experience, and was dismayed when they ran past a distant signal at danger without any reaction from the driver. He called across the cab; but when they got the green light at the home signal and the driver was still hesitating, it became all too clear what was amiss—a driver who could work safely at night only with his own fireman, *who knew his driver was colour-blind.* This incident led directly to the periodical eye-testing of footplate staff.

In 1874 Ivatt took charge of the locomotive department at Holyhead, and in 1876 he was promoted to Chester. More: on 20th September 1876, at Hampstead, he married Miss Margaret Campbell. He was 25, she 28; they had first met in Ely eight years before.

Rather unexpectedly there came a serious edge to the Ivatt proficiency with a revolver when, in late October 1877, he took over an office in Cork, had the desk moved squarely opposite the door, and kept his revolver ready, and known to be ready, in the top right-hand drawer. It was never used, but a useful deterrent, as they might have argued, locally. They were troubled times in Ireland; remnants of the Fenian gangs, and tenants revolting against the landowners, might drop in unexpectedly and decide to shoot first and ask afterwards. The job was Southern District Division Superintendent of the Great Southern and Western Railway: but in 1882 he was appointed Asst. Locomotive Engineer at Inchicore, Dublin, and four years later, consequent upon Aspinall's move to the Lancashire & Yorkshire, he was appointed Locomotive Engineer. He was rather serious, and aged 35.

Fig. 2. Ivatt's 4-4-2 tank for the G.S. & W., 1893. With 16 sq. ft. grate area, 150 psi boiler pressure, 5 ft. 8½ in. wheels, and cylinders 16 by 20 in., they had a tractive effort of 9,530 lb.

Unquestionably Ivatt found the Inchicore job much to his taste. Dublin is an attractive city, even after Cork, and when he became " head man " of the loco and carriage and running departments he moved into the ugly but comfortable house that went with the job—St. John's,

Island Bridge. There was plenty of work, but no major upheaval—partly on account of consistent previous Crewe influences at Inchicore. Alexander McDonnell had been Locomotive Superintendent from 1864 to 1883 and in addition to many Crewe items reminiscent of Ramsbottom had introduced swing-link bogies and Webb's cast-iron wheels for goods engines. Aspinall had made no marked changes in designing two classes of 4-4-0s, construction of which was less than half finished when Ivatt took over. The larger ones had 18 by 24 cylinders and worked the Dublin–Cork mail trains, covering the 165 miles in 4 hrs. 5 mins. including three stops.

The Ivatt designs for the Great Southern and Western included 0-6-0 tanks, to replace some unsatisfactory 0-6-4s, and 2-4-2 and 4-4-2 passenger tanks. The 2-4-2s built in 1892 had 16 by 20 cylinders, 5 ft. 8 in. driving wheels, boiler pressure 160 psi, and total heating surface about 850 sq. ft. Some of them achieved sixty years' life. Inchicore Works turned out a good job and had considerable prestige. Ivatt's first pupil had been persuaded by his father first to take a law degree, to sustain him in a career when he got over his craze for engineering: his name was Richard Maunsell.

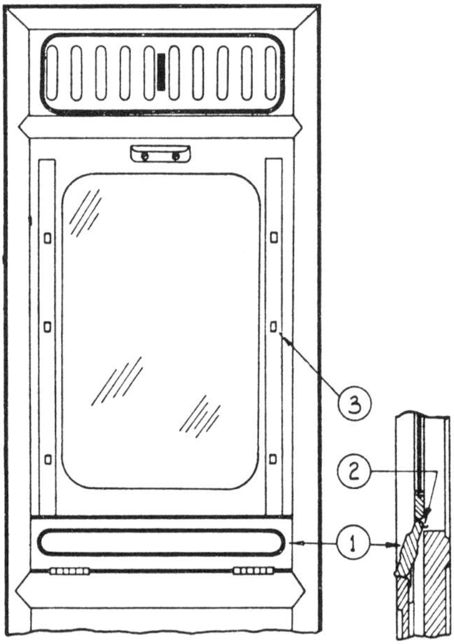

Fig. 3. Ivatt's carriage window patent, 1888. The sprung, hinged flap 1 supports the sash closed as shown; or intermediately by pegs 2 engaging in any of the slots 3.

Ivatt took all his duties and responsibilities very seriously and conscientiously. He would sit in his cosy study at St. John's, smoking thoughtfully and sketching slowly, pad on knee. Thus emerged, in 1888, his first patent—the well-known sprung flap to support carriage-window sashes. The tempo of work was civilized. His anxieties were for the most part pleasurable technicalities. He may have been preoccupied at times: on one occasion as a dutiful father and F.Z.S. he was strolling round Dublin Zoo with his three elder daughters when he noted a loose end of wool from Maude's skirt. He absently wound up a good ball of wool and she lost several inches of skirt before he was alerted: it was late 1890, and Maude was six. About that time one might find Ivatt laughing aloud at *Three Men in a Boat;* he bought his copy soon after publication. His sense of humour allowed him to laugh also on the occasion when all the family assembled on the lawn to watch his demonstration of a new penny-farthing bicycle. After a cool straight run he made a decisive application of the brake and landed suddenly and unexpectedly but approximately feet-first having passed right over the front wheel.

Of course Ivatt had not forgotten about railway matters across the Irish sea. He had many ties in England, he kept up with Aspinall and others, and he watched with interest the Railway Race of 1888, being impressed by the performances of locos from his old L.N.W.R., and the G.N.R. on the East Coast route. He was a man who strongly felt the need for discussions on current technical and administrative problems with his opposite numbers, and this need was interestingly filled.

On 21st January 1869, at Perth, the five Scottish Loco Superintendents formed The Association of Locomotive Engineers in Scotland. This seems to have fizzled out in 1876, but two of its members, W. Stroudley and James Stirling, met with some others in London in 1889 and invited all their opposite numbers to a meeting: and so, on 15th January 1890, at the St. Pancras Hotel, was formed the Association of Railway Locomotive Engineers. The twenty-five present included:

W. Adams	London & South Western
J. A. Aspinall	Lancashire & Yorkshire
W. Dean	Great Western
J. J. Hanbury	Metropolitan
J. Holden	Great Eastern
M. Holmes	North-British
H. A. Ivatt	Great Southern & Western of Ireland
S. W. Johnson	Midland (called to the Chair)
W. Kirtley	London Chatham & Dover
J. Manson	Great North of Scotland
J. C. Park	Great Northern of Ireland
J. Stirling	South Eastern (elected Secretary)
M. Stirling	Hull & Barnsley
P. Stirling	Great Northern

And seven apologies were received including:

D. Drummond	Caledonian (elected Deputy Chairman)
L. Longbottom	North Staffordshire
J. C. Park	North London

T. H. Riches	Taff Vale
J. G. Robinson	Waterford & Limerick

They decided to hold two meetings each year: a winter meeting at the St. Pancras hotel and a summer meeting in the country. The second meeting of the A.R.L.E. was in Edinburgh and there the first item of business was transacted:

> Mr. Ivatt called attention to the Engines and Boilers Act, 1890; and it was resolved that each Locomotive Engineer should call the attention of his General Manager to this Act with a view to oppose the passing of the Act.

The rather formidable party of twenty-eight then went by special train for a tour of the Forth Bridge, visited the Edinburgh Exhibition, and dined together. The A.R.L.E. was truly launched, and Ivatt became a staunch supporter, seldom missing a meeting. He arranged for the Summer meeting of 1893 to be held at Killarney, and acted as host on behalf of the Great Southern and Western Railway. The only notable abstainer from A.R.L.E. membership was F. W. Webb, who refused to join on principle: he would not tolerate a group discussion, but was ready to help individually, and Ivatt occasionally saw him at Crewe. This may have catalysed Ivatt into compounding an 0-6-0 and a 4-4-0 at Inchicore in 1894. Both originally had a pair of 18 by 24 cylinders, and he fitted them both with a high pressure 18 by 24 and a low pressure 26 by 24 cylinder. The driver could work the 4-4-0 simple or compound by operating a simple change valve, whereas the 0-6-0 automatically compounded after starting, by means of a flap valve developed by Worsdell on the North-Eastern. The 5 ft. 3 in. Irish gauge facilitated this experiment, but

Fig. 4. The G.S. & W. Compound 4-4-0, No. 93, designed and built by Ivatt at Inchicore in 1895. [*The Engineer*

the low boiler pressure of 150 psi may have reduced its effectiveness. It amused Ivatt by showing neither gain nor loss from compounding.

Examination of engines in for repair too often revealed incipient cracks in their crank-shafts, and this worried Ivatt although he knew that the spread of such cracks was slow. He rigged up a full-size fatigue tester to study the propagation of the cracks in a crank-axle, and when reporting the experiments in *The Engineer* in April 1891 he called special attention to the likelihood of cracks starting from sharp corners as in keyways.

Inchicore was no great cradle of experiment, however, nor was the work particularly exacting; and Ivatt found life spacious around Dublin. Sport was good, he was able to devote time to his hobbies including astronomy, and his skill as a conjuror grew apace as it was called upon more and more to entertain a considerable circle of friends.

The Doncaster enginemen and firemen had a drinking fountain erected to honour Patrick Stirling's 70th birthday on 29th June 1890; but the old man ignored all hints about retirement. When his Assistant and Works Manager, Shotton, died in May 1895, he merely said at the next Locomotive Committee meeting, " In view of my own increasing years, I feel we must engage, as his successor, a man capable of taking over from me in due time." But there was far too much at stake for the Great Northern Railway to be caught napping with no Locomotive Superintendent; and so, having engaged D. E. Marsh from the Great Western as young blood to replace Shotton, the General Manager and one of the directors, Sir Henry Oakley and R. Wigram, journeyed discreetly to Dublin on 27th August to see Ivatt. They liked what they saw, reported back to their Board, and on 9th October Ivatt visited the Rt. Hon. W. L. Jackson, Chairman of the G.N.R., at King's Cross. Jackson, who became Lord Allerton in 1902, was very far-seeing and had a clear and concise manner: without much ado he said, " We are looking for a good man, and are offering £1,750." " Why yes, " Ivatt replied, " You should certainly get a good man for that salary." " But we are offering the job to *you*," said Jackson. Ivatt looked at his pipe, and thought about the Dublin setting of his work and his home, and quietly answered, " I could not consider such a move for less than £2,500."

At the G.N.R. Board meeting on Friday, 1st November 1895 it was reported that enquiries made of Messrs. S. W. Johnson, J. A. F. Aspinall, F. W. Webb and W. Dean indicated that Mr. Ivatt's standing in his profession, his character, his knowledge and his practical experience left nothing to be desired. The Chairman said he had had an interview with Mr. Ivatt and gathered that he would be willing to accept the position of Locomotive Superintendent if the Board were willing to agree to a salary of £2,500. After considerable discussion it was Resolved to offer £2,500, it being however stipulated that he be not allowed to receive pupils. The chairman handled what was probably a typically difficult discussion in a shrewd and statesmanlike way: he knew, and with hindsight we can agree, that it was worth paying an extra £750 to get the real McCoy—it always is. The pupil embargo was G.N.R. policy, but within a few months it was agreed that the Locomotive Superintendent could take up to eight apprentices at a premium of £50.

Ivatt received his formal offer of the job on 2nd November and formally accepted it on 4th November, the starting date being purposely left vague: why worry about time, thought Ivatt, full of Irish experience, as he strolled back to his office after lunch on Friday, 11th November 1895. But two telegrams awaited him. One was from his friend Wilson Worsdell, for information:

> " MR STIRLING OF DONCASTER DIED THIS MORNING WORSDELL GATESHEAD "

The other was from a new employer, for action:

> " COME OVER TONIGHT IF POSSIBLE SEE ME TO-MORROW KINGS CROSS CHAIRMAN WILL BE THERE POSITION VACANT BY DEATH OAKLEY KINGS CROSS "

And so in March 1896 whilst his family rather gloomily moved into Leicester House, Regent Square, Doncaster, a re-vitalized and challenged H. A. Ivatt began looking round the G.N.R. arena.

He found traffic growing in volume and weight and the Stirling singles coping only under the best drivers: he found loco repairs being done at the five main sheds, with attendant diffuse technical control: and for good measure in between his shed and works inspections and his footplate rides he walked the track from King's Cross to Doncaster and duly reported that it was inadequate for the large engines which would soon be required. The recent serious derailments at St. Neots in November 1895 and at Little Bytham in March 1896 vividly coloured his arguments, and he finally stung the Chairman with the disconcerting remark, "Had I known the condition of the track I would not have come." " I will have the track made second to none," said W. L. Jackson, " You just design the engines." The resulting track and locos are historic.

Ivatt's modest expenses from these travels worried his chief Clerk-Loco Accountant, Matthewman, who had been with Stirling, and he took one claim back with a remark that immediately entered the list of family sayings: " Haven't you forgotten something, Sir?" Ivatt was generally ready with a neat riposte on such occasions, and one finds a casual turn of phrase in his comparatively rare writings. In his First Half-yearly Report, dated 24.7.1896 to the Locomotive Committee covering the previous six months' working of the Locomotive Department he wrote " I would remind you that the half-year includes one extra working day in consequence of 1896 being a leap year." In fact the expenditure was £475,000, a pretty tidy sum in those days and, compared with the same period the year before, this extra day represented over £2,000—about the price of an engine. Loco coal was a major item, though reasonably priced at 8s. per ton.

It is a pattern of life that a delayed change causes a rush, and Ivatt was immediately faced with demands for more and larger engines. Not only were amenities increasing so that passenger trains were becoming heavier as 4- and 6-wheel-bogie stock replaced the six-wheelers, but additional workings were introduced, such as the King's Cross–Manchester expresses. In parallel, goods traffic was on the increase. The situation was complicated by the other railways also finding themselves short of motive power, so that all the contractors had full order books.

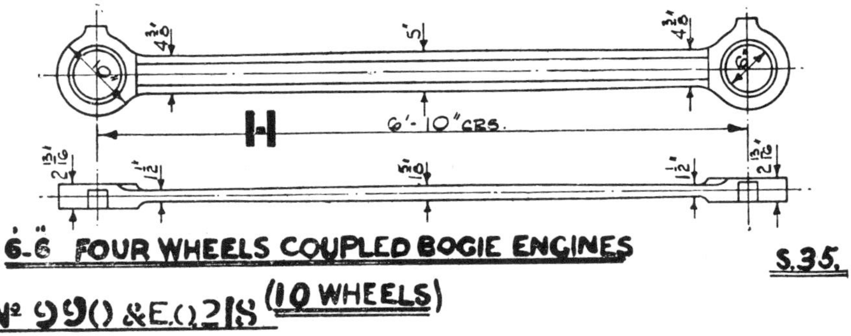

Fig. 5. Coupling rod for No. 990 and No. 251 — a facsimile of the Doncaster drawing with wheels wrongly given as 6ft 6in. Bulleid saw these being milled by supporting the ends only and allowing them to deflect under the cutter for the increased thickness at centre.

Ivatt had taken over a range of good class and well-maintained but essentially small engines. For express passenger working there were 53 of the famous 8-foot Stirling "Singles," supported by the equally fast 2-2-2s, mostly with 7 ft. 7 in. wheels. Then for branch passenger and mixed traffic working there were numerous 2-4-0s and 0-4-2s, mainly built between 1867 and 1874. Freight was handled by 0-6-0s with 17½ in. by 26 in. cylinders. Suburban 0-4-4 tanks and shunting 0-6-0 tanks, both fairly well up to their jobs, completed the picture: and these two were the only types built by Stirling after 1885 except for the last six "singles", built in 1894, which he provided with larger cylinders and increased grate area.

Most urgently needed were 0-6-0s, for goods and shunting, and medium-powered four-coupled passenger engines. Ivatt directed his drawing office effort first to the boilers and front-ends: his boilers had increased heating surfaces and grate areas, and they also had domes, much welcomed by the enginemen because they allowed more latitude in water level with less risk of priming. Some economy gestures were appropriate, and the brass safety-valve cover was replaced by an iron casting. Stirling's standard 17½ in. by 26 in. cylinders were retained, but the steam and exhaust passages improved. At this stage, orders were placed for about 70 0-6-0 saddle tanks and tender engines. Except for a batch of ten 2-4-0s, Ivatt decided to supply the four-coupled passenger engines as 4-4-0s, and the first of these, No. 400, was actually completed by Doncaster Works in 1896.

This concentrated design effort had still left Ivatt time to get round his main Running Sheds, and he was impressed by the admirable work of the footplate crews, which Stirling had largely inspired. It was more rigorous than either current Great Southern and Western working or his own firing experiences. He was always a champion of his enginemen, urging that everything possible should be done to facilitate their task—from engines to rules. Unworkable rules outraged his keen sense of fair play, and at the A.R.L.E. meeting in November 1896 he pointed out that distant signals were treated simply as indicators of the positions of their home signals, and that therefore the present rule, which required a driver to be prepared to stop at any obstruction between the distant and the home signal, was unfair to enginemen. " When new rules are being introduced, " he said, " We must ensure that those affecting the Locomotive Department are such as can be approved by the Locomotive Engineer." This was agreed, but S. W. Johnson pointed out that the rule as it stood was essential when Permissive Block Signalling was in operation.

In February 1897 Ivatt obtained sanction to build an experimental passenger engine of weight about 52 tons. He had found out that even the best drivers of the famous " singles " lost the necessary delicate touch, to avoid slipping, after a spell on 4-coupled engines; and this emphasized that the days of the " singles " were numbered. He felt Stirling had already gone to the limit with his 19¼ ton axle-loading on the last six " singles ". Ivatt the eminently practical knew well that a machine is far from ideal if it needs humouring. He also sharply understood from his own experience the nightmare of all footplate staff—shortage of steam. He thoroughly approved the basic simplicity of the Stirling designs: but already he was a veteran at interpreting the demands of his Operating and Commercial opposite numbers—they would always demand something in excess of their stated maximum demand. He therefore planned his new express engine not as a 4-4-0 but as a 4-4-2, treating the pair of coupled wheels as a direct replacement of Stirling's single drivers and retaining the advantage of the trailing wheels, namely plenty of room around and below the firebox and plenty of scope for boiler and firebox enlargements.

To these basic design considerations Ivatt added several detail refinements. His balanced slide valve, with Richardson's strips, permitted an ideal exhaust passage besides reducing the load on the valve-gear and wear on the valves. Sharing Stirling's rooted dislike of coupling rods swinging about on fast engines, he made them short by placing his coupled wheels as close together as possible, and took advantage of the bending-moment diagram to use stepped crank-pins which gave 11½ in. throw to the coupling rods compared with 12 in. for the connecting rods. Ivatt discussed all his earliest thoughts of a 4-4-2 and many of the subsequent details with his friend Aspinall, who also decided upon a 4-4-2 for the Lancashire and Yorkshire Railway. There was not a great deal in common between the two engines, except the wheel arrangement and the very large boiler, but suddenly great rivalry developed—which Works would turn out the first English Atlantic—Doncaster or Horwich?

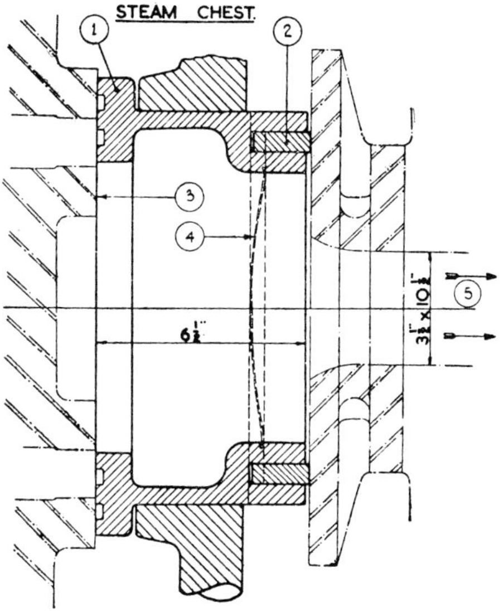

Fig. 6. Balanced slide-valve for Atlantics. The slide-valve 1 carries four Richardson's strips 2 held against the steam-chest walls by springs 4. Exhaust steam passes directly from the cylinder 3 to the blast pipe connection 5.

Ivatt was indignant that his idea might first appear on another railway, and so were his directors—there was considerable prestige to be gained in such matters. Aspinall also wanted the prestige and could see no harm in pressing Horwich to the utmost—after all, Ivatt had started his design earlier. In the event Horwich was unplaced and Doncaster scored the victory when the Ivatt Atlantic, No. 990, was completed in June 1898. It gained considerable publicity as "the largest and heaviest express engine in the Kingdom."

No. 990 was an immediate success from the driver's viewpoint—though it had no greater tractive effort than a Stirling "single" this effort could be applied at starting with far less fear of slipping; the adhesive weight was up from 19¼ to 32 tons. It had about 30 per cent more heating surface and grate area, and it steamed admirably. Ivatt had already tried his balanced slide-valve arrangement on a Stirling engine and "proved" it, and there were no other major changes: but he determined on rigorous trials before duplicating his first Atlantic.

He also wanted convincing that there was no more to be had from the " singles ", and so he designed and built a 4-2-2 with 7 ft. 7 in. wheels, 18 by 26 cylinders, but larger boilers than Stirling's: see table, page 28.

Meantime Doncaster were turning out more 4-4-0s and the contractors were supplying more 0-6-0s. There were plenty of queries, and Ivatt moved with the times and reluctantly had his office and house connected to the national telephone in November 1898. This novelty made quite a talking point at the complimentary dinner given by the A.R.L.E. to S. W. Johnson as President of the Institution of Mechanical Engineers, on 24th November. One special guest was present—A. Sturrock, who had given Johnson his first job.

Parliamentary influences required an investigation into automatic couplings about this time, and in April 1899 Ivatt led a party of four, including loco and traffic men from the Midland and Great Eastern Railways, on a three-month American trip, unofficially accompanied by one of the G.N. directors, R. Wigram (always referred to as " Old Wiggy " by the Ivatt daughters). This added up to a routine step in the adoption of the Buck-eye coupling, but Ivatt inwardly digested American locomotive trends, though luckily he avoided copying their external appearances. On his return to the Works he was annoyed to find that 990 had spent almost the whole time resting in the shed at Grantham, because the District Loco Supt. did not hold with coupled driving wheels for fast passenger work—any more than Stirling had done. Ivatt decisively " promoted " this officer to the smaller shed at York, and 990 got back to work. This is the rare case of Ivatt being unable to overcome prejudice by persuasion; and it points the moral that persistent saboteurs of improvement must ultimately be regarded as technical obstructions and correspondingly removed or circumnavigated.

Although Ivatt had placed one order for goods engines in America—twenty 2-6-0s from Baldwin—he had found in America the same shortage of locomotive building capacity as existed in this country. Ably assisted by Marsh, he was increasing the Doncaster Works output by improved machines and extensive use of pneumatic tools, but pressure for new engines was relentless and in November 1899 he put forward a scheme for building a large new erecting and repair shop at a cost of £294,000. When completed in 1901 it was at once christened " The Crimpsall "—you entered from Crimpsall Road. Ivatt made this large enough for all major repairs to be done at Doncaster, where technical control would be more reliable and more consistent. With engine sizes and speeds increasing, and likely to increase further, and with sometimes only rudimentary control over material specifications, Ivatt was worried about safety and reliability.

So the five main running sheds, King's Cross, Peterborough, Ardsley (Leeds), Lincoln, and York, ceased to do general repairs and were limited to bearing failures and routine attentions. Though unquestionably sound, this decision caused some upsets from loss of local prestige and by severing the practice of drivers " keeping an eye " on their own engines whilst undergoing repair. But Ivatt was quick to debunk the latter claim, and made no secret that he preferred drivers not to worry about sizes and fits and how things were manufactured; he simply wanted them to be good drivers.

It is so fatally easy to drift away from sharp and clear realization of what the operators of machines require, and Ivatt was determined not to fall into this error. Hence his sustained shed interest—facilitated of course by the running being directly his responsibility. Nor did he neglect social occasions: his yearly attendance at the King's Cross Good Friday dinners became traditional, and he had a fund of suitable stories. It was said that this fund was not only inexhaustible, but permitted accurate matching to any occasion: from Running Shed dinners to gatherings of Pillars of the Church in Cambridgeshire. In contrast to this ability in semi-formal circles, he never formally addressed any of the Learned Societies; though he was elected to the Council of the Institution of Mechanical Engineers in 1900. In March he and Churchward both gave some sound advice in a discussion on pneumatic tools, Churchward recommending that the compressed air main should be large enough for future needs, and Ivatt both advising 100 rather than 80 psi, and regretting that he had been too busy to take measurements of the air consumed.

In June 1900 Sauvage gave a paper on French Locomotive Practice, and in the discussion Ivatt said:

> " The thing that strikes me about the Paper is the great increase in the power of locomotives which has taken place in France during the last ten years. The measure of the power of a locomotive is the boiler. Mr. Sturrock, who left the position which I myself now occupy on the Great Northern Railway over thirty years ago (and who, I am glad to say, comes to see me at Doncaster and talk locomotives now and then), says that the measure of the power of a locomotive is ' its capacity to boil water.' It will be seen from the Paper that a great many of the boilers of the French locomotives are quite up to 2,000 ft. of heating surface, and a great many of the fireboxes have over 20 ft. of grate area, and in many cases the pressure is over 200 lb. It is no use having large cylinders, and figuring the power of the engine from the cylinders, unless one has a boiler that will keep the cylinders properly supplied. A large purse is not of much advantage unless the bank account is capable of keeping it well filled.
>
> " One of the difficulties which locomotive engineers have to deal with is trying to pull very big trains at very high speeds. When a locomotive engineer makes an engine that is capable of pulling a church, he is at once asked to hitch on the schools as well! What is required for running heavy fast expresses is to start with an engine of the dray-horse type, capable of exerting great tractive force, and quickly getting up the speed to about 50 miles an hour; then to take that engine off, and put on another of the quick trotter or high-flyer type.
>
> " Of course that is impossible in practice, but it seems to me that the four-cylinder compound, with plenty of adhesive weight, is likely to be a solution of the difficulty. A four-cylinder compound, with a boiler big enough to allow all four cylinders to work by high pressure, not for a short distance only, but for

many miles when necessary, fitted with a simple arrangement which will allow the engine to be worked compound at will, might perhaps assist in the direction I have tried to indicate.

" The author is quite right when he says that there are two sets of opinions on locomotive matters; sometimes the drawing-office size of a blast-pipe is not the same as the steam-shed size."

Sheds *v.* Works *v.* Drawing Office; then, as now . . .

Taking part in these discussions further convinced Ivatt that larger boilers were an advantage and that there were still many rewards in locomotive design to be had by careful experimentation. The large boiler on his 4-2-2 was proving its worth and he built eleven more of these engines in 1900. There was also the growing experience from the Stirling engines he was rebuilding with larger boilers, increased grate areas, and domes—their performance and their service reliability were much improved. The Atlantic No. 990 had satisfied him and he was building a further ten of these: they were able to take a 200 ton train out of King's Cross and accelerate to 60 m.p.h. by Hornsey with ease. With heavier trains it was still the boiler that limited performance, Ivatt noted, the driver having to notch up and partially close the regulator to conserve steam.

Fires near railways were automatically blamed on steam engines, and Locomotive Engineers tended to lower their voices when they said " spark arresters " because their Solicitors claimed that the use of this expression implied that engines emitted sparks, a well-known truth which they did not wish to endorse. Another perennial irritation was that deflector plates to arrest sparks were disliked by the Sheds because they hindered tube cleaning, and so they tended to get " lost. " Drivers thought they impeded steaming—which was certainly true if they resulted in tubes not being properly cleaned. Ivatt felt that all this might be eased by simply increasing the length of the smokebox and so allowing the offending larger cinders to gravitate harmlessly to the bottom. The subject was lengthily discussed at the A.R.L.E. meeting on 30th November 1900, W. Dean in the chair: he said the G.W.R. fitted a corrugated deflector plate, but that he had found no advantage in extending the smokebox length from 3 ft. 9 in. to 5 ft. S. W. Johnson said that his representative had travelled on these G.W. engines and had observed that those with the longer smokeboxes threw rather fewer sparks. Most members agreed that the best way to avoid sparks was to use boilers of adequate size to avoid forcing; some came up with pet ideas, including McIntosh, who said the blast-pipe should lean towards the smokebox door—not less than 1/8th in. for goods engines and 3/16 in. for fast engines. No one demanded an explanation of this, at any rate during the meeting. Ivatt said he had consulted the G.N.R. Solicitor to be sure there was no risk in conducting experiments with a longer smokebox and had got the all clear, but would like further views: all agreed Ivatt need have no hesitation in experimenting, and Johnson gloomily added that in case of a fire it mattered very little whether the engine was fitted with a spark arrester or not: if fitted, it would be alleged to be defective, and if not fitted, exception would be taken. Ivatt, still cautious, formally reported the proposed experiment to his Loco Committee in December 1900.

With the anxieties of the larger passenger engines mostly past at this time, Ivatt was engrossed in designing a more powerful freight engine, and in progressing work on the Crimpsall, whilst suffering the usual distractions from queries on the numerous engines still being built by outside contractors. This pressure of work rather curtailed his sporting interests, but it was not uncommon to see him, of a week-end, shooting clay pigeons in that part of the wagon works area still known as "the decoy," the name coming from earlier and more truly sporting activities. Marsh shared this interest, and the two would be seen at it together, interrupting themselves now and then to discuss Works problems. Marsh was an admirable Works Manager and Chief Assistant, and made major contributions to the design and layout of the Crimpsall.

Fig. 7. "Long Tom," 1901. [*The Engineer*

Early in 1901 "Long Tom" appeared, Ivatt's 0-8-0 coal engine, designed to handle the ever-growing mineral and coal traffic. It had a boiler similar to that of No. 990 but with slightly less grate area. With 4 ft. 8 in. wheels and 20 by 26 inside cylinders its tractive effort at 85 per cent boiler pressure was 27,600 lb. It weighed 54½ tons and had a 41 ton tender. Again these engines were cordially received by footplate staff; they were powerful brutes with plenty of steam and no nonsense, and though rather uncomfortable on account of the cab being excessively encroached upon by the back of the boiler this was a "good fault" in firemen's eyes as it resulted in a short firing swing. Fifty 10-ton trucks with 20-ton brake van was their normal loading on the Peterborough–London run, and they comfortably handled these 700-ton trains. On a Sunday, one could see them resting, at Hornsey (Ferme Park) or Peterborough (New England). Forty years earlier Archibald Sturrock had bought the first 0-8-0 for the G.N.R., and he paid Ivatt and Doncaster one of his periodic visits to look over his recent and much-publicised eight-coupled goods loco. Ivatt remarked with truth that there was nothing very special about it, and that everyone was doing it: indeed, Worsdell's slightly heavier and similarly-dimensioned outside-cylinder 0-8-0 appeared only a few months after " Long Tom." The older hands about the Works remembered the previous 0-8-0; so this visit was much discussed and among those who by a strange coincidence found they had pressing business near the weighbridge, and thus saw Ivatt and Archibald Sturrock together, was one of the premium apprentices, O. V. Bulleid.

Spring 1902 found things in good fettle at Doncaster. The first ten Atlantics were fully upholding G.N.R. fast-running prestige. The general signs of larger engines were propitious with booming traffic, and more " Long Toms " were being turned out from the works, nice-looking jobs in Great Northern green. As did many C.M.Es. Ivatt would walk round the Works on a Sunday, occasionally with one or more of his children and very occasionally with his wife. Once Mrs. Ivatt, trying in vain to push in a loco buffer with her parasol, looked round to find her husband watching with considerable interest. On formal Works tours with the directors, then more frequent than normal with the increased activity and the Crimpsall coming up to full capacity, Ivatt would let them go where they wished, prepared to answer questions: " Very different from Mr. Stirling," a fitter was heard to comment, " He told them which way to go and walked in front."

But Ivatt could be very firm when the occasion demanded. It was common for suppliers' tenders to be considered by the Locomotive Committee, and of course the directors concerned had strong trade interests. This once led to a positive demand for Ivatt to place an order for axles with a certain supplier, which he refused to do. At this moment of impasse Lord Allerton entered the room, to receive the complaint that " Ivatt was being very awkward." " You must remember that Ivatt is responsible for these components," said the Chairman, without hesitation, " And so if he decides upon a certain source of supply for technical reasons, his decision must be accepted." This wise reply now has its place among the text-book axioms, and it set a pattern of buying behaviour of great value to succeeding engineers. But Ivatt's thinking was even more subtle than at first appears; the *reason* for using a named supplier was and sometimes still is that one cannot fully specify the technical details of the job. Ivatt recognized that under such circumstances it is useless to build up more and more details and clauses in a specification; far better to get close to your technical " opposite number " in the supplier's organization and agree the common goal. Accordingly one found Ivatt writing the very simplest letter to his suppliers of axles: " Please supply so many to the enclosed drawings, the axles to be to my satisfaction." Wisely exploiting Doncaster's geographical convenience, he supported his laconic letter-writing by visiting his suppliers regularly.

Though almost painfully scrupulous in placing his own convenience second to the job in hand, he preferred visiting Kitsons at Leeds on a Tuesday, when they normally lunched off his favourite cold sirloin.

Though Ivatt clearly saw that a more powerful engine than 990 was required, he was not certain whether a larger boiler would meet the case or whether an improved front end and cylinder arrangement were needed. He had decided upon a longer smokebox after his spark-throwing experiment, and to decide about the cylinder arrangement he built another small Atlantic, No. 271, with four cylinders, 15 in. by 20 in., all driving the leading coupled axle. The engine had piston valves and inside valve gear. Ivatt soon reached the conclusion that any improvement was marginal and certainly did not justify the extra cost, complication and maintenance.

" It's no use having a large purse and nothing to put in it," Ivatt repeated towards the end of 1902 when the new, large Atlantic No. 251 put in its appearance and caused a profound sensation. The frames, wheels, motion and cylinders of the 990 class had been designed to take something more, and they certainly got it; the boiler diameter was increased by 10 in. to 5 ft. 6 in. and the longer smokebox gave a business-like balance to the wide firebox. The engine followed the admirable tradition of letting the appearance stem from the functional parts without disguise: compared with the " singles " it looked less elegant—but very formidable.

251 had the same tractive effort as 990 and thus again less than the latest 8 ft. Stirling singles. One result of this came nearly 50 years later when British Railways, using Midland terminology slightly out of context, gave these Atlantics the class " 3P " classification, whereas in fact they could beat the living daylights out of a Midland Compound, if it came to a display of steam-raising.

How important is it that an engine should still do its allotted task even if it has a load of duff coal on the tender, or if the fireman has strained his arm, or a washout is overdue? How many pounds of coal per mile is it worth, to put down 100 passengers one minute early rather than a few minutes late? These questions are still lacking clear answers, but 251 was intended to reduce the uncertainties, and it certainly succeeded in doing so. The engine was used by the advertising people as the G.N.R.'s image, in modern parlance; and as a symbol of power, speed, and reliability it contributed nobly to G.N.R. prestige.

When Ivatt first came to Doncaster he found the London suburban traffic being worked by Stirling's 0-4-2 and 0-4-4 tank engines, and in 1899 he designed and built some 4-4-2 tanks which did not really improve on Stirling's for all-round performance. Towards the end of 1902 the growing successes of electric traction, on tramways and railways, was being seen as a real challenge to steam, and the task of accelerating the normal 150-ton suburban trains of the period to 30 mph in 30 secs. on the level was taken up by several designers. Notably, Holden produced

COMPARISON OF STIRLING AND IVATT EXPRESS PASSENGER ENGINES

Class	No.	Type	Date	Cylinders dia. × stroke in. in.	Coupled wheel diameter ft. in.	Boiler pressure lb/sq. in.	Total heating surface sq. ft.	Grate area sq. ft.	Tractive effort (at 85 per cent pressure) lb.	Weight in working order: Engine tons	Weight in working order: Tender tons
Stirling Single*	1	4-2-2	1870	18 × 28	8 0	140	1045	17¾	12,600	45¼	26½
Stirling Single	1003	4-2-2	1894	19½ × 28	8 0	170	1032	20	16,100	49½	41¾
Ivatt Single	266	4-2-2	1898	18 × 26	7 7	170	1270	23.2	13,620	48½	41
Ivatt Atlantic*	990	4-4-2	1898	18¾ × 24	6 8	175	1442	26.8	15,850	58	41
Ivatt Atlantic*	251	4-4-2	1902	18¾ × 24	6 8	175	2500	31	15,850	68¼	41

* Preserved at York

the Decapod 0-10-0 tank on the Great Eastern in February 1903; it could produce the necessary acceleration with a 200-ton train but was too gross for the track. The G.N.R. must have been bitten by a similar bug, and Ivatt's solution was an 0-8-2 tank, very largely based on " Long Tom ", which came out in November 1903. It weighed 79 tons of which all but 13 were on the coupled wheels, and with tractive effort 30,000 lb. at 160

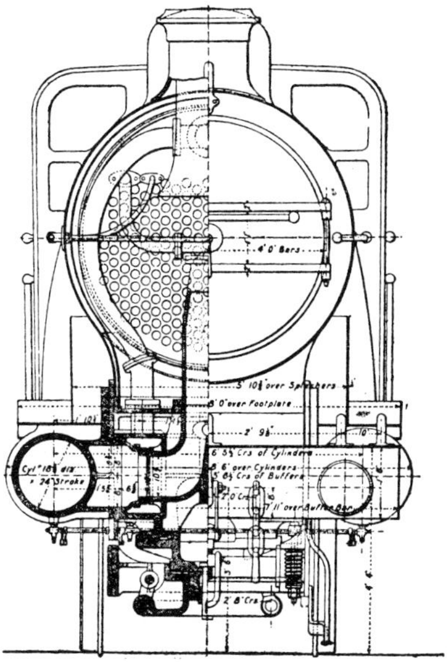

Fig. 8. The robust and uncomplicated front-end of No. 251. Note the single swing-link bogie, and the simple exhaust path, of which Ivatt said, " The exhaust goes through the back of the valve and straight up the chimney." (Barrow, 31:7:1901)

psi boiler pressure it theoretically could and in fact did achieve the necessary acceleration. But these engines were not sufficiently fast runners and so, in spite of their excellent acceleration, they were little if any better than the 4-4-2s built five years before: and their bulk frightened the Civil Engineer, specially when he thought about the notorious curves around King's Cross. Ivatt disliked the whole performance—the bulk of the engines, the lack of guiding wheels in front of the coupled wheels, and most of all the puzzle why top speed was so disappointing.

With larger freight engines available and correspondingly heavier trains, it became clear that despite traffic increases the total requirements of foot-plate hours were decreasing. A warning of the reduced promotion chances was given, but with natural reluctance to see their numbers reduced the foot-plate staff petitioned the Board for a hearing. Grievances were duly aired, but the proceedings were naturally an anxiety to Ivatt, torn between some hardship cases and the clear need for economies in working. He could see that many such economies, all to the public good, must come from reducing wasteful use of labour which meant cutting some jobs. Then, as now, such corrective action is essential if further waste and far more serious consequences are to be prevented. Ivatt found these problems worrying, and must have been turning them over in his mind one evening as he left his office, walked into Regent Square, entered the house, hung his hat on the hall stand, wheeled right and opened the drawing-room door. He then found he was in the next-door house.

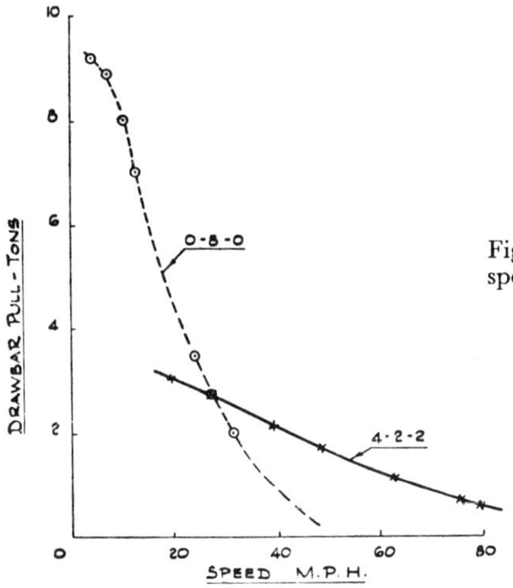

Fig. 9. Reduction of drawbar pull with speed. Dray-horse 0-8-0 compared with quick trotter 4-2-2.

Economy drives also re-kindled the compound controversy: Johnson had achieved considerable success with his Midland Compound during its first year of running, and compounding successes in France were impressively put over by M. Sauvage in a paper to the Institution of Mechanical Engineers in April 1904. Simple *v.* Compound became a grand debating arena, especially as Whale had just pulled off a decided hit in reversing the Webb compound policy with the almost aggressively simple *Precursor*. As so often in such controversies, fed briskly by Press and non-technical opinion, the rather obvious fact that the two contestants must therefore be about equal is overlooked, and so is the obvious conclusion that the decision taken hardly matters, one way or the other. Ivatt staunchly supported the Simple school, but was unusual in emphasizing how little it mattered: he opened the resumed discussion on the Sauvage paper, 15th April 1904, and related how in 1895 he had compounded an 0-6-0 and a 4-4-0 engine on the Great Southern and Western Railway, the result being that the engines were no better and no worse than before. He had since heard that they had been re-cylindered as simples when the cylinders wanted renewing.

Ivatt was in excellent form at this discussion. He went on to compare the drawbar pull at various speeds of single-wheelers and eight-coupled locos (still thinking about his suburban tanks) and pointed out that the indicated cylinder horse power could be disproportionately greater than the effective drawbar horse power, especially at high speeds. His final remarks admirably convey his views on complications and on handling engines, but hint at an area of doubt:

> " Every driver acquires skill in the best way of converting the energy of the coal into drawbar pull. The text books indicate that he should run with the throttle wide open, and regulate the steam required in the cylinders by altering the point of cut-off with his reversing gear, or in other words that he should work the steam as expansively as possible; but the driver knows that if he does this he will use more water (and consequently more coal) than if he runs with the cut-off at the point which the engine *likes best*, and he regulates the supply of steam by wire-drawing at the throttle.
>
> " I do not profess to explain scientifically the reason for this, but the fact remains, and it may help to reconcile people to the failure of various improved valve-gears (so-called) which have been tried at various times. A loco fitted with complicated gear, which produces diagrams with beautiful square corners, is, I believe, no better in practice than one with the old link-motion, which very possibly turns out a diagram shaped like a leg of mutton."

" The fact remains," Ivatt had said, admitting the area of doubt which included the puzzle about the lack of top speed on the 0-8-2 tanks. He could see with crystal clarity the importance of a good front end, and in particular he recognized the vital need of large, unencumbered exhaust passages. But he never spotted in cold isolation that with short valve travel it was impossible to get ample steam and exhaust openings when notched up. It is easy when one knows: whilst in the dark the myriad alternative reasons for a shortfall in performance cloud perception and take so long to eliminate. Even on the large Atlantics exhaust steam could not get freely away when the motion was notched up beyond about 30 per cent, but with the colossal boiler capacity this was no embarrassment at all to the footplate staff who could run at 30 per cent with full regulator indefinitely: to reduce speed they simply eased the regulator appropriately. The sheer performance of the engines seemed fully to vindicate the adequacy of their front end and their valve gear: the 0-8-2s were not so well off in comparison, having larger cylinders and rather less favourable steam and exhaust passages.

Just at this time the directors of the " Old G.N. " (as Mrs. Ivatt persisted in calling the G.N.R.) decided that it would at least do no harm to buy a compound passenger engine from an outside locomotive builder and, accordingly, they instructed the General Manager, Oliver Bury, and Ivatt to discuss the matter with five firms. All the locos offered were either too heavy or too long or insufficiently powerful: Ivatt in his report on 28th June 1904 advised taking no further action owing to the work involved in re-tendering to suit length and weight limitations. But Bury disagreed: he was a competent engineer himself, he liked the possibilities of economy from compounding, and he even quoted Ivatt's own hint that a compound might combine the dray-horse and the quick trotter. Technically fascinated, his judgment was blunted and he made the classic error of forgetting that if simples and compounds have about equal claims after thirty years of arguments and trials, and if at the same time you possess only simples and have a loco engineer who has tried both and prefers simples, then you are sure to be wasting money and effort in buying a compound. On 1st July 1904 Bury overruled Ivatt's advice and specifically recommended the Board to approve purchase of one compound Atlantic from the Vulcan Foundry Co.; and this recommendation was accepted.

Ivatt was philosophical about this decision: he knew perfectly well that the grass is greener beyond the fence, and that however much one admires and appreciates one's colleagues there are moments when their performance seems less attractive than some much publicized external (so-called) achievement. But prestige demanded that he should also design a compound, which he proceeded to do under considerable stress, which was not much relieved by the successes of 251, and her sister engines now emerging from Doncaster Works. Besides, it distracted from more pleasurable and inventive work, such as his patented water-scoop and built-up crank-axle. Moreover, there were other design headaches afoot: the first suburban stock electric lighting, and first thoughts about superheating, though this was still confined to the stationary boilers in the Works. Then there was a sudden serious upsurge in cases of hot axle bearings. This became alarming and culminated in terse comments and a demand for monthly statistics, when the Chairman had to change carriages twice between Leeds and King's Cross on account of hot boxes. The Midland had an enviable reputation for freedom from this trouble and, accordingly, Ivatt arranged with S. W. Johnson to obtain not only the standard whitemetal used by the Midland but also their special lubricating oil mixture: and right into the 1920s G.N.R. and L.N.E.R. carriage axle boxes were marked M.M.—Midland Mixture.

These pressures in mid-1904 put Ivatt " under the weather " for the only time in his career, the symptom being an emotional scene at a high-level meeting when he failed in an appeal to increase the labourers' wage rate. Doctors, including his wife's brother, looked at him and shook their heads and said that the terrific pace of twentieth century industrial life was to blame: the Edwardian era was proving even more hectic than the strenuous 1890s: he needed a long rest. Again the Chairman appears to have weighed up form and taken decisive action, and the result was three months' sick leave. Ivatt went off to Italy with his wife and daughter Dorothy and her friend Dorothy Harrison, comfortable in the knowledge that loco affairs were left in the capable hands of D. E. Marsh. He benefited enormously from this break: increasingly prone to worry, he had got too close to the limitless worries of his job and temporarily lost his perspective. Luckily he had regained it when a telegram arrived from Marsh, saying that he had accepted the job of C.M.E. on the L.B.S.C.R. and could he start on 1st January 1905? Ivatt finished his lunch, cabled agreement, and enjoyed the remainder of his leave as though nothing had happened. He returned to Doncaster fully refreshed and with the added satisfaction, echoed by his family, of moving into Avenue House, just beyond the terminus of the Avenue road tram.

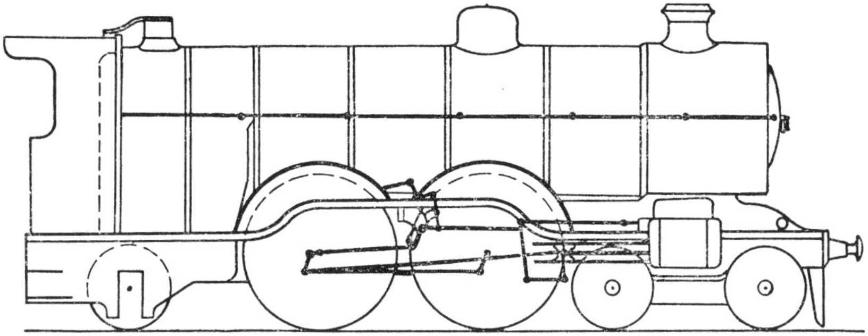

Fig. 10. Ivatt's 4-cylinder compound large Atlantic with Walschaert's valve gear, G.N.R. No. 292.

Marsh had certainly kept things ticking whilst his chief was absent and the 4-cylinder compound large Atlantic, No. 292, was well under way. Ivatt, who sorely missed Marsh, personally introduced him as a new member of the A.R.L.E., and sent him off with a complete set of drawings for 251—they both preferred this to the new compound. Rumour had it that R. E. L. Maunsell was to be the successor, but in fact the job went to none of the very numerous outside applicants but to Ivatt's own District Loco Superintendent at King's Cross—F. Wintour. Ivatt favoured Maunsell but the chairman favoured Wintour. He at once set about finishing No. 292, which emerged from Doncaster Works in March 1905. Ivatt used Walschaert's valve gear on this engine, but with a valve travel of only $4\frac{3}{8}$ in. compared with $4\frac{1}{8}$ on the simple Atlantics. The engine took readily to the road and repeated history for Ivatt by seeming to him no better and no worse than the simple engines. In July the compound Atlantic from the Vulcan Foundry was delivered, but due to minor teething troubles it only fully took to the road (and had its full purchase price of £4,000 released) in October.

All the Railway Boards were getting involved with heavier trains and demanding engines to work them on less coal per mile. Ivatt lobbied some of his opposite numbers and arranged with seven of the leading railways to produce overall statistics of coal consumption against engine miles and ton miles, and other ratios. These figures became available in May 1905 and the G.N.R. showed up about 3 per cent better than the average of the other seven.

Even so, the big thing was to test the Vulcan compound and the Ivatt compound against a standard simple Atlantic, and this was duly and carefully done in 1906. Ivatt's characteristically brief report on this trial was accompanied by the King's Cross to Grantham track profile, an outline diagram of each engine, and tables of dimensions and results. It

Fig. 11. Vulcan 4-cylinder compound Atlantic, G.N.R. No. 1300.

constituted his one and only formal contribution to the proceedings of the Institute of Mechanical Engineers. The full text (excluding a few notes) and the main points in the tables are reproduced below:

NOTES ON ROAD TRIALS OF THREE EXPRESS PASSENGER-ENGINES, CARRIED OUT ON THE GREAT NORTHERN RAILWAY IN 1906

The three Engines tested were, No. 1300, Four-Cylinder Compound; No. 292, Four-Cylinder Combined Compound or Simple; and No. 294, Two-Cylinder Simple. No. 1300 was designed and built by the Vulcan Foundry Co., Newton-le-Willows; in general arrangement and dimensions it resembles the Four-Cylinder Compounds of the Northern Railway of France. Nos. 292 and 294 were designed by the author and built at Doncaster. The leading dimensions and ratios of the Engines are given in Table 1.

The trials from London to Doncaster were so arranged that each driver and fireman, of three sets of men selected, should run each engine for three weeks with the same group of trains (mostly express) in regular rotation. By this means it was intended that each driver should make the same number of trips with each engine on each train; thereby eliminating the personal equation and equalizing all conditions as far as possible. The drivers and firemen took great interest in the trials, and, as an additional stimulant for them to make each engine show to the best advantage, prizes were arranged *based on the aggregate performance of the men*, and not on that of any engine. The men ran each of the engines for one week prior to commencing each three-weeks' trial, in order to get thoroughly familiar with them.

The engines were put into the same condition of repair before the trials, and were treated in the same way throughout, and were supplied with the same quality of coal, namely, Yorkshire from the Barnsley bed. Careful account was taken of coal and oil used, time lost or made up, state of weather, weight and composition of trains, and cost of running repairs. An inspector rode with each engine during the trials. The results are shown in Table 2.

G.N.R. 1906 TRIALS—TABLE 1

Dimensions		*Engine No. 1300*	*Engine No. 292*	*Engine No. 294*
Makers		Vulcan Co.	G.N.R.	G.N.R.
Date first into Service.. ..		July 1905	March 1905	May 1905
Weight in working order ..	lb.	159,040	153,440	152,990
Weight on drivers	lb.	82,880	80,640	80,640
Tractive effort	lb.	14,869	8,994	16,875
Tractive effort No. 292 working simple	lb.	—	20,070	—
Cylinders		4	4	2
Type		Compound	Comp. or Simp.	Simple
Diameter and Stroke, H.P. ..	ins.	14 × 26	13 × 20	18¾ × 24
Diameter and Stroke, L.P. ..	ins.	23 × 26	16 × 26	—
Maximum valve travel ..	ins.	5⅜	4⅜	4⅛
Driving wheels diameter ..	ins.	80	80	80
Working pressure	psi	200	200	200
Heating surface ..	total sq. ft.	2514	2500	2500
Grate area	sq. ft.	31	31	31
Ratios:				
Cylinders		1:2.7	1:2.0	—
Weight on drivers ÷ Tractive effort		5.5	9.0	4.8
Weight on drivers ÷ Tractive effort, No. 292, as Simple		—	4.0	—
Tube heating surface ÷ Fire-box heating surface ..		13.8	16.7	16.7
Volume of cylinders in cubic feet		17.1	9.1	7.7
Total heating surface ÷ Volume of cylinders ..		146	274	326
Grate area ÷ Volume of cylinders		1.8	3.4	4.0

It will be seen that the standard simple Atlantic won by a very small margin. Or, as had been said before, it was " no better and no worse! " Ivatt chuckled to himself and wondered how much he ought to worry about improving 251 and her sisters. After all, the Vulcan engine incorporated the very latest French practice including a longer valve travel. One can imagine informal discussions on the subject after Council meetings of the Institution of Mechanical Engineers—S. W. Johnson was still on the Council as a past President, Aspinall was a Vice-President, and George Whale and G. J. Churchward were also members of Council.

The traffic department of the G.N.R. rightly looked further than its main line passenger and freight services, and one such look embraced the 14-mile Louth–Grimsby line. This had four intermediate stations, and

TABLE 2

Results of Trials		*Engine No. 1300*	*Engine No. 292*	*Engine No. 294*
Miles run, Engine		11,286	11,670	11,673
Speed, Average miles per hour		49.02	49.9	49.58
Weight of train, average tons		229.98	238.03	234.29
Total train ton miles		2,540,130	2,717,112.5	2,674,420
Coal used (includes lighting-up)				
Per engine-mile	lb.	44.86	43.02	44.31
Oil used				
Per 100 engine-miles	pints	7.34	7.18	6.22
Cost per engine-mile				
Coal	pence	2.4	2.3	2.37
Oil	pence	0.165	0.16	0.14
Repairs	pence	0.56	0.45	0.37
Total cost per engine-mile	pence	3.125	2.91	2.88
Total cost per ton-mile	pence	0.0092	0.0085	0.0085

in the rail-car boom period of 1905 six additional halts were built and a rail-car service planned. Ivatt designed a little steam rail-car, the coach of which was one of the first jobs of his new Carriage side assistant, H. N. Gresley. The engine had 9½ sq. ft. grate area, 175 psi boiler pressure, 3 ft. 8 in. wheels, and 10 in. by 16 in. outside cylinders with Walschaert's gear, giving a tractive effort of about 5,400 lb. The coach seated 53 passengers. It had first been proposed to order these rail-cars on outside builders, but Ivatt reported he could save £1,000 by building the first two at Doncaster. Ivatt was having to account carefully for any moneys required, to get sanction from first the Loco Committee and then the Board. Sanctions in 1905 ranged from a modest £250 for the first trial superheater from the American Locomotive Company to £37,680 for twelve coaches and six dining cars for the new Sheffield expresses.

The Works were pressing on with more large Atlantics, and all was well except for those wretched suburban trains, with which the various four-coupled engines were still struggling. Ivatt saw he must take some action, and felt that a move from his rebuilt Stirling 0-4-4s to a larger 0-6-2 might be the solution: one always wanted some reserve power. This was again brought home on the Grimsby line, where on market days and special occasions traffic demanded an extra coach to be tacked on, and this defeated the little rail-car engines. Vans and horse-boxes were also tacked on—operating afterthoughts, never mentioned when the rail-cars were first proposed, as Ivatt pointed out when challenged that he had not provided adequate power for the job.

A good example of ample provision for the job came up in Ivatt's three new trains for the Sheffield and Manchester services. Four seats only per first class compartment! Concealed electric lighting behind the cornices was a feature of the first class diners, and the Press was very favourable about the large windows. The coaches were all steel-framed, with six-wheel bogies, buck-eye couplings and elliptical roofs. Gresley delighted in these technical improvements and in the general elegance, and so did Ivatt, although he had already expressed concern at the extreme luxury then demanded, involving heavy construction and maintenance costs and far more tare weight per passenger: but these were the standards demanded. During construction the Board descended to inspect the new trains and in particular to decide upon the best of several different seats which Ivatt had contrived. After rigorous practical testing of these seats opinions became strongly divergent and the Chairman, who had had enough, wisely announced " We feel we had better leave it to you, Ivatt." As they withdrew, Ivatt, still tall and slender, eyed their variously portly frames and remarked *sotto voce* to Wigram " It is a good thing we do not have to fit their fronts also."

Wintour, as chief Assistant and Works Manager, and with great first-hand experience of the suburban working, took a special interest in the proposed 0-6-2 tanks. Ivatt chose a 5 ft. 8 in. wheel compared with 5 ft. 7 in. on his own 4-4-2s and on the very successful re-built Stirling 0-4-4s. He also retained the cylinder size of the latter, 18 in. by 26 in., a useful half-inch larger than the 4-4-2s. Haunted by maintenance costs he retained the boiler pressure of 175 psi, but he made a decided increase in grate area to $20\frac{3}{4}$ sq. ft., and in total heating surface to 1,250 sq. ft. At this period it was common for the Works to possess a great deal of unrecorded know-how. Clearances and tolerances were not usually shown on drawings—for example, the drawing would simply call for a 1 in. pin in a 1 in. hole. The works were also left a fairly free hand to arrange pipe-runs, the drawing following-up as a copy of the first engine. The mock-up element in this old procedure was wise. But of course when a drawing came back from the drawing office to the Works instructing them, in effect, to carry out their own proposals, they managed to take umbrage: and both sides were sometimes guilty of sabotaging communications.

The interests of the business in hand and the sirloin steak were joined by a third interest when Ivatt visited Kitsons in 1906—they were building five Atlantics for Marsh, identical to No. 251, save for their 26 in. stroke cylinders and external fittings and finishes. These duly did the Brighton run with considerable abandon, and Marsh was most careful to credit their design to Ivatt. Their success and the equal performances of the three Atlantics in Ivatt's comparative trial all redounded to the general glory of the standard G.N.R. large Atlantic, " 251 " class.

The three-month rest cure of 1904 had proved to Ivatt the necessity of applying adequate time to relaxation, and possibly the autumn of 1906 found him at his peak as an amateur magician. Using simple home-made apparatus, finished with exceptional craftsmanship, he presented a deadpan or slightly astonished air whilst things miraculously appeared or became substituted. The act normally included a horrible accident, apparently involving some relative's treasured pocket-watch. Ivatt was also mildly addicted to practical jokes: he had a masterly knack of so starting a champagne cork that it would blow out unexpectedly during the soup. His wife reacted with astonishment or horror as appropriate, expert through long experience. The day before their thirtieth wedding anniversary she was in good form, preparing things, particularly as her youngest daughter was rather starry-eyed about Oliver Bulleid and she approved—it was his 24th birthday. But at 11 p.m. the down mail crashed at Grantham, and in the early hours before dawn on 20th September 1906 Ivatt stepped off a special train into the forlorn drizzle to examine the engine. It was No. 276, a large Atlantic built in 1904, lying on its side without its tender. The brake was on, the blower partly open, the regulator closed; indicating, as far as damage would allow, a correct though late brake application. On re-railing the engine the brakes were found still to be in working order, and Ivatt was at least spared the anxiety that some engine defect might have contributed to the accident. He always thought there was insufficient evidence to speculate on the cause of this accident, in which the death roll included both the driver and the fireman, young Talbot, who had been one of his premium apprentices at Doncaster.

Films, plays, novels and TV with home-spun wisdom always appeal: Jerome K. Jerome did it in palatable disguise and so did Charles DeLano Hine in *Letters from an old Railway Official* published in 1904. Ivatt found this book delightful, and marked several passages in his copy including:

> " The temptation of a legislator is to make too many laws; of a doctor, to prescribe too much medicine; of an old man, to give too much advice."

And again:

> " The greatest of executives are those who can make men think for themselves, who can work men and have them believe they are playing, who can suggest a new thought to a man and leave him with the idea that he originated it himself."

Every executive must know these: Ivatt observed them.

They involve spade-work. Ivatt did lots during 1907; he got Gresley's new coaching stock accepted as the new standard for the East Coast Joint Stock; he persuaded the Loco Committee to make proper provision by amortisation for keeping tools and machinery in the Works up-to-date; and he persuaded the Board to step up the building programme at Doncaster from 35 to 45 new engines a year.

This was the busiest period of the Crimpsall. With passenger trains established at their heavier loads, almost all the " singles " had been scrapped except those rebuilt with larger boilers and the few built by Ivatt: even these were being relegated to softer duties as the stud of Atlantics increased yearly. And then there appeared from Doncaster

Works another shape, which was to become inseparable from King's Cross suburban working for over fifty years—the first 0-6-2 tank. It certainly looked, and proved to be, a great deal beefier than the 0-4-4s and the 4-4-2s. Ivatt still didn't like this comparatively high-speed large-wheeled engine having no leading truck or bogie, and he devoted

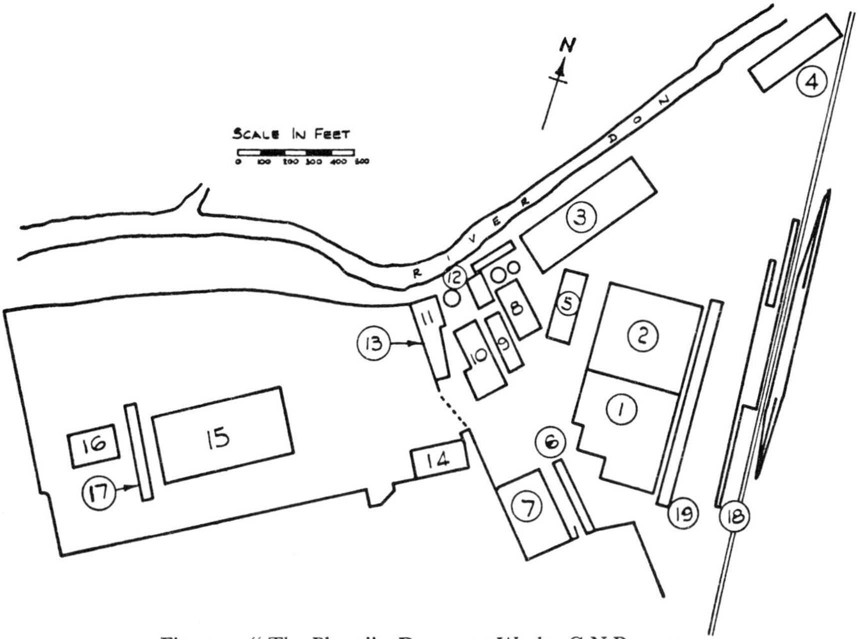

Fig. 12. "The Plant"—Doncaster Works, G.N.R., 1905.

1 Loco shops.
2 Carriage shops.
3 Carriage shops.
4 Carriage shed.
5 Timber drying shed.
6 Joinery.
7 Stores.
8 Erecting shop.
9 Forge
10 Boiler shop.
11 Iron foundry.
12 Gas works.
13 Works boundary until 1900.
14 Paint shop.
15 Erecting and repair shop—The Crimpsall.
16 Tender shop.
17 Electric traverser.
18 S. end, Doncaster Station.
19 Offices.

further drawing office time to attempts at a suitable 2-6-2 design. Wintour took a real paternal pride in the 0-6-2, and thought it could not be improved. "That's what I call a good engine," he once confided to Ivatt, and spoilt the effect by adding "No drawing office nonsense about it."

The longer wheel-base of a tank compared with a tender engine inevitably causes difficulty: for example, flange wear is affected by both the wheel-base and the amount of guiding permitted by leading and trailing bogies or trucks. With every sign of the 0-6-2 tank proving a success and the continuous double cry in the background from the traffic people for 0-6-0s and for a mixed traffic engine, Ivatt turned out a medium-sized 0-6-0 in 1908. With the same 5 ft. 8 in. wheels and 18 in. by 26 in. cylinders as the 0-6-2 tanks, they had slightly smaller boilers but turned out to be the type of engine " beloved of operating departments."

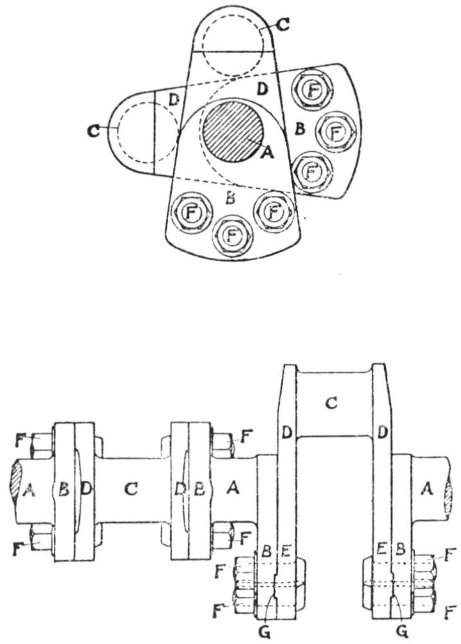

Fig. 13. Ivatt's patented built-up crank axle, 1908. Each section of the crank shaft A has an extended cheek B mating with the crank C by the extended crank arms D, E. Bolts F secure the sections in position, as located by keys G.

Paradoxically, the Atlantics with their outside cylinders threw into sharp relief the perpetual troubles from crank axles—particularly on larger, heavier, and faster locomotives. Apart from the stresses due to their function, crank axles have to stand blows of considerable magnitude and undesirable direction when inequalities in the rail place a guiding load on the flange. Creeping cracks result, starting from flaws or stress-raising corners or even from rough machining. Ivatt had become more alive to this by continued observation since the days of the Inchicore fatique experiment: and as a good engineer he noted the force-resisting techniques in nature—ranging from massive rock through deep-rooted oak to flexible reed. " We must try the reed-in-the-wind rather than the oak-in-the-storm," he said, when he developed two types of built-up crank axles which allowed axial flexibility whilst preserving torsional stiffness. The design also allowed some internal balancing and reduced maintenance costs.

Sometimes there were distinct clashes of opinion at A.R.L.E. meetings. T. Hurry Riches remarked that he had been trying spark arresters for about 30 years, and he had never found one worth being put in an engine. J. Holden said that all Great Eastern engines had been fitted with spark arresters, and that they had been most effective. Ivatt said nothing at the time; but at the next meeting, in November 1908, he took the Chair as President. Mellow, 57, and not averse to leg-pulling, he started by looking innocently around and asking, "Will members, when they have anything particular to say, please speak one at a time and thus give all a chance of hearing." The inflexion of the voice can make these suggestions extremely telling. Ivatt added that much of what was said by the older members was of great use to the younger members, and moved briskly on to the first item of business—choice of venue for the summer meeting. The younger members probably grasped the point he was making—the various reactions of a group of experts assist the individual expert in his own task and decisions. Ivatt also used, and advised using, ratios to help in weighing up situations. He used them freely in arriving at design fixes and in comparing his engines with those of other designers. He also used them as ammunition in, for example, a successful attack on the Traffic Department for excessive shunting by quoting trends in the ratio shunting mileage to total engine mileage.

Ivatt spent a lot of time on detail design improvements, and initialled most new loco drawings. Further thoughts about the compounds, and discussions with Worsdell and Hughes made him wonder if he had provided large enough low-pressure cylinders on 292, and he set out another engine with the low-pressure cylinders increased from 16 in. to 18 in. This appeared as No. 1421 in 1909, by which time there were eighty large simple Atlantics, in addition to the three compounds. No. 1421 did seem to have a little something extra, but not such as to justify the extra first cost and maintenance, Ivatt decided once again.

The year 1908 was notable for a distinct advance in the application of superheating. The theoretical advantages were perfectly clear, the lubrication problems though serious were known to be tractable if care was exercised, and from numerous experimental shapes the Schmidt superheater was emerging as an eminently practicable proposition. The £50 royalty per engine was infuriating to all Loco Engineers but, reflected Ivatt, let us find out if it does all it claims before worrying too much about the cost of extending its application. Accordingly he had one of the 0-8-0 "Long Toms" fitted; it was successful beyond doubt, and so he proceeded to build five new superheated 0-8-0s in 1909. Because his overriding objective was to reduce operating and maintenance costs, the performance of the engines already being fully adequate, he reduced the boiler pressure from 175 to 160 psi and restored the tractive effort by increasing the cylinder diameter from 20 to 21 in. Ivatt similarly superheated one of the small Atlantics in 1908, and achieved similar success. Wintour spoke for him at the discussion on George Hughes' paper, "Compounding and Superheating," in March 1910: after saying the G.N.R. experience was limited to seven engines but 10 large Atlantics were now being built with Schmidt superheaters, Wintour added, "As Mr. Churchward has stated, it is absolutely necessary there shall be some check on the lubrication which, if it once gets slack, will cause a great smash on the engine. In one case where the lubrication failed, the piston and the cylinder were quite broken up, and we find it very necessary to have a reliable lubricator and a good cylinder oil, with steam superheated to 650°F. If these precautions are not taken, more cost may be incurred in five minutes than will be saved in two years."

Like many others, Ivatt patented an arrangement of steam pipes in the smokebox, to provide a low degree of superheat in older engines where new tubeplates were hard to justify: but their complication militated against their advantage—they were mounted on trunnions to permit swinging them clear for tube-cleaning.

The last new Ivatt engine was a superheated version of his 0-6-0 with 5 ft. 2 in. wheels: again he went for the economies of a lower boiler pressure and larger cylinders than on the previous, saturated engines of the same type. These engines appeared in 1911, when Ivatt was mopping up before retirement. He had long publicized his intention to retire at age 60, holding this as a goal in civilized living. He wanted a real break from job pressures: so much so that when the Council appointed him in his absence a Vice-President of the Institution of Mechanical Engineers in October 1910 he declined the appointment. He kept up minor improvements in his Department, adding a Mutual Improvement Class room and a Stores extension to Doncaster running shed in June 1911. He retired at the end of September, but stayed on till the year end, to help Gresley in taking over: the time was spent largely in discussions with Gresley, punctuated by leave-taking parties at a number of places, and presentations. Ivatt was probably the most affectionately regarded of all the illustrious C.M.Es.

With a pleasant house and grounds at St. Clair, Haywards Heath, and with hobbies stretching wisely from craft work to revisiting old friends in London and beyond, Ivatt enjoyed a text-book retirement. From his workshop emerged numerous delightful items in wood, including a yo-yo and a casket with little radial plungers locking the lid to the body: it could only be unscrewed after twirling the box to disengage the plungers. He was approached again and duly elected a Vice-President of the Institution of Mechanical Engineers in 1922: but his health failed a year later and he died in October 1923.

The large Ivatt Atlantic is an admirable illustration of a first-class basic design permitting the successful exploitation of subsequent technical improvements. Ivatt himself had been able to reduce the boiler pressure with his first application of a superheater: in due course Gresley restored the pressure and brought up the superheaters to a nicely-chosen optimum. The engines then put up a number of positively heroic performances—writing and re-writing an exciting epitaph to their designer. A feat of L.N.E.R. No. 4404 in 1936 might have been discredited had not Fate placed on the train a reliable recorder in the person of Cecil J. Allen.

It was the 1.20 p.m. King's Cross–Edinburgh, with 17 coaches = 585 tons, whose " A3 " Pacific ran hot at Grantham, so that No. 4404 was substituted at a moment's notice. The Gateshead crew, driver Walker and fireman Barrick, cheerfully set out to see whether they could *recover* any of the time lost: having to set back twice to get the huge train started, they lost a couple of minutes over the fifteen miles to Newark, but gained a minute to Retford and another three minutes to Doncaster. The first 68 miles were covered in 68 minutes, and Allen had to look out of the window at the Selby curves to convince himself that No. 4404 was unaided and that the huge train was still intact! York was reached 2½ minutes ahead of the normal Pacific schedule. When Allen went along to applaud the performance, Walker merely remarked " Grand engines, these."

CHAPTER 2

H. N. Gresley's follow-through to the L.N.E.R.

The Reverend Sir William Nigel Gresley was the ninth holder of a hereditary baronetcy conferred in 1611. One of his sons in turn entered the Church and became rector of Netherseale, Derbyshire. His fifth child, Herbert Nigel Gresley, was born in Edinburgh on 19th June 1876.

Younger sons of rectors solved a grave parental problem by indicating what they wanted to do when grown up, and young Gresley did this by showing a consistent interest in railway engineering whilst at Marlborough College. You had to live very close to Derby not to be influenced by the tremendous Crewe reputation in the 1890s; and it was natural and expected when Gresley started as a premium pupil at Crewe under Webb in June 1893.

A boy with an enquiring mind must have been impressed, and rightly, with some of the current ideas and action at Crewe. In April 1893 Webb had made his 2-2-2-2 express compound *Greater Britain* work trains from Euston to Carlisle and back daily for a week, covering 3,600 miles in a well-publicized reliability trial. The second engine of the class, *Queen Empress,* was displayed at the Chicago Exhibition in the autumn of 1893. These 52-ton engines with their 25-ton tenders were impressively large and long: their boilers had an intermediate combustion chamber about a third of the way between firebox and smokebox. For the Diamond Jubilee these two engines were respectively painted bright red and pale cream. The red caused *Greater Britain,* which had a very fair turn of speed, to be called *The Scarlet Runner.* Gresley laughed at this rather typical joke, which might equally well have come from Marlborough or Crewe. Equally typical were many verses of The Crewe Song, composed for and sung at the February 1894 Crewe Dinner: the seventh verse went to the tune of " In the Gloaming,"

> In the firebox, Oh! my foreman,
> You may look in vain for me,
> For I am inside the boiler,
> And my feet you cannot see.
> T'will be best to leave me there, sir,
> Best for you and best for me.

Gresley was a careful and thorough, if rather ponderous, apprentice. He had the usual inauguration in the bolt shop, and did not suffer the tribulations outlined in another verse of the Crewe Song, which went to the tune of " A Miner's Dream of Home,"

When first in the bolt shop I worked on a lathe,
I spoilt about six bolts or more,
And just as I was trying to smuggle them away,
The foreman walked in at the door.

Then he quietly gazed upon them,
And turned round and asked me for my check.
I said to my mate, " He has sent me home "
And he murmured, " Oh, bleeding Hec."

From a Works slant, Gresley also saw some remarkable and rather exotic experiments, including a triple-expansion engine, a figure-8 firebox, and a steam-controlled friction-wheel to link the engine driving-wheels instead of coupling rods: all failed; the first departing with the nick-name Ichabod, and the last emitting a shower of sparks. But Crewe Works techniques were notably advancing, and to complete his grasp of them Gresley spent nearly a further year in the fitting and erecting shops as an Improver.

It may well have been young Gresley's first important moment of perception, when he realized that Crewe drawing office lacked the progressive flair of the Works; so he entered the L & Y drawing office at Horwich as a pupil of Aspinall in 1898. Just as he had seen larger boilers taking shape in Crewe Works, so he found Aspinall and the Horwich drawing office involved with the larger boiler for their Atlantic. These engines also had swing-link bogies, and a low-degree superheater in the smokebox.

After a spell of looking after the Materials Test Room at Horwich, Gresley was sent to Blackpool as Running Shed Foreman: energetic, twenty-four, and busy in the summer of 1900—but not busy enough to prevent him becoming engaged to Miss Ethel Fullagar of St. Annes-on-Sea. They married in 1901, just as Gresley was appointed Assistant Manager of the Carriage and Wagon Works at Newton Heath. Normal promotion opportunities were enchanced by Aspinall becoming General Manager of the L & Y and his successor, Hoy, soon leaving to join Beyer, Peacock. The nett result was that in 1904 George Hughes became C.M.E. and Gresley became Assistant Superintendent of the Carriage and Wagon Department. At this point he could well be pleased with his experience and progress: aged twenty-eight, with deep and detailed knowledge gained by hard work on the loco, carriage and wagon, and running aspects of two leading railways, well-connected and well-married, personality developing strongly, and master of a comparatively senior job. But he had a second important moment of perception, when he realized that further promotion was baulked by young seniors and that, in particular, the departmental head, Hughes, was not due to retire for twenty years. He wanted further promotion, and to a railway with an older C.M.E.

It came barely a year later, in March 1905, when H. A. Ivatt appointed him, at age 29, Carriage and Wagon Superintendent of the Great Northern Railway at Doncaster. Ivatt's recognition of his potential, and Gresley's insistence on his place in the hierarchy, are both illustrated in Ivatt's formal report on the appointment—" Salary £750, not to be considered final if his work justifies more; and he shall not be subordinate to anyone at Doncaster except the Locomotive Superintendent."

Though Ivatt must have found Gresley cocksure and pushing, and though Gresley must have found Ivatt cautious and slow, they soon generated considerable mutual respect. Their paths did not cross as much as on some railways, because traditionally the G.N.R. Carriage man had practically a free hand in design, which was done in the shops supported by a small shop drawing office. Gresley's predecessor, Howlden, had worked in this way with conspicuous success, the clerestory-roofed East Coast Joint Stock carriages being one of his notable designs. Corridor carriages of this type were being turned out at the time Gresley took over.

The steam rail-car boom had hit the G.N.R. just before Gresley's arrival, and Ivatt soon called on him to design the coach. This he did in the form of a fifty-seater with elliptical roof: and the success of the roof in appearance, lightness, ease of manufacture and cost led to his adopting it when, early in 1906, he built a prototype bogie luggage van for the E.C.J.S. With its bowed ends, buck-eye couplings, all-steel underframe, and teak body it made important design advances, which Gresley incorporated again in a set of new carriage for the Manchester expresses. These also had electric lighting, and carriage warming apparatus taking low-pressure steam from the engine.

A natural result of this progress was the selection of Gresley's exterior design as the standard for future E.C.J.S. carriages. On the wagon side there were also progressive ideas, including vacuum-braked bogie goods wagons and 50-ton well-wagons for girders: these got due publicity in the technical press.

When Ivatt visited his Carriage side he greatly liked these improvements, but he did not altogether like the state of the shops, which tended to have piles of dubious material in the corners, rather reminding him of Inchicore and Horwich, neither of which were noted for their tidiness. So, as they walked through the shop, he asked casually, " Gresley, do you know why God made the world round? " Already better at asking such questions than answering them, Gresley admitted that he did not. " Well," said Ivatt, " It was so that there wouldn't be all sorts of odd corners." Nothing more was said at the time, but it was characteristic of Gresley that he took the hint and thereafter the shops became and remained subject to the inestimable discipline of tidiness.

1907 saw the introduction of what became a Gresley speciality—articulated carriages. He took his first step by mounting pairs of non-bogie Howlden coaches, notorious rough-riders, on three bogies: the one between the coaches was designed with three bolsters to provide pivoting and bearing surfaces. Several such pairs were re-built from the older coaches, whilst at the same time new conventional 4-wheel and 6-wheel bogie coaches were being turned out, including a set of six to make up a new train for the 5.30 King's Cross to Newcastle. Gresley maintained an intense interest in every new carriage and, his mind trained by studious note-taking during pupil days and catalysed by sheer interest, he remembered for years afterwards the numbers and peculiarities and construction dates of every coach he built.

Among technical improvements came the Spencer Moulton double-bolster bogie with pressed steel frame and rubber buffing springs. After successful trials, Gresley adopted it as standard for the G.N.R. This decisive action epitomizes the Gresley approach, learned by having got around and applied by moral courage, of basing your designs upon a synthesis of the best techniques available at the time. The circumstances of the 1910s were entirely different from those of the 1960s in that industry, particularly the railways, had virtually no middle-level technical staff: the Chief personally met suppliers and discussed such technicalities as bogies, forgings, steel specs. Unlike Churchward, Gresley regarded these external contacts as more important than internal technical advances, and this in turn made him increasingly approachable by and sympathetic to his opposite numbers, but rather distant and autocratic to his own staff: deep down, he felt it unlikely that they could think out anything better than he could. Against this he was, of course, an excellent leader and decision-taker, and his staff enjoyed the satisfactions of success. So, with mainly estimable qualities, a successful record, a powerful personality, and well spoken of in circles concentric with the G.N.R. Board, it came as an easy decision to appoint him, despite his meagre 35 years, to succeed H. A. Ivatt as Locomotive, Carriage and Wagon Superintendent, on 1st October 1911.

Ivatt agreed to stay on until the end of 1911 to assist the take-over, and Gresley was wise enough to take the fullest advantage of this, whilst keeping an eye on the carriage side and getting closer to Wintour, the Loco Works Manager and Webster, the Running Superintendent, both of whom felt they had prior claims to be the new Chief. Ivatt still found Gresley rather over-confident, and Gresley still found Ivatt rather slow and cautious: but they were technically *en rapport*, as they discussed locomotive design trends; room for improvement in the large Atlantics with better superheaters and piston valves; logical extension from 4-4-2 to 4-6-2 when necessary, and hopes of doing it better than Churchward's recent *Great Bear*; two of Ivatt's convictions, the undoubted advantages of big boilers and the wide firebox, and " Don't go to three or four cylinders if two will do the job." They discussed Ivatt's patents for improved crank axles, and agreed the advantages of outside cylinders driving the coupling rods almost directly: and they debated Ivatt's mixed-traffic 0-6-0 against Churchward's new 2-6-0, both having 5 ft. 8 in. wheels. Ivatt introduced Gresley to important suppliers and attended the A.R.L.E. dinner after Gresley's first attendance; the two other new boys were Maunsell, and Vincent Raven—Gresley's North-Eastern opposite number.

So Gresley settled in with expected efficiency as 1911 drew to a close, and the only problem was to secure for himself a really top class technical personal assistant. At this point O. V. Bulleid, a well-qualified G.N.R. man, applied to re-join the Company after a spell abroad, and the problem was solved.

Though Gresley had had no connection with the running side since his spell at Blackpool, he now found himself in full charge—and at a time when the one-man-one-engine tradition was having to give way to a more productive use of both men and engines. Pushing Webster, who was no lover of change, he got the rosters re-arranged throughout the system, thereby incidentally getting to know the District staff. This sharpened his realization that his first locomotive design work would have to be directed to the mixed traffic and the freight side, where traffic demands were as usual on the increase.

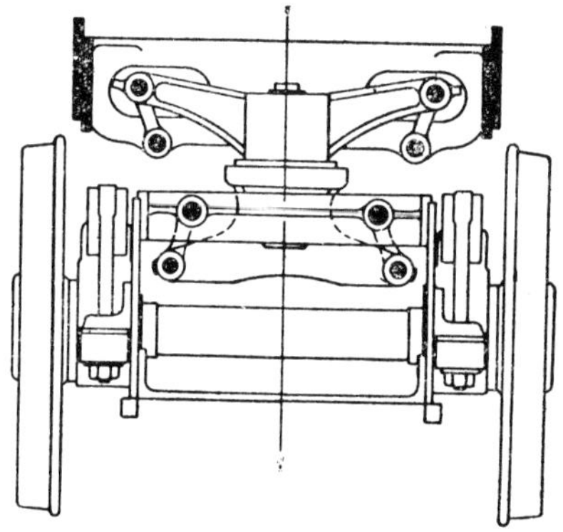

Fig. 14. Gresley's double swing-link pony truck, patented in 1912.

There was no dramatic call for new engines; at his first few attendances at Loco Committee meetings he was mainly concerned in coping with routine requirements—machine tools, improvements to Works services, additional Running Shed facilities, Staff matters, and the usual comparative cost statements. Then came an authorization for what Gresley referred to as an express goods engine, for which he visualized a modern version of Ivatt's 6-coupled engine with 5 ft. 8 in. wheels.

It was a brisk performance, showing Wintour and Doncaster plant works at their best, to get out the first new Gresley design, 2-6-0 No. 1630, by the late summer of 1912. As will be seen from the table of leading dimensions on p. 52 this engine marked a definite step forward in superheating and piston valve developments, and it had a "modern" look, with its outside Walschaert's valve gear and 4 ft. 8 in. diameter boiler. Design points of note were the valve travel, $5\frac{3}{8}$ in., and Gresley's patented swing-link pony truck. No. 1630 was a distinct size larger than Ivatt's mixed traffic 0-6-0s of 1908.

Meanwhile there was a demand for a freight engine one size larger than Ivatt's "Long Tom," and Gresley met this late in 1913 with a 2-8-0,

No. 456. Dimensions are given on p. 52. These engines had the sloping external steam pipes to the steam chests, a feature that gave the engines one detail of characteristically Gresley appearance. They clanked, particularly when coasting, on account of the coupling rods touching the wheel centres, and thereby evoked their name of "Tangoes."

"Remember," Ivatt had said late in 1911, "that you need several months trial of a new design before building a batch—don't let the General Manager or the Traffic people push you around." Gresley followed this advice, No. 1630 appearing well before the rest of a batch of ten, and No. 456 being later followed by a further four. Then Gresley built a second batch of the 2-6-0s, but with boilers 5 ft. 6 ins. diameter—the same as the 2-8-0s, and Ivatt's large Atlantics. This made a good engine excellent.

Though the cab layouts of these first Gresley engines were little changed from Ivatt layouts, Gresley started his admirable procedure of having the proposed arrangement mocked-up in wood, and getting some of the drivers to look it over and comment.

Gresley was also getting to grips with the costing arrangements at Doncaster—partly of necessity, because the G.N.R. Board was keenly cost-conscious and would not tolerate any "extravagant nonsense" from the new, young, Loco Superintendent. It may have been merely as an appropriate gesture to them that Gresley decided, in December 1912, to paint all goods and shunting engines dark grey instead of Great Northern Green, at an estimated annual saving of £1,000. He was a staunch believer in charging full on-costs when estimating for any jobs done in the Works. The A.R.L.E. in 1913 were faced with this problem for the new statutory form of Railway accounts, and Hill and Gresley proposed that full overheads should be charged for both capital work and renewals. Pettigrew (Furness Railway) thought the matter should be brought up at some other meeting and discussed in detail, instead of picking out one item only. Gresley remarked that they had all received the report, Mr. Hill had raised one question, and if there were any other points with which Mr. Pettigrew did not agree, it was for him to raise them at this meeting. The resolution was then put to the meeting and carried unanimously. This little incident is an admirable example of Gresley preventing a clear straight decision being put off by vague peripheral doubt: all executives, please copy.

Then came the 1914–18 war.

Too old for oversea drafting, and in any case too useful in his job, Gresley was very soon immersed in munition work at Doncaster, under conditions of considerable difficulty as he lost his staff to the Colours and had additional traffic to handle. But there were lulls, and some design work could proceed. War time traffic underlined the ever present hint that a larger express passenger engine was wanted, however valiant the Ivatt Atlantics. So a Pacific was got out, with four 15 by 26 cylinders, 5 ft. 6 in. diameter boiler, grate area 36 sq. ft., 2,500 sq. ft. heating surface plus 730 sq. ft. of superheater. The proposed cylinder arrangement and outside Walschaert's valve gear with rocking levers was given a try-out by so rebuilding one of the large Atlantics. This trial was rather inconclusive as the resulting engine was under-boilered—though with over 2 tons more tractive effort it was a good starter. Seeing no particular advantage in the 4-cylinder arrangement, then so fashionable, and remembering Ivatt's advice, Gresley became extremely interested in solving the problem of designing a 3-cylinder engine with two sets of valve gear. He could visualize clearly that two phased motions could be combined to give a third, similar motion, phased equally between them; but how to achieve a simple linkage to do it for a given cylinder layout? With one clue missing, but something good to be going on with, Gresley patented in 1915 two suitable linkages: the now well-known, simple two-to-one lever, applicable to three valves in the same horizontal plane; and a rocking-shaft analogue which would transmit the appropriate motion irrespective of valve plane.

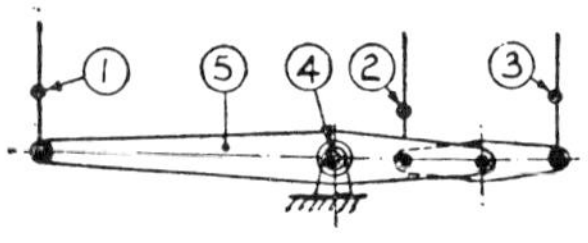

Fig. 15. Gresley's simple two-to-one lever. Items 1, 2 and 3 are the valve-spindle extensions; item 4 is the pivot for the two-to-one lever 5.

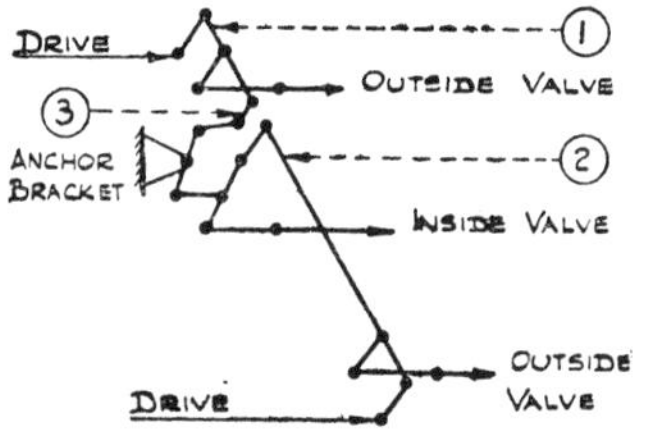

Fig. 16. Gresley's two-to-one rocking-shaft arrangement, as applied to his first 3-cylinder engine, No. 461. The rocking shafts 1 and 2 transmit the drive from the outside valve gear to the outside valves. Lever 3 is half the length of the other rocking shaft levers.

The latter arrangement appeared on the first Gresley 3-cylinder engine, No. 461, a 2-8-0, in May 1918. Details duly appeared in the technical press, and Gresley was not surprised at the considerable adverse criticism of the number of pin-joints involved in his first conjugate valve gear: as far as he was concerned there were two sprats in engine 461, and they caught two mackerels. First, the engine fulfilled his hopes of the advantages to be gained from a 3-cylinder engine. Secondly, Holcroft, holder of a 1909 conjugated valve-gear patent, wrote to him and the resulting collaboration gave Gresley the key to his future use of the simple two-to-one lever: it was only necessary to keep the three valves horizontal and displace the centre crank by an angle equal to the inclination of the inside cylinder. This cylinder had to be inclined to prevent fouling the leading coupled axle.

Back in 1917 the A.R.L.E. had appointed a committee under Churchward, on which the leading Loco Superintendents including Gresley served, to design standard locomotives for manufacture after the war. Gresley was a party to the outline design, but all the main design work was done by Maunsell and Fowler and completed in June 1918—details on p. 52.

When Gresley accepted an invitation to become the first Chairman of the new Leeds Branch of the Institution of Locomotive Engineers, he first had to join the Institution which he did by election in March 1918, and he then had to give his Chairman's address, which he did on 11th May. Offering some of his experiences on debatable points in locomotive design, he said:

On Boilers:

" The power of an engine depends upon its capacity for boiling water. The boiler is therefore without question its most important feature. A boiler which will supply steam when an engine is notched up to 20 per cent cut-off, and which fails to do so when the engine is let out on a long incline and has to work at 50 or 60 per cent cut-off, is too small for the cylinders on that particular work.

On fireboxes:

" The wide fireboxes of the 'Atlantic ' engines introduced by my predecessor, Mr. Ivatt, are more economical from the point of view of life, and I think also from the point of efficiency, than the narrow ones. Recently I had to condemn one of these large fireboxes which had run 420,000 miles. Although the first engine of this type was built sixteen years ago, none of the boilers have been scrapped. The work done by these engines is as heavy as that done by any passenger engines in the country, and the trains hauled by them often exceed 500 tons behind the tender. They have the biggest boilers and smallest tractive power of any working on the principal railways of this country.

On Belpaire boilers:

" In the case of almost every railway which has adopted the Belpaire box, the firebox roofs of their old round topped boilers were stayed by roof bars, which are well-known to be objectionable on account of the difficulty in keeping the firebox top free from dirt. Naturally, when they introduced Belpaire boxes with direct roof stays, many of the troubles disappeared, and the improvement was put down to the adoption of the Belpaire type boiler . . . I have come to the conclusion that, from a maintenance standpoint, the Belpaire boiler offers no advantage over the direct stayed round topped boiler, whilst undoubtedly its first cost is greater.

On the proposed standard locomotives:

" The present is, in my opinion, the most inopportune moment for the introduction of the standard engine. After three and a half years of the greatest war the world has ever known, we are hard put to it to carry on the railway transportation of the country. To add to the difficulties by the introduction of several new types of standard engines, having new standards for such parts as brake blocks, firebars, valves, piston rings, and a hundred others, which constantly require renewal, and of which stocks have to be kept in the various depots all over the country, would be the height of folly and could only result in disaster.

Replying to the vote of thanks:

"Colonel Kitson Clark, Mr. Stamer, and Gentlemen, I thank you very much for the way in which you have received my address. Several points were raised but, of course, the Chairman has the power of exercising his right of directing the proceedings of the meeting, and I am not going to be drawn into a discussion.

"There is just one point. It is in reference to an observation of my friend on the left (Stamer). He asks, 'Why not a wide firebox?' The answer is that we have not had an engine to build which was big enough. If, and when, it is necessary to build an engine of that type it will certainly be considered. I thank you very much for your attention."

LEADING DIMENSIONS OF
CHURCHWARD, GRESLEY, & A.R.L.E. 2-6-0s AND 2-8-0s

		Churchward 2-6-0	*Gresley* 2-6-0	*A.R.L.E.* 2-6-0	*A.R.L.E.* 2-8-0	*Churchward* 2-8-0	*Gresley* 2-8-0
	date	1911	1912	1918	1918	1903/5	1913
Boiler pressure	psi	200	180	180	180	225	180
Combined heating surface	sq. ft.	1479	1080	1568	1802	1842	2032
Superheater	sq. ft.	192	230	254	268	262	430
Grate area	sq. ft.	20.6	24.5	25	30	27.1	27.5
Wheel diameter	ft.-ins.	5-8	5-8	5-8	4-8	4-7½	4-8
Cylinder diameter × stroke	ins.	18½ × 30	20 × 26	20½ × 28	21½ × 28	18½ × 30	21 × 28
Piston valve diameter	ins.	10	10	10	10	10	10
Valve travel	ins.	6¼	5⅜	6¾	6¾	6¼	5⅜
lap	ins.	1⅝	1¼	1½	1½	1⅝	1¼
Total weight in working order, tons	engine	62	61¾	65	75	75½	76¼
	tender	40	43	44	44	40	43
Tractive effort	lb.	25,670	22,100	24,918	33,282	35,380	33,736

Gresley was clearly stung by Stamer into saying something on fireboxes, without giving away his previous and current "Pacific" thoughts. Equally, his dislike of the standard engines was clearly coloured by a fear that developments of his 3-cylinder 2-6-0s and 2-8-0s would be inhibited. A railway crawling with engines designed by others was not in the Gresley scheme of things: he had the clear ambition of designing the *best* engines.

In his year as Chairman of the Leeds Local Centre Gresley amply demonstrated his dislike of evasion. Once Pegler, the quite redoubtable Midland Railway District Loco Superintendent at Leeds, asked a question and added "There are several other points, but I did not get the paper in time to go thoroughly into the matter." Gresley: "We shall be glad to have the benefit of your experience, Mr. Pegler. There is such a thing as correspondence." But Pegler never wrote.

In July 1918, the end of the war in sight, Gresley promoted Wintour to Assistant Locomotive Engineer and Works Manager. His assets were twin: great ability as a Works Manager, and hailing from Horwich.

A month later Webster retired, and Gresley replaced him by promoting Groom, an experienced and co-operative running man and, incidentally, a scratch golfer. Both these moves potentially strengthened Gresley's position in any pending grouping or nationalization of railways. It was well into 1919 before war time distractions fell away and allowed real design effort to re-start. Gresley got Bulleid back as Personal Assistant in April, and they hotted up preparatory work on the 6 ft. diameter boiler, the nickel-chrome steel connecting and coupling rods, and the simple two-to-one conjugated valve gear. " And get the balancing worked out, the Drawing Office don't know how to do it properly," commanded Gresley—enthusiastic and unintentionally brusque.

	CONNECTING RODS			COUPLING RODS		
SECTION	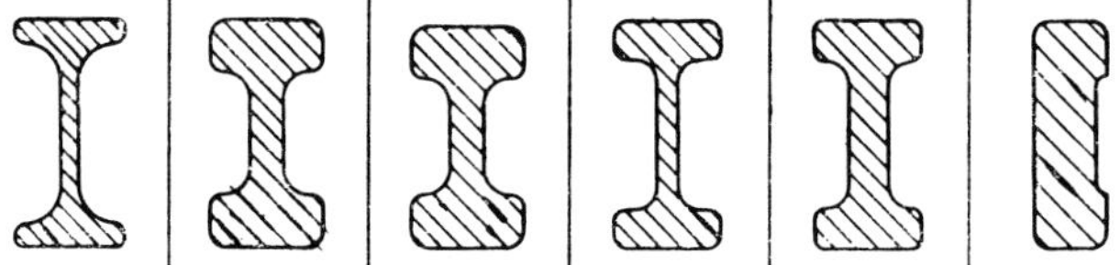					
OVERALL DIMENSIONS, INS	2½ x 5	2½ x 5	2½ x 4⅜	2⅜ x 5	2⅜ x 5	1⅜ x 5
ENGINE NO	1000	1640	251	1000	1640	251
TYPE	2-6-0	2-6-0	4-4-2	2-6-0	2-6-0	4-4-2
CYLINDERS	3	2	2	3	2	2
ROD LENGTH	8'-1"	8'-1"	10'-0"	8'-9"	9'-0"	6'-10"
ROD WEIGHT PER FOOT, LB	16 4	27 7	27 1	17 0	25 3	25 4

Fig. 17. Gresley's lighter rods for engine No. 1000, made possible by using nickel-chrome steel.

This work saw the light of day in March 1920 on 2-6-0 No. 1,000, and in 1921 on a batch of 2-8-0s built by North British. The success of these led Gresley to standardize on the simple version of his conjugated valve gear. Compared with the rocking-shaft arrangement it was delightfully simple. It literally delighted Gresley, and during its arduous conception he acquired a paternal blindness to its shortcomings. And when, as expected, the ever-growing traffic demanded an engine bigger than the " Atlantics," he naturally applied it to his first " Pacifics." Details, p. 68.

It is a measure of a good designer that he can improve upon what he's got as wholeheartedly as he can produce new pet designs. Gresley made giants of the large Atlantics by further increasing the superheaters. For the suburban services he was thwarted in a proposed 2-6-2, as Ivatt had been, so he set about the Ivatt class " N.1 " 0-6-2 design, and came up with the decidedly improved " N.2 " whilst retaining the 5 ft. 8 in. wheel size:

		Ivatt " N.1 " *0-6-2, 1907*	*Gresley " N.2 "* *0-6-2, 1919*
Boiler pressure	psi	170	170
Grate area	sq. ft.	20¾	19
Total heating surface	sq. ft.	1250	998
Superheater	sq. ft.	—	207
Cylinders	inches	18 × 26	19 × 26
Tractive effort	lb.	17,900	19,945

Rather unfortunately, Gresley lost his one assistant who brought out the whole truth, however unpalatable, when Bulleid took over the Carriage side late in 1920—he could not get really close to his other assistants. Still enraptured with his conjugated valve gear, he too lightly dismissed the snags. . . .

Overrun of the inside valve damaged the steam chest covers, so the pivot was strengthened; it was not realized that overrun was inherent in the design as soon as wear started. The geometry prevented the use of a piston valve larger than 8 in. diameter on the " Pacifics." Worse, far worse, the geometry made a short valve travel simpler and this unfortunate step was taken. The running sheds disliked having to dismantle the levers for valve maintenance, such as ring renewal; this disadvantage was probably raised by Groom and flattened by Gresley. And always there was the characteristic, slightly uneven beat, noisily proclaiming that the inside big-end was taking more than a third of the duty. Called in as an outside consultant to weigh this evidence, Gresley would certainly have voted for a third set of valve gear. But of course the valve gear was only one design feature: his new engines showed design advances superior to those seen on the other Railways, and the same could be said about his carriages.

So Gresley emerged powerfully from any assessment. His design work was among the very best. His stature was still growing and he was already an established figurehead. For his war work at Doncaster he had been awarded the C.B.E.

As the year 1922 unfolded, J. G. Robinson of the Great Central Railway was offered the job of C.M.E. of the L.N.E.R., but he was close to retirement, and declined. This merely brought forward the inevitable appointment to the post of Herbert Nigel Gresley.

Eleven Works and nearly 7,500 engines came under Gresley's control with the L.N.E.R., not to mention 21,000 carriages and vans, and over 300,000 wagons. He reported to Sir Ralph Wedgwood, ex-N.E.R., and covered the whole system, second only to the L.M.S. in size: all the other chief officers were appointed on a regional basis, reporting to their Area General Managers. He lost executive control of the Running Department: but he naturally obtained excellent collaboration from Groom. He had Wintour comfortably in charge at Doncaster and he appointed Stamer at Darlington to be his Principal Assistant. Most of the displaced C.M.Es. were near retirement. On the whole he was spared the worst difficulties that come from a grouping, though there was undoubtedly a hard core of older hands who would rather do something wrong than seek advice. They coloured his natural inclination to proceed mainly upon Great Northern lines.

It is sometimes forgotten, amid the sad retraction from the kaleidoscope of the pre-grouping railways, that grouping was done to try and make the railways pay. An already financially-embarrassed Company, awaiting take-over, does not rush out and spend all its spare cash on improving its plant and equipment: sure enough Gresley found at least part of his newly-acquired loco stock in a very run down condition, and in parallel Bulleid was finding the same about some of the coaching stock. So the first year or two after the Amalgamation found Gresley sometimes on tour but mainly at his King's Cross Office coping with his paperwork, whilst loco and carriage construction in the various works was proceeding on orders placed before he took over. He was happiest about Doncaster where Wintour was making hearty progress on the batch of ten " Pacifics " ordered by the G.N.R. after *Great Northern* had shown her paces, and on a batch of fifteen 3-cylinder class " O2 " 2-8-0s.

Gresley was meticulous about paperwork to an extent rather out of keeping with his character. The main part of the mail was placed on his desk each morning, fully supported by the file of previous papers on each subject. He methodically gave full attention to each letter or report and this system of working commonly kept him occupied most of the day. Correspondence relating to the Carriage side, Electrics, and Accounts, was passed respectively to Bulleid, Richards, and Rogerson: they brought in for discussion anything of a major or particularly interesting nature. A large quantity of drawings came in for approval, and Gresley personally approved the majority of those dealing with engines. He never objected to a decision being taken and passed on in his absence, but sometimes the local chiefs demurred at receiving the resulting decision over any signature junior to Gresley's: at which he simultaneously felt how stupid they were being and how important he was—emotions which are common enough but should never be fostered by ponderous procedures.

Simultaneously the A.R.L.E. was suffering slightly from the effects of the Amalgamation, its membership comprising a collection of C.M.Es. and ex-C.M.Es. which from the new angle looked horribly heterogenous. George Hughes, always inclined to be mellow, could see nothing to worry about, but Gresley made a characteristic move to secure proper hierarchical order, in a letter dated 17th January 1923, which was read out at the meeting on 19th January:

" Dear Sir,

Meeting at St. Pancras Hotel
Jan. 19th, 1923.

Referring to your letter of the 13th inst. I am very sorry that I shall not be able to be present at the meeting on the 19th inst. particularly as the matter to be raised concerns the future of the Association and the amendment of the rules.

I have read through Mr. Hughes' suggestions, but I regret that I cannot agree to them. I much prefer the scheme which was outlined by Sir Vincent Raven at the last meeting under which the Chief Mechanical Engineers of the four Groups would have the final decision in all recommendations made by the Association after having the benefit of the recommendations of their principal Assistants, who would be members of the Association.

So far as I can understand from Mr. Hughes' recommendations all members would be in the same position, therefore the Chief Mechanical Engineer of a Group could be outvoted by his own Assistants.

Apparently under Rule 2 membership is to be thrown open not only to the Assistants of the Chief Mechnical Engineers, but to the Assistants of the Assistants, whoever these may be; also, as worded, Electrical Engineers, who are not under the Mechanical Engineers would qualify for membership.

With regard to Rules 3 and 4, we know how in the past the Institution has suffered from electing their Presidents according to seniority only, and if these rules were adopted it would be possible for the Chief Mechanical Engineer of a Group to be presided over at the meetings by one of his own junior Assistants.

If such a constitution as that suggested by Mr. Hughes were adopted I could not continue as a member of the Association.

Yours faithfully,

(Signed) H. N. Gresley."

These views prevailed. At the meeting on 11th October each C.M.E. listed those of his assistants whom he felt were eligible, and all were elected without comment. On Gresley's list were Stamer, Wintour, R. A. Thom (in charge at Gorton as Asst. C.M.E.) and C. W. L. Glaze (Works Manager, Stratford). Subsequently, T. Heywood was elected in April 1925 and Bulleid in October 1925.

Gresley was faced with considerable motive power shortages, which he met by some *ad hoc* cross-posting of engines and by placing orders for selected types, such as " Director " class 4-4-0s ex G.C.R. Of his own designs, further batches of " A.1 " Pacifics and " K.3 " 2-6-0s were built, some by outside contract. Some of the former were to take the Newcastle and Scottish expresses beyond York: they were fitted with Westinghouse brake equipment. Different enough to cause annoyance to North-Eastern drivers, to whom no attempt was made to " sell " them, they provoked complaints to which Gresley responded effectively but not brilliantly at a meeting in York.

In 1925 two new Gresley designs appeared, and both had about them a slight air of giving the Traffic people *more* power than they could exploit. One was the 2-8-8-2 6-cylinder " Garratt," based on the class " 0.2 " 2-8-0s. With a firebox having 56 sq. ft. of grate area, and tractive effort nearly 73,000 lb., it applied its own bulk of 178 tons to banking duties on Worsborough bank—3 miles at 1 in 40. The other was the first Mikado in this country—with the standard " A.1 " Pacific boiler applied to the

2-8-2 wheel arrangement, driving wheels 5 ft. 2 in. diameter and three cylinders 20 by 26. In addition the trailing wheels were driven by a booster, consisting of a 2-cylinder engine used at starting and to improve acceleration after checks. These engines more than met the culminating demand from the Operating Department, to haul trains of 100 wagons, i.e. 1,600 tons, between Peterborough and London: such trains proved an embarrassment, taking too long to marshall and divide.

A nostalgic haze drifted around Darlington in July 1925 with the exhibitions and procession for the centenary of the opening of the Stockton and Darlington Railway: many notable old engines paraded, and among the modern engines were the latest Gresley Pacific, a 2-6-0, a 2-8-0 and, of course, the 2-8-2 and the "Garratt." They quite well summarized the Gresley designs to date, and all sported their two-to-one valve gears.

Comparisons have to be close to be fully effective. At Darlington several notable engines from the other railways appeared; but it was at the British Empire Exhibition at Wembley in 1924 that considerable comment had resulted from Gresley's "A.1" Pacific *Flying Scotsman* and Collett's *Caerphilly Castle* being seen side-by-side. The point was that Gresley's engine weighed twelve tons more than Collett's; with tender it weighed twenty-two tons more, and was five feet longer; and it looked decidedly beefier. But its tractive effort was 29,800 lb. against *Caerphilly Castle's* 31,600. Gresley's reaction was that for the tractive effort comparison to be meaningful the boilers must be able fully to support the cylinders: and he simply could not believe that the Great Western boiler could raise steam at the rate his could. Yet he did not want to shut his eyes to realities: the Belpaire boiler might have something special, and he recollected Churchward's experimental work. Again, he would have to design a 4-6-0 for the old Great Eastern section in a year or two. Besides, other engineers must be making the comparisons he was making. And so, as often before, he approached the G.W.R., but this time for a full comparative exchange. On G.W.R. metals Pacific 4474 competed with *Caldicot Castle*, and on the L.N.E.R. *Pendennis Castle* competed with Pacific 2545—after the first choice had failed from a hot box.

The Great Western engines scored a triple first. They got away with less slipping, they maintained higher average speeds, and they used significantly less coal. Gresley's staff were horrified at the results, and it is an interesting aside to their loyalty that they reacted with various "explanations"; but Gresley was rightly pleased at his wisdom in arranging the trial and hastened to find how his engine could be improved. With his usual perception he also saw the immense value of a stationary locomotive testing plant.

Both Gresley and Ivatt had provided such large boilers that their engines could be worked with full regulator and late cut-off at comparatively high speeds, successfully enough to blind their eyes to the fact that the expansive properties of the steam were not being properly exploited. But one of the technical assistants, B. Spencer, looking with a new eye, did not like seeing Pacifics worked for long spells at late cut-offs, often with the regulator partly closed. He knew that the steam could be used more expansively by increasing the lap and the valve travel. Gresley had turned down this idea in 1924 but now accepted it for trial; the outside valves were given $1\frac{5}{8}$ lap, and the centre valve an additional 1/16th to make some compensation for overrun. Travel was increased from $4\frac{9}{16}$ to $5\frac{3}{4}$ in. The results converted Gresley, and his acknowledgment is on p. 132. As so often happens to a designer when he drops the last piece of the jig-saw neatly into place, the result was unexpectedly rewarding: coal and water consumption were down by over 25 per cent, and the class " A.1 " Pacific was transformed.

The summer meeting of the Institution of Mechanical Engineers was held at Newcastle-on-Tyne in July 1925. This meeting being on the home ground of the Institution's first President, and the already-eminent Gresley being in the same line of business and a Member of Council, he naturally presented the technical paper which opened the proceedings. He took as his subject " The Three-Cylinder High-Pressure Locomotive," and fell into the unexpected error of over-playing the case for the three-cylinder arrangement. After pointing out how his conjugated lever saved a set of valve-gear and thus removed the main objection to three cylinders, and supporting this by examples of similar gear used in Germany and the U.S.A., he went on to discuss and then summarize the advantages:

(1) Less coal consumption.
(2) Increased mileage between general repairs.
(3) Less tyre wear.
(4) Lighter reciprocating parts, consequently reduced hammer-blow.
(5) More uniform starting-effort.
(6) Lower permissible factor of adhesion.
(7) Earlier cut-off in full gear.

Of these, item (7) merely repeats item (1), and item (6) repeats item (5). Item (3) is a detail of item (2). Moreover, item (4) sins by omission: with four cylinders hammer-blow can be nil. Frankly the case for three cylinders is marginal, and Ivatt was probably right once and for all when he advised using the least number of cylinders that would do the duty. But when a leading designer overstates a marginal case it shows emotion at work—not necessarily a bad thing, so long as speaker and audience recognize it. Gresley, fresh from seeing a " Castle " walk away from a Pacific, could not resist a vague gesture of defiance in his penultimate paragraph:

" Undoubtedly a four-cylinder engine can be designed, the power of which will exceed that of a three-cylinder within the same gauge limits, but the construction of such an engine at the present moment would be premature, in the same way as the construction of three-cylinder locomotives nearly eighty years ago was unnecessary for the requirements of the times."

There was a lively discussion. Clayton, Maunsell's Assistant, said that the two-to-one lever had the inherent defect of lost motion, hence inadequate control: Gresley replied that the trouble had been overcome by the use of grease-packed ball-bearing joints. Beames challenged the statement that " With the present type of locomotive boiler it is neither practicable nor economical to make any considerable increase in boiler pressure." Sir Vincent Raven, President, who was in the chair, said " I always adhered to the Stephenson valve-gear, because I believe in simplicity. I used three sets of valve-gear, and if I went back to rail-work today, I should do the same again . . . I really think the distinct advantage of the three-cylinder engine for locomotive purposes has been proved." Holcroft's contribution to the two-to-one lever was also raised, but Gresley, out of character, dismissed it in a rather cavalier fashion.

A factor which may have contributed to Gresley's tendency to over-sell three-cylinder engines was the shrewd look permanently turned by the L.N.E.R. Board on loco costs. When further medium-sized 0-6-0s were needed in 1924 he came up with a three-cylinder 2-6-0 design having 5 ft. 2 in. wheels, 18 by 26 cylinders and the standard boiler from the " K.3 " 2-6-0s. Not surprisingly, authority for this rather extravagant design was withheld, and Gresley was forced to bring out an 0-6-0. Here he was making an error to be repeated in the fullness of time by Fowler, and Bulleid: it was H. G. Ivatt years later who at last demonstrated that a modern 0-6-0 was " Not on," by producing an advantageous 2-cylinder 2-6-0, whose accessibility and reduced maintenance amply justified the higher first cost. The Gresley 0-6-0s, class " J.38 " with 4 ft. 8 in. wheels, and " J.39 " with 5 ft. 2 in. wheels, had large boilers, Stephenson valve-gear with 1½ in. lap, 8 in. piston valves, and 20 by 26 cylinders—with the attendant maintenance trouble on the driving axleboxes. Design was done at Darlington, and many of the better North-Eastern Railway features were incorporated, including a cab to North-Eastern standards, which had long been cosier than those of the G.N.R. Austerity is a matter of fashion, and enginemen almost always preferred what they were used to: when Sir John Aspinall gave the Thomas Hawksley lecture to the Mechanicals in November 1925 he remarked, " I can well remember the time, about 1872, when Mr. Webb put the first cab on to a London and North-Western engine. As these cabs were added to other engines, much indignation was expressed by the drivers, who had from their daily exposure to the weather become very hardy, whereas when they worked on an engine with a cab they were kept much warmer while there, but were much more affected by the weather on account of the changes of temperature when they were off the engine." Wisely, Gresley let his cabs evolve gradually.

For 1926 and 1927 Gresley was elected President of the A.R.L.E., and his innovation, to crispen discussions, was to have short papers on each subject circulated before each meeting. Some were inconclusive, including that by Stamer on the Booster: but Gresley interestingly remarked that he had considered the question of fitting boosters to locomotive bogies. Thom launched a paper on comparative maintenance costs of boilers with 180 and 200 psi pressures; this again brought a discussion full of conflicting experiences, the only data given on a practical cost basis coming from Stanier, who said he had recorded 0·7d. per mile over the whole life of a large boiler, and 0·3d. per mile whilst it was comparatively new. He said that there was no appreciable maintenance cost difference between 200 and 225 psi boilers—just as Thom and Beames had found between 180 and 200. Fowler said that a great reduction in maintenance had been obtained when the pressure was dropped from 220 to 200 psi on the Compounds: but he hinted that excessive maintenance was due to the engines being worked hard by tough ex-L.N.W.R. drivers on the Birmingham 2-hour expresses. Gresley certainly obtained what he wanted from this discussion—the all clear for a move from 180 to 220 psi as required. But the effects of heavy working and of different sources of water were still in doubt, and discussing the matter again with Bulleid one afternoon, Gresley asked, "Thom said repair costs were less in the London area than Doncaster—how much less?" "I don't know," said Bulleid. "Oh, don't you," exclaimed Gresley, momentarily forgetting the query, "and you're the only assistant I've got who ever admits it."

The value of a stationary loco testing plant became clearer and clearer amid uncertainties about boiler pressure, valve travel, etc.; Gresley devoted his Presidential Address to the Institution of Locomotive Engineers in September 1927 to the need for such a plant which he suggested might be set up as a Government research establishment for the contractors as well as for the railways.

September 1927 also saw another new Gresley design emerge from Darlington works, the "D.49" "Shire" class 4-4-0 for light passenger working. With a 4-4-0 Gresley had to relinquish his tenet of not driving the leading coupled axle. This in turn permitted him to arrange the three cylinders in line above the bogie centre, and to place his two-to-one lever behind the cylinders where it enjoyed the double advantage of being unaffected by valve rod expansion and undisturbed during valve maintenance.

Gresley never lost his apprenticeship-acquired sketching skill, and when a new idea came to him he would sketch it out, roughly to scale, to satisfy himself whether or not it justified a more serious exploration. One such idea—whilst laying out the cylinders for the Shire class—a little more than a year after his pronouncement about limiting cylinders to three—was a 6 cylinder "uniflow" engine with three cylinders each side of the smokebox in V form. Drive was by bevel gears to the leading coupled axle, and it was here that difficulties arose which killed the scheme. It is rather curious that, having considered applying a booster to a bogie and a 3-cylinder engine through gearing, Gresley never integrated these ideas and tried his hand at the ideal of an engine with its boiler carried on two power bogies.

The good designer does some hard thinking when one adverse detail is found to have been spoiling his results. After the interchange of 1925 had shown up the deficiencies of short valve travel, Gresley revised and re-applied a basic design lesson—the tabulation of the data to make absolutely certain that everyone in the design team clearly understands the data and the target. This pin-pointed his boiler pressure as being below average, which now seemed slightly ludicrous when read against the title of his 1925 paper. So he fitted two Pacifics with 220 psi boilers, lined the cylinders of one only to retain the original tractive effort, and acquired enough comparative data to make his design fixes for the class " A.3 " Pacifics—cylinders 19 by 26, tractive effort 32,900 lb. compared with the 29,800 lb. of the class " A.1 " and boiler modifications to allow the higher pressure and more superheater area.

Meanwhile Gresley was well immersed in a major experimental venture, built round a Yarrow water-tube boiler, with working pressure 450 psi. Two high pressure cylinders 12 by 26 drove the leading coupled axle, and two low pressure cylinders 20 by 26 drove the middle axle. Two sets of Walschaert valve gear were used, the H.P. valves being operated by rocking shafts from the outside motion, with means for separately adjusting the cut-off to the H.P. cylinders. Two trailing axles were needed to carry the weight at the firebox end, and there were numerous refinements including heated air feed to the firebox. The height of the steam drum imposed a boiler casing of the " streamlined " type, left no room for a chimney, and enforced wind-tunnel work on deflector plates, in which Professor Dalby collaborated. In spite of persevering follow-up work, the 4-6-4, No. 10,000, used more coal and performed less effectively than a standard Pacific.

When it became urgent to provide a new 4-6-0 for the Eastern section in 1928, Gresley placed the design work and the construction of the first ten on the North British Locomotive Company. He gave general design directions, and of course standard parts had to be used and appearance had to conform. By allowing the inside cylinder to drive the leading coupled axle, it was again possible to place the two-for-one lever behind the cylinders.

Gresley's achievements on the L.N.E.R. loco side from taking over in February 1923 till the appearance of No. 10,000 in December 1929 were remarkable whether seen in isolation or in comparison with the achievements of the other Groups. Like most eminent men, he took trouble to secure adequate rest and recreation, and in the former he was helped by an ability to snatch a quarter or half-hour's sleep at any time, and awake feeling extraordinarily refreshed. For holiday he went shooting in Scotland every year for the full month from early-August. During these absences Bulleid signed all the accounts, and Gresley sometimes came back to London for a day or two and looked briefly in to settle any queries.

Rather in contrast to this planning of rest, Gresley shared with Bulleid a boyish delight in stepping on to a train just as the whistle blew. He would walk down the steps from his office at King's Cross to the over-bridge, get delayed by someone accosting him with a last-minute query, and step on board just in time. One day he reached the over-bridge only to see his Edinburgh train pulling away, and had to return to Bulleid's office, looking glum and crestfallen, to admit this gaffe. " What else can you expect, cutting it so fine " said Bulleid, rather maddeningly, from amid a pile of interesting drawings.

No similar risks were taken when they set off, with a party of British railroaders including Sir Henry Fowler, to attend the International Railway Congress at Madrid in May 1930. They had their own carriage throughout and took the journey very comfortably, sometimes stopping for an hotel meal. One can visualize the sprawl of hats, coats and cases strewn round the compartments. After a leisurely meal at Miranda de Ebro they strolled back to their comfortable disorder, and were astounded when Gresley asked the guard why their carriage had been changed. It reluctantly transpired that an axlebox had been running hot, the train had been re-marshalled with an identical coach, and the disarray of personal belongings had been scrupulously copied. But Gresley had noted the serial number.

The Congress resolved upon international collaboration on Locomotive Experimental Stations, and this was quoted in the Department of Scientific and Industrial Research report dated 27th June 1930. A committee of thirteen, including the four C.M.Es., had been set up in December 1928 after successful lobbying by Gresley: they recommended a stationary test plant costing £90,000, gave an outline design based on proposals by Gresley and Fowler, and found a suitable site near Crossgates Station on the Leeds–Selby line. But there were signs of a slump, and of course it was hopelessly out of character to push ahead with anything important and fundamental when time is on your side and labour is otherwise unemployed. Gresley kept plugging, and in July 1931 gave a paper on stationary testing plants and techniques to the Institution of Mechanical Engineers. Again technical response was good, financial response negligible.

No such frustrations faced Gresley as he tore through job after job with Bulleid on the L.N.E.R. carriage side. Besides, there was an inspiring mixture of the technical and the decorative, the latter helped by Gresley's friend, Sir Charles Allom. Stylish painted interiors were adopted for the new train, to inaugurate the non-stop *Flying Scotsman,* and both Gresley and Bulleid were equally pleased with the train, which took a lot of thought, and with the corridor in the tender, which permitted a change of engine crews. Painted interiors present hazards, however, and Bulleid nearly had a fit when a person sitting opposite struck a match on his new paintwork. He protested vigorously, and the person said what could he expect, if he failed to provide striking plates. Bulleid just had enough strength left to point out that it was a non-smoker. Similar trouble attended the new painted sleeping cars in 1930–31, but here Bulleid adroitly countered by reproducing the decor of Sir Charles Allom in rexine, after which his indignation at paint-scratching passengers subsided.

Buffet cars were introduced in 1932 for the Cambridge run, and there was a wave of technical improvement, from new ventilating systems to experimental light-alloy carriage construction. Gresley was also full of support for the gimmicks: radio was made available by earphones in July 1932, and there were hairdressing facilities and a cocktail bar. They looked a long way ahead on 1st February 1932 when a TV picture was received as far as Huntingdon on a King's Cross–Peterborough train. Fairly successful, but not much use, was the photo-electric device, novel in 1932, for switching on carriage lights when the train entered the dark of a tunnel. Gresley never lost his enthusiasm for innovations, and Bulleid would report, as of old, when there was anything new to be seen: when he and Newsome had finished one of the new sleepers incorporating all the latest gadgets including the trousers-on-top hanger, and he duly told Gresley the new sleeper was ready, Gresley simply said, " So you want me to come and see your new coat-hanger."

It was an interesting feature of the long Gresley–Bulleid collaboration that they never seemed either to get in each other's way or to duplicate effort: yet the collaboration was not limited to the carriage side. Bulleid put over some fundamental technical advances such as welding carriage frames, which needed Gresley's conversion and approval. He provided items which Gresley only indicated in outline, such as the larger hopper wagons and the 50-ton brick wagon—the latter they found pleasing as it taxed the efforts of the Traffic Department. Bulleid had also taken some design interest in the series of engines fitted by Gresley with poppet valves, but by 1931 they both felt that on balance they preferred conventional valve year. Gresley said, at Leeds in February 1931:

> " It is a fact that savings have been effected by the Caprotti gear on the L.N.E.R., but it was fitted on an engine which was previously very heavy on coal consumption. I do not think a similar economy can be effected on the performance of an engine fitted with modern long-travel valve gear."

All C.M.Es. suffer the annoyance of some designs never coming to fruition, and in Gresley's case this centred around tank engines. In addition to the 2-6-2 tank design of 1919 and a three-cylinder 0-8-0 tank of about the same period, a three-cylinder 2-6-4 was schemed in 1925, and a two-cylinder version for Southend in 1927. Then in 1930 a three-cylinder 2-8-2 was set out, to replace Ivatt's 0-8-2s on colliery working around Colwick. But they came to nought, and the first and only Gresley tank design appeared from Doncaster in October 1930, in the person of No. 2900, class " V.1. " This was for heavy suburban work around Edinburgh and Glasgow, and at last Gresley got his three-cylinder 2-6-2 arrangement, with 5ft. 8 in. wheels, and a tractive effort of 22,460 lb. compared with the 19,945 lb. of the 0-6-2s.

Another Scottish operating problem was presented by the ever-increasing weights of the Edinburgh–Aberdeen trains. On this difficult road, the Pacifics were rostered to take 480 tons without a pilot; but now came a request for a locomotive to haul 550 tons—and one might assume that, as soon as the engine was designed and construction put in hand, a reduction of the booked times would be nonchalantly proposed. Gresley was determined to provide adequate power, which would involve eight coupled wheels; and to remove elementary doubts he had one of his 1925 2-8-2 freight engines working a passenger train, and maintaining speeds up to 65 mph in spite of its 5 ft. 2 in. wheels. So with a 6 ft. 2 in. wheel it should be quite practicable to maintain 75 mph; and design work proceeded at Doncaster. Gresley regarded this design as a special challenge: it would be the first eight-coupled passenger engine in the country, and his own first major design after the unsuccessful 10,000. For the boiler he copied his own successful practice, extending the barrel diameter to 6 ft. 5 in., and using 220 psi pressure with a wide firebox having a grate area of 50 sq. ft. Three 21 by 26 in. cylinders, all driving the second coupled axle, gave him a tractive effort of 43,462 lb. The boiler size left no chimney headroom, and after wind tunnel experiments the boiler sheeting was carried forward and the smokebox top lowered so that the chimney front protruded about 2 ft. Gresley had a number of discussions with Chapelon and incorporated the double chimney and the large, carefully smoothed steam and exhaust passages that had been proved so successful in France. He also imported the wedge-shaped cab front, to throw the exhaust clear and improve visibility. The first of the new engines, *Cock o' the North*, was completed in May 1934, with Lentz rotary cam poppet valves. The second, *Earl Marischal*, had 9 in. piston valves operated by Walschaert–Gresley gear. Gresley's words of 1931 came back with a rush as the poppet valves gave trouble. Due to wear the continuously-variable cut-off had to be restricted by stepped cams to only six settings—12, 18, 25, 35, 45 and 75 per cent, which were too coarsely spaced in such a powerful engine. Again, the poppet valve arrangement necessitated excessive clearance volumes—up to 16 per cent for the inside cylinder compared with 7·8 per cent with piston-valves. However, these were coal-wasting rather than performance-wrecking disadvantages; and, heralded by the admirable sound of the Canadian Pacific whistle presented by the Romney, Hythe and Dymchurch Railway, *Cock o' the North*, could turn in an electrifying performance on a train longer than any platform. On a test run from King's Cross in June 1934 with 19 coaches and dynamometer car, total weight 650 tons, the average speed was 59·3 mph for the 11½ miles from Essendine to Stoke summit: the train went over the summit at 56½ mph with 30 per cent cut-off. This would have been 35 per cent cut-off and perhaps 60 mph after the cam modification, probably over-stretching the fireman but not the engine! On the short level stretch before Corby a drawbar-horsepower of 2,100 at 57½ mph was recorded. Luckily *Cock o' the North* performed equally and consistently well on the summer and autumn holiday traffic north of the border: and then proceeded, in December 1934, to Paris.

Following up the resolution of the 1930 Madrid Congress, Gresley had kept up his keen interest in stationary locomotive test plants, and he attended the opening ceremony of the plant at Vitry, near Paris, in September 1933. Now he had arranged for his new engine to be tested there, and in fact Bulleid ran the tests and stayed throughout. *Cock o' the North* was unhappily plagued by hot boxes, and gave its most exhilarating result on a run to Orleans when 2,800 draw-bar horsepower was developed. Paradoxically, this was the only engine Gresley ever tested on the stationary type of plant he so strongly advocated. He showed no great interest in the results and never followed up Bulleid's theory that the damper areas were inadequate. When four more engines of the " P.2 " class were built and *Cock o' the North* was converted to Walschaert–Gresley gear in 1936/7, the only changes made were to the steam passages and the streamlined front.

Whilst the *Cock o' the North* design was taking shape in Doncaster drawing office, and later whilst the engine was showing its paces, Gresley was weighing up two advances indicated by this design—increased power and the undoubted practicability of progressing from the smooth external casing to more complete streamlining which would save power at high speeds. He accordingly pointed out to his Chief General Manager, Sir Ralph Wedgwood, that there was scope for an extra-high-speed train on the King's Cross–Newcastle run—averaging, say, 70 mph so as to cover the 268 miles in four hours with a stop at Darlington. He visualized the project as a complete train, and he visited Germany to obtain first-hand experience of a similar project, the *Flying Hamburger.* In October 1934 this was a well-established high-speed diesel train, booked to average 74 mph on the comparatively easy road between Berlin and Hamburg: Gresley was most impressed by the smooth running at 100 mph and he placed a firm enquiry for the supply of a complete train for the Newcastle run. Detailed proposals for a 115 ton diesel-engined train of three articulated coaches with 140 seats came back, with calculations suggesting a booked time of 4 hrs. 15 min. for the journey. "Interesting", said Wedgwood, " but you could operate a more comfortable train with more seats to a faster schedule with one of your ordinary Pacifics". He well knew how to exploit Gresley's hunches by supporting the main idea and slightly enlarging the target. In this case there were admirable fourfold results: the Pacific was improved, streamlining was introduced, an excellent special train was designed, and the four-hour run to Newcastle became an everyday occurrence.

The improved Pacific was classed " A.4 " with boiler pressure increased to 250 psi cylinders reduced to 18½ by 26 in., piston valves increased to 9 in. diameter, and special attention paid to the size and smoothness of steam and exhaust passages: all these made for greater power and freer running. Standard Pacific valve gear was fitted, with the 65 per cent limit to cut-off in full gear, and 40 per cent of the reciprocating weight was balanced. Brake power was increased from 66 per cent on class "A.3" to 93 per cent of the adhesive weight.

The streamlining was based mainly on the shape of Bugatti rail-cars running between Deauville and Paris: Gresley and Bulleid travelled on these, and noted the significantly reduced air disturbance. So the wedge-shaped front was decided. No inspiration about streamlining the lower parts of the engine came until they stood in the erecting shop at Doncaster when the cylinders had been fitted to *Silver Link*, and Gresley said "What are we going to do about the running boards?" Bulleid suddenly saw in his mind an aerofoil shape extending from well in front of the cylinder to the back of the cab, and without saying anything he sketched it on a piece of sheeting. "That's just about right," said Gresley. A model was sent to the National Physical Laboratory for wind-tunnel tests, and here are some of the results:

Horse-power Saved by Streamlining

Speed, mph		60	70	80	90	100	110	120	130
Horse-power required to overcome head-on air resistance	standard Pacific	97	154	231	328	451	599	778	989
	streamlined Pacific	56	89	134	190	261	347	451	573
Horse-power saved by streamlining		41	65	97	138	190	252	327	416

The *Silver Jubilee* train differed from standard L.N.E.R. design by using steel exterior panels covered with silver rexine. The spaces between the bogies were faired with panels to within 10 in. of the rail, and rubber sheeting smoothed the gaps between the carriages. The noise level at 70 mph was reduced from the normal 65 decibels to 60 decibels by fitting double windows and filling the floor, roof, and side air spaces with insulating material. Triangular rubber bolster stops were fitted to the bogies for improved suppression of the side lurches which sometimes occurred on striking a curve at speed.

The order for *Silver Link* and its train reached Doncaster in April 1935, and was completed in five months. There was a dramatic Press run on 27th September, and the *Silver Jubilee* service was successfully started on 30th September.

New-look, fast trains which keep time probably do more for an engineer's reputation than the best of engines alone. For Gresley, growing in reputation but mellower at 60, the year 1936 brought many satisfactions. He received his Knighthood: he gained an honorary D.Sc. from Manchester University; and he was elected President of the Institution of

Mechanical Engineers. Naturally he devoted his Presidential address to High Speed, describing the *Silver Jubilee* and some of its sources. He said there had been only one engine failure during its first year of service, just completed, during which it had run 133,464 miles and carried about 68,000 passengers. The seven coaches and streamlined locomotive cost £34,000, gross receipts were 13s. 11d. per mile, and operating expenses 2s. 6d. per mile excluding track charges and return on capial. He pointed out that extra high-speed running was not necessary: the train did not normally exceed a speed of 90 mph, but ran fast uphill. He indicated the growing demand for other inter-city high-speed trains, explained the operating difficulties on lines already congested and clogged by slow-moving non-fitted freight trains, and in a table of mixed-traffic engines included his own recent 2-6-2 class "V.2" *Green Arrow*.

The year 1936 also found Gresley starting another 2-year spell as President of the A.R.L.E., and after the meeting on 28th February he took members to King's Cross to see the *Silver Jubilee* arrive, and to inspect the train and engine: among those present were H. G. Ivatt and D. C. Urie. These were pleasurable, railway-based duties, in contrast to chairing a Board of Trade committee to enquire into steering gear for steamships: but as demands on his time grew, Gresley found his railway work also increasing, with numerous improvements resulting from experiments inspired by his staff who were wisely proliferating the ingenuities of the maestro. There were also demands for new locomotive duties, often involving two or three quite advanced exploratory designs. In March 1937 the class "K.4" appeared, and successfully handled 300-ton trains on the West Highland line from Glasgow to Fort William and Mallaig. With engine weight 68 tons compared with the 93 tons of a class "V.2" and with the same cylinders but 5 ft. 2 in. wheels, it had a tractive effort of 36,600 lb. About this time, too, Gresley was looking at the inevitable reply to possible demands for general passenger train speed increases—a 4-8-2.

On the whole Gresley found 1937 rather an anti-climax after the successes and pleasures of 1936. It brought the satisfaction of a joint L.N.E.R.–L.M.S. decision to build a locomotive testing plant, and he cordially welcomed R. C. Bond who was proposed by Stanier to be its superintendent; but the international situation was murky, and Gresley wondered if any new engine of his would grace it. Then, doubly annoying as it had not occurred to him, Bulleid was spirited away, to replace Maunsell on the Southern. He found such incidents more tiring than of old and was reluctantly reminded of a recent warning by his specialist that he was working harder than was good for his heart. Luckily Gresley was full of other friends, other interests: but within his own Department he tended to be a long way above his staff, and only Bulleid had got close enough for free discussion and the occasional, sobering, terse rejoinder. Moreover the other assistants were exceptionally competent and growing more independent with age:

LEADING DIMENSIONS OF GRESLEY LOCOMOTIVES

Engine Class	Engine type	Date	Cylinders Dia. × stroke in. in.	Coupled Wheel dia. ft.	Coupled Wheel dia. in.	Boiler Pressure lb./sq. in.	Total Heating Surfaces sq. ft.	Supr. sq. ft.	Grate Area sq. ft.	Tractive Effort lb.	Weight in working order Engine tons	Weight in working order Engine and Tender tons
G.N.R.												
K.3	2-6-0	1920	3 18½ × 26	5	8	180	1901	407	28	30,031	71¾	114¾
O.2	2-8-0	1921	3 18½ × 26	4	8	180	2032	430	27½	36,470	75¾	119
A.1	4-6-2	1922	3 20 × 26	6	8	180	2930	525	41	29,835	92½	148¾
L.N.E.R.												
P.1	2-8-2	1925	3 20 × 26	5	2	180	2930	525	41	38,500	100	151½
J.38	0-6-0	1926	2 20 × 26	4	8	180	1454	289	26	28,414	59	103
D.49	4-4-0	1927	3 17 × 26	6	8	180	1397	271	26	21,556	66	118
A.3	4-6-2	1928	3 19 × 26	6	8	220	2692	706	41	32,909	96¼	152½
B.17	4-6-0	1928	3 17½ × 26	6	8	200	1676	344	27	25,380	77¼	116¾
V.1	2-6-2T	1930	3 16 × 26	5	8	180	1325	284	22	22,464	86¾	—
P.2	2-8-2	1934	3 21 × 26	6	2	220	2714	776	50	43,462	107	167½
A.4	4-6-2	1935	3 18½ × 26	6	8	250	2576	748	41	35,455	103	168
V.2	2-6-2	1936	3 18½ × 26	6	2	220	2431	679	41	33,730	93	145
K.4	2-6-0	1937	3 18½ × 26	5	2	200	1421	310	27	36,599	68½	112½
V.4	2-6-2	1941	3 15 × 26	5	8	250	1444	355	28	27,420	70½	113¼

and some were a lot older than should be the case for properly-planned progression—Thompson 56, Thom 64, and Peppercorn already 48. Stamer and Glaze had recently retired. So a cold wind seemed to roam through the familiar office at King's Cross when Bulleid left at the end of September 1937: Gresley did not replace him, Spencer and Newsome sharing the work.

Though he successfully exploited the very real advantages of fast uphill running in the attainment of fast average speeds, Gresley had never lost his enthusiasm for high speed, which possessed him as a schoolboy when he drew out a Stirling single, and as an apprentice during the 1895 Railway races. He had consistently encouraged bursts of high speed in the various preludes to the faster trains, and *Silver Fox* had attained 113 mph in August 1936: but, since 29th June 1937, the British record of 114 mph rested with Stanier's Pacific. The world record of 124·5 mph had been set up by a German 4-6-4 in June 1936.

Of these, the L.M.S. record was both the more annoying and the easier to top: not only did L.N.E.R. Pacifics commonly run faster than those of the L.M.S., but the L.N.E.R. possessed between Stoke summit and Essendine an ideal length of track for high-speed tests—straight, free from junctions and subsidence, and with ruling gradient 1 in 200. But rather typically Gresley did not order an immediate reply to the L.M.S. record: he bided his time, determined to beat the Germans also. The opportunity would present itself during the brake trials he was continually arranging, which were aimed at reducing the time taken for a full application of the vacuum brake on the engine to be effective at the rear of the train. This took about 10 seconds on a train 674 ft. long weighing 333 tons, but had been reduced to as little as 3 seconds with a Westinghouse Quick Service valve. Typically, such a train running at 90 mph on the level would stop in about 60 seconds (1,250 yds.) with normal equipment. Often a distant signal is only 1,000 yds. from its home signal, so one can appreciate the importance of effective braking as speeds increase. Gresley fitted the Westinghouse valves to the high speed trains in 1938, and started another series of brake tests. For the tests on 3rd July 1938, class " A.4 " Pacific No. 4468, *Mallard* was chosen. She was only a few weeks old, her free-running capabilities had the help of the Kylchap double blastpipe and chimney—and besides Gresley had an affection for the common wild duck. Newsome was as usual in charge of the tests and driver Duddington was on the engine. Gresley rode in the ex-N.E.R. dynamometer car; the train weight was 240 tons gross. Setting off south from Grantham, they made good speed up the bank and passed Stoke summit at 74½ mph. Then driver Duddington continued with full regulator and 40 per cent cut-off, and speed increased rapidly to 100 mph down the 1 in 178 bank to Corby, and further to 112 mph at mile post 95, where the 1 in 200 gradient down to Essendine starts. Duddington tried lengthening the cut-off to 45 per cent, but judged that *Mallard*, to use H. A. Ivatt's expression, liked 40 per cent best. At Little Bytham the speed had crept up to 122 mph and at mile post 91 it was 124. The L.M.S. record was pulverised, but all thoughts were now on the German record; and time seemed to stand still whilst the train leapt forward under a plume of steam. Then the speed indicator swung to 125 mph; and then for each of a few jubilant seconds 185 ft. were covered—126 mph. It was 4.36 p.m. Only minor pleasure showed through Gresley's normally confident and impassive appearance, but suddenly he felt much less tired.

Apart from the satisfaction that the L.N.E.R. and L.M.S. were together proceeding with the locomotive test station, Gresley found 1939 a frustrating year. He had foreseen the war, and disliked the inevitable repercussions on the railway—the extra work, the worries of the Executive Sub-Committee of which he was first Chairman, and the curtailing of locomotive design development. Though becoming easily tired, he kept up his fighting spirit; it was in his blood. Taking the chair at the February 1939 A.R.L.E. meeting in the absence of Stanier, he said after completing the rather meagre agenda, " We have not been discussing fresh subjects. I wish the Hon. Secretary would take steps to ensure that the subjects put on the agenda relate to matters upon which up-to-date information is required." The Hon. Secretary and Vice-President, Bulleid, agreed and hoped members would suggest items for future meetings. But the next meeting was not held till six years later.

The war, which put paid to the 4-8-2 express passenger engine which Gresley had outlined, brought a number of demands for special wagons: but the only notable locomotive design permitted to proceed was the class " V.4 " 2-6-2. As the larger new engines had spread throughout the L.N.E.R. system, it had been the common and obvious procedure to relegate the displaced engines to secondary jobs. Then Gresley pointed out that there could well be a useful measure of economy in providing an engine specially for this secondary working—a modern, efficient engine with of course great route availability. The " V.4 " was the result, with three 15 by 26 cylinders, 5 ft. 8 in. wheels, and boiler pressure 250 psi giving a tractive effort of 27,420 lb. This engine, if compared with, say, a class " K.4 " at once puts over Gresley's message—provide the best practicable motive power. One can argue that a cheaper 2-cylinder engine with similar performance would be almost as good, but it all comes back to the values of being able to recover lost time, of flexibility, and of that extra margin for emergency. Gresley was determined to provide the best tool for the job, as the current slogan went, and he succeeded in spite of two grave hazards: demands on him for war work were a real burden, and in November 1940 his specialist issued an uncompromising warning about his heart. But those about him were all pulling their weight in the war struggle, and Gresley had no intention of relaxing: and that fine bird the class " V.4 " 2-6-2 *Bantam Cock* perhaps also included a gesture of defiance at the enemy when it made its bow in February 1941.

It is a long haul, to be the militant head of a locomotive department for 29 years, specially when 18 of them are with so large a Company as the

L.N.E.R. Some of the triumphs bring strains greater than their rewards. Sir Nigel walked to his train with a slow and tired step one evening in February 1941. He was due to retire in June, but to the dismay of the Office a message came that he had died, from heart failure, on 5th April.

The Engineer for 11th April 1941 carried a balanced appreciation by the editor, L. St. L. Pendred:

> " The railway world can ill afford to lose a man of the ability of Sir Nigel Gresley, whose death on 5th April at the early age of sixty-four we mourn to-day. For many years he was pre-eminent as a British locomotive designer, and not even the historic figures of the past have more famous engines to their credit than he. Trained under such masters as Webb and Aspinall and Ivatt, he combined the experience gained under them with a natural aptitude for design which he fostered and enlarged by the careful study of foreign, particularly French, developments. He never hesitated to embody in his own engines the good things he found in others, and was always ready to make practical tests of promising inventions. But despite this broadness of outlook there is not one of his many designs that is not essentially British, both in characteristics and appearance. They carry on the great tradition of British locomotive engineers, but always adding to and improving on what had gone before."

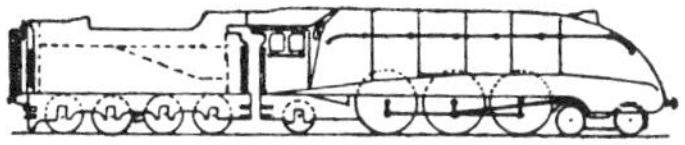

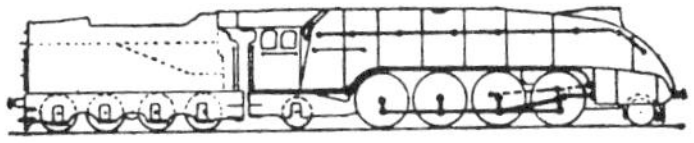

CHAPTER 3

O. V. S. Bulleid; Great Northern to Southern

When Mr. and Mrs. Samuel Bulleid of North Tawton, Devon, died suddenly within a few months of each other in 1862, they left two sons, William and John. Their uncle, Samuel Snell Lee, charitably took them into his home and his business at Teignmouth; but they learned the business the hard way, and by 1875 had both emigrated to New Zealand.

William's success as a merchant permitted a business holiday in England in 1878, and at a musical soiree in London he re-met a childhood friend, Marian Pugh. She was from Llanfyllin, from the rail-head, descended from several generations of local lawyers and erstwhile landowners.

William and Marian married promptly, in August 1878, and sailed the next month to set up home in Invercargill, South tip of the South Island: and of their three children the eldest, O. V. S. Bulleid, was born on 19th September 1882. But in 1889 William died and the young widow with her three children returned reluctantly to Llanfyllin. Here she lived with her widowed mother, two younger children, and two nieces; whilst Oliver lived mainly at Accrington with uncle, aunt, and two cousins. This rather cold-blooded apportioning was typically arranged by Marian's dominating elder sister: it gave Oliver the company of a cousin of his own age for holidays and for schooling—first at Bridge of Allan and then at the new Accrington Municipal Technical School. Success in the London Matriculation at age 16¾ led to the decision that he should be a lawyer and join his uncle John in New Zealand. With clothes bought and passage booked, Oliver was taken on a round of good-byes which included his cousin Edgar Lee, then Vicar of Christ Church, Doncaster. " Rubbish," cried the Vicar, " He's staying in England and he's going to be an engineer," and without more ado arranged for him to start a 4-year premium apprenticeship under H. A. Ivatt at the G.N.R. Works on 21st January 1901.

This mixed upbringing undoubtedly made young Oliver independent, unemotional, hard-working, and tough—mentally as well as physically. And so, perhaps helped by the comparatively late starting age of 18¼, he really waded into his apprenticeship. The first 2½ years were spent in the shops, including work on the Atlantics, the 4-4-0s and the 0-8-0s.

The enquiring mind of 19 asks questions: Bulleid's questions, thanks to an economics slant in his schooling, ranged into costing. Receiving poor replies, he sought and obtained permission, through Clayton, Ivatt's chief clerk, to see the accounting procedures. Similarly, he recognized his academic limitations, took immediate action by increasing his technical reading, including the American magazines, and resolved to shift his evening class work from Doncaster to Sheffield University as soon as his posting to the Drawing Office with Staff hours made this practicable. This came in September 1903, and he went to Sheffield three nights per week. About this time, basking in the Press glory of 251, the G.N.R. directors arranged an essay competition among the apprentices for the best essay on locomotive design. Bulleid put in a reasoned case for a 2-6-2, which was adjudged promising but unorthodox, and J. R. Bazin won the modest prize with, strangely enough, a 4-4-2 arrangement.

Early in 1904 Bulleid obtained and read Dr. Goss's work on loco front end design, and set out the appropriate chimney and petticoat shape to suit the large Atlantics. To his surprise this scarcely differed from the existing design. He asked how this particular design had been worked out, and learned that Ivatt had had the Drawing Office proposal, which was in turn based closely on previous practice, drawn out full size in thick line and set up against the office wall. He had looked it over, and had made a number of alterations to the sweep of the petticoat and the chimney taper and outline. These were then faithfully dimensioned on the drawings, and the engines so built—though Ivatt put a stove-pipe chimney on 251 till he was satisfied that the design was correct. Bulleid got Ivatt's permission to try one engine exactly to the Goss formula; for cheapness the new chimney was again wrapped from plate and finished with a simple ½-round beading. The engine had a distinctive beat, but no difference in performance could be detected. And because it looked so frightful, it was soon given back its normal chimney.

Ivatt did not always agree with these suggestions, however brilliant; once Bulleid commented on the Chief's short-sightedness to Clayton, who replied "You should try to realize the difference between seeing something from above and from below."

In September 1904 Bulleid switched to Leeds University for three nights a week, and this became doubly hectic when, still nominally an apprentice but now just 22, he was sent to inspect all joints as made on a new 15 in. water main being laid by the G.N.R. from Bawtry to Doncaster to supply Works and loco water.

There was great interest in rail cars at this period, and in addition to those designed by Ivatt and those bought out the General Manager, Oliver Bury, arranged (without consulting Ivatt) to buy a Daimler-engined petrol rail car. Ivatt sent Bulleid as observer on the trials of this car on the Hertford branch in the summer of 1905: he found this rather frustrating, and soon realized that trials carried out by makers interested mainly in their engines have less short-term value than trials carried out by a user determined to keep the machine running. In spite of some dramatic all-night repair feats, they suffered a breakdown on the curve approaching Hatfield one warm evening, which had three interesting results: an infuriated stranded passenger; a discovery by Bulleid that it is easier to walk two miles than learn to operate a platelayer's trolley; and a summons to see Mr. Ivatt. Bulleid explained the frustrations of being a mere observer without authority, and so Ivatt promptly put him in charge: adequate spares and operating discipline did then, in fact, enable the car to perform its intended duty between Hitchin and the new Garden City at Welwyn for three months without a service failure. Bulleid stayed at Hitchin, freely using both the Running Shed and the Stationmaster's offices. And since the Stationmaster was off duty daily from 2 p.m. till 3.30, casual enquirers who would normally have found the office shut and gone to ask the porter naturally addressed their enquiries to Bulleid, who cheerfully dealt with them all, and freely used the stationery provided by the two Railways concerned—the Great Northern and the Midland. The latter were delightfully old-fashioned, thought Bulleid, because they provided un-gummed envelopes and separate sealing wafers.

Appointment as Assistant to Webster, the Loco Running Superintendent, brought Bulleid back to headquarters at Doncaster and to a variety of typical maintenance problems. One day Webster asked for a report on the abnormal number of failures experienced with the standard G.N.R. screwed coupling between engine and tender, and Bulleid wrote this up, attaching the blame to a sharp-cornered undercut provided at each side of the centre boss where the dienuts ran out, a typical Works problem. Only a week or so later, in January 1907, Bulleid was transferred to be Assistant to Wintour, Locomotive Works Manager. As he entered the office for duty, "You might just deal with this," said Wintour, rather sardonically, tossing back the screwed coupling report. Unabashed, Bulleid did so; and very soon got from Wintour a free hand in the major job of mechanizing the Smith's shop.

A battery of drop-hammers was decided upon, and an American forging machine—the largest in the country. With it, the makers offered one free tool, to choice. Naturally looking for the most difficult component against which to choose this tool, Bulleid selected the clutch end of the 10-ton wagon hand-brake lever. "Impracticable," came back word from America. "Nonsense, similar jobs already being done," retorted Bulleid. The Americans duly produced a tool which would do the job, after doubling over the bar ends, in two strikes; and the technically correct piece price for the machine operator would then have been ½d., compared with 1s. 3d. paid previously for hand work by a smith and his striker. Bulleid proposed 1d. under the rather difficult circumstances of a large shop completely mechanized: Wintour decided to pay 4d. So though the new operation seemed to quarter the previous cost, the return on capital was poor, and the resulting productivity was only about one-eighth of what it could have been. The scars of such errors persist today. But selling ideas is as important as having them, and Bulleid failed again when lobbied by the loco accountant to do a clean-up of the shop order paperwork. They collaborated on a scheme, worked it out in detail, and got from Wintour a gruff "No." He added that he was not having his Works managed for him by the Loco Accountant. Ivatt might have been more sympathetic: about this time his chief clerk tentatively hinted at a salary rise on account of the many extra letters being handled in the Department. "*Fewer* letters in the Department would be a good reason for an increase," said Ivatt.

Spurred by the limitations of an " assistant to . . . " job, and by thoughts of career, marriage, and the boss's youngest daughter, Autumn 1907 found Bulleid furiously learning French ahead of his appointment in December as Assistant Works Manager and Chief Draughtsman of the French Westinghouse Company's Works at Freinville (i.e. Braketown, near Paris). His tour of leave-taking of Doncaster Works included Gresley, who added to the flood of good wishes but remarked "It is very easy to leave a Railway, but very hard to get back on it." Apart from the shock of discovering the difference between French as gleaned in Doncaster and as spoken in France, Bulleid did admirably at Freinville, and life was rose-tinted when he returned to Doncaster for his marriage to Marjorie Ivatt on 18th November 1908. Asked if she minded settling in France, Mrs. Bulleid (aged 20 and fortified by fluent colloquial French picked up in Paris and Brussels) replied that it ought to be more exciting than being the youngest of four daughters living at home.

The job at Freinville taught commercial manufacturing methods, showed the latest thinking on signalling and brakes and steam heating equipment, and introduced French railway engineers as the customers. Then came a rather unexpected change to a better job when, through the agency of Wintour's brother, Bulleid became Mechanical Engineer to the Exhibitions Branch of the Board of Trade. This job was for the Brussels and Turin Exhibitions of 1910 and 1911, but it then folded up: and so in December 1911, aged 29 and with young wife and year-old daughter, Bulleid returned to Doncaster to seek a railway job again. H. N. Gresley was in the process of taking over as Locomotive, Carriage and Wagon Superintendent, and he at once offered a choice of jobs: District Loco Superintendent at Grantham, or Personal Assistant to Gresley. The former was essentially a routine job in which Bulleid would show little inspiration and would find little interest, particularly under Webster who was nicknamed " Mr. No " and was not an enthusiast for innovations: the latter was at the hub of the G.N.R. and would cover a wide field, and had the single disadvantage that the boss would be only six years older than his P.A. What Bulleid saw as an open choice probably appeared to Gresley as a polite way of signing up, without apparent persuasion, the most experienced and potentially valuable P.A. he would be likely to acquire anywhere. So on 1st January 1912, settling into a small office beside the Drawing Office, Bulleid began his association with Gresley that was to last over 25 years.

The reason why Gresley appreciated Bulleid from the start was simple: he was ready at hand to assist when required, but when not so required he was out and about finding things that needed doing and getting them done. A good example was the lighting in King's Cross shed, a scene of important round-the-clock activity and yet, in 1912, lit only to candlelight standards. When the new gas lighting on Derby station rightly hit the news, Bulleid went to collect all the data from Henry Fowler who though C.M.E. of the Midland was also the master-mind on any gas project. The resulting application at King's Cross shed was a dramatic improvement duly appreciated by Webster.

As is common when a new C.M.E. takes over, Gresley became involved in discussions with the Traffic Department as to the maximum loadings of various engines, and this led in the middle of 1912 to a lengthy job in which Bulleid collaborated with Attwood, of the Superintendent of the Line's staff, on the classification of goods trains by type and speed, and the appropriate loading of each type for the various classes of engine available. Thus they compiled the new Loading Circular: the nett result was an annual saving of 3 million train-miles. Of course the Sheds were decidedly lukewarm: it meant increased engine-loadings, and thus less margin, more trouble. Some of the increases were hotly contested, so Bulleid carried out practical trials, some of which interestingly proved the Sheds right. The reason was that the gradient profiles were those of the original track surveys; they had not been modified—either where the actual site work had differed from the survey, or where there had been alterations with the passage of years.

This work naturally included corresponding braking tests, and Bulleid and Attwood verified their recommendations for various classes of brake van by carrying out tests on the 1-in-50 incline where the Great Northern line joined the Midland near Shipley. The procedure was to have an engine push off the particular brake van and its rake of trucks down the incline at 4 mph, which they measured in a rough and ready way as being a brisk walking pace alongside the brake van; and when this speed was attained the guard applied his brake to confirm that the wagons could be brought to a satisfactory stop. On one occasion, Bulleid watched with some trepidation when the brake van picked up its wheels and disappeared into the mist down the incline, heading for the Midland main line only about a mile-and-a-half away. Fortunately, the guard succeeded in halting the trucks before they reached the catch points. These tests also uncovered a curious error in thinking on the part of Gresley who had designed some 8-wheel 20 ton brake vans in the persuasion that they would have better braking characteristics than the standard 4-wheel 20 ton brake. This would have been so if the brakes had been perfectly balanced, but in practice when the brake was applied it connected first on one pair of wheels which, only carrying 5 tons, immediately picked up, and the same thing usually followed only too soon with the second axle. Bulleid reported this to Gresley, who at once saw the point, withdrew the vans, and expressed the wish that people would tell him when equipment was unsatisfactory.

About this time the first large boiler for the class "K2" 2-6-0 was completed, and during its pressure test the boiler shop foreman noticed a slight bulging at each side, between the horizontal and vertical firebox stays. When this was reported, Bulleid designed a framework with a series of fixed points from which distances could be accurately measured to corresponding points round the periphery of the boiler over the firebox: the test was repeated, and the movement confirmed; and it was this test which led to the fitting of the rather crude transverse boiler stays and which years later made Bulleid sympathetic to the Belpaire arrangement for the Merchant Navy boilers.

The Bulleid war service was marked by a powerful patriotic feeling and a sincere liking for the French. He was commissioned in the Army Service Corps and went to France in January 1915. He spent most of his time organizing railway transportation of troops and munitions, and suffered such irritations as marked the final offensive at Amiens in August 1918. An ammunition train preceding the vital trains of tanks was standing in the tunnel at Amiens station in the black-out when it was run into by a light engine. The force of the collision derailed the engines and so smashed the first wagons that their load was spilled around the track in the tunnel. The load was cases of handgrenades, which in turn burst open. There was nothing for it but to re-route the tank convoy. In August 1918, and with sad effect on his gratuity, Bulleid was posted as Works Manager at Richborough, as Major, R.E. Within weeks of this return to England he was busy learning Portuguese from the Portuguese Vice-Consul at Ramsgate because Oliver Bury, who had interests in the San Paolo Railway of Brazil, arranged for him to go there as Chief Mechanical Engineer. But the local General Manager persuaded Bury to retain the present incumbent and so, in common with all Railway staff, Bulleid returned after demobilization in April 1919 to his pre-war job as P.A. to Gresley.

He, and the others, were warmly welcomed back. Colleagues left at home had been short-staffed, rationed, and under heavy pressure for munition work. They had also possibly suffered more mental uncertainty than civilians in World War II because they had entirely escaped participation in danger. There were no great changes at Doncaster, except the appearance of the first G.N.R. 3-cylinder engine which struck Bulleid as being slightly odd because the adjacent rivals, the North Eastern Railway, had been leaders of the 3-cylinder vogue, whereas the well-known Ivatt dictum was " Don't go to three or four cylinders if two will do the job." Talk of nationalizing the railways was waning in front of amalgamation rumours. Standards seemed to Bulleid to have deteriorated: this was probably partly true, partly an effect of the sheer volume of work done by the railways during the war on reduced maintenance manpower, and partly Bulleid being old enough at 36 to magnify the quality from a gold-lit past.

There were several interesting design problems waiting to be tackled, one of which was the balancing of the 3-cylinder 2-6-0. Bulleid did nearly all the calculations, based on the recently published work by Professor Dalby. There were also some practical problems in acquiring design data, one of which concerned the two-to-one lever for the same engines. The

Drawing Office were unwilling to assume a maximum deflection, so Bulleid empirically chose 1/16 in. and they then designed a lever which would give no more than this amount of deflection assuming an unyielding pivot, and the design was proved by a lash-up in the shops. When, later, suspicion that the inner piston valve was moving too far was confirmed by placing lead markers inside the covers, it was correspondingly easy to diagnose that the pivot was deflecting; and the pivot support was accordingly strengthened.

General Managers were finding their feet after the war just as actively as Chief Mechanical Engineers, and Oliver Bury was rather envious of the successful Central Train Control system recently instituted by Sir John Aspinall on the Lancashire and Yorkshire Railway. Bulleid and Attwood therefore moved in again, to collaborate with the other departments concerned in applying C.T.C. This was started in the West Riding section of the G.N.R., and included the design of the train control board at Leeds.

Sometimes Gresley called on Bulleid for specific trouble-shooting, as when they were troubled by excessive wear and play in side rod bushes. There was a quartering machine used in Doncaster Works for boring the side rod pin holes accurately at right angles, and Bulleid checked this machine, using a portable French device which he could apply to the wheel centre and read off angular settings with considerable accuracy. He found the quartering machine inaccurate, and was collecting his gear when Wintour came into the shop and sharply said that if Mr. Gresley wanted his machines checked he should ask the Works Manager. Bulleid, equally sharply, reported to Gresley that the quartering machine was inaccurate. The following day he was summoned by Gresley and found him obviously in the throes of a tough argument with Wintour. Asked what he meant by the report, Bulleid—maddeningly right—probably annoyed them the more by pointing out that they had no more to do than simply correct the machine. He then drew out a graph showing the play necessary to allow rotation at various angular errors, and sent this to the *American Machinist*, who duly responded with a cheque for $7.50.

Gresley would always support any practical experimental work, and early 1920 found Bulleid delighted with a recording accelerometer he had obtained from Elliott Bros. He even took it to show Burrows at Swindon—Gresley would arrange with Churchward to borrow the Great Western Railway dynamometer car rather than that of the North Eastern Railway, which was inquisitively close, and Bulleid and Burrows would fix up the details. By disconnecting the clockwork time-scale drive from the accelerometer and instead driving it on a distance basis from a pulley fitted to the axle of a van, Bulleid made a number of road tests. One interesting result was that the large Atlantics settled down to a free coasting speed of just over 30 mph on a down gradient of 1 in 200.

A serious epidemic of golf hit the Plant Works about this time, probably started by Groom who took over from Webster, and fanned by the first post-war cars—Bulleid's an air-cooled and Peppercorn's a water-cooled Morgan, both with preoccupying acetylene lighting. Groom's handicap was +1. Peppercorn was a cheery and vigorous player, said to have deepened the large bunker on the 8th at Rossington by several inches. Bulleid was so bitten by the golf bug that he dropped his keen interest in photography. He applied his usual technique of reading, study, practice and concentration, and remained a dim golfer; in contrast to considerable successes achieved by his wife, who simply played. But Peppercorn and Bulleid enjoyed their one big moment: starting early in a flag competition, they astoundingly had four strokes each in hand after holing out at the 18th, and were able to pitch their flags on the green of the 1st. Two hours later the expected winner was passing flags along the 16th, 17th, and 18th, and having got round with one stroke in hand he was striding down the first fairway to flag his last shot when he spotted the unbelievable two flags on the green. And then, backwards along the first fairway and into the clubhouse rang his turbulent comments on flag competitions and on long-handicap railway golfers.

In late 1920 E. Thompson was transferred to York and Bulleid succeeded him as Assistant Carriage and Wagon Superintendent, reporting to Gresley and doing Gresley's old job of carriage and wagon design, manufacture, and repair, including road vehicles—horse and motor.

Gresley retained a great interest in the carriage side, and always came at once when phoned by Bulleid that a new carriage was finished and ready for him to inspect. Gresley had a keen eye for detail, and would throw out some slightly critical comment: once, striding into the shop and looking apparently straight up and ahead he said "Those split pins in the spring hangers are too long." Bulleid glumly found the criticism valid. Works standards were generally high, and once at the end of inspecting a hitherto flawless carriage Gresley felt round a high moulding and discovered a small gap where it should have been hard up against the panel. "A fault here," he commented. Bulleid never shone at the slick riposte, but the Head Foreman unhesitatingly replied, "But we always leave something for you to find, sir." Of course Bulleid could be just as maddeningly brisk and observant. Though basically free from affectations he was inclined, under stress, to walk a pace ahead of his staff and ask a second question a shade ahead of the first being answered. He avoided colloquialisms: engines were locomotives and carriages and wagons were rolling stock—however stationary. He was a born taker of short-cuts and when visiting Swindon to call on G. H. Burrows always walked straight from the station platform across the track to the Drawing Office. Only years later, in L.N.E.R. days, was he challenged, and his previous immunity was ascribed to his purposeful walk and to the fact that the attache-case he carried was a replica of the G.W.R. type.

In 1920, pre-war late Edwardian lushness was slow in giving way to what opponents of the newer fashions were calling stark unadorned "functionalism." Bulleid recognized that railway carriage interiors must move with the new fashions, to avoid rapidly acquiring a dated appearance. Accordingly, he halted the interior work on a set of new carriages, and substituted a far simpler design and finish in one compartment—aiming at being rich in quality but essentially plain, and incorporating concealed panel fastenings. He then called in Gresley for a verdict, explaining that the change would mean scrapping materials and some work done on three carriages: characteristically, Gresley gave an immediate and unhesitating O.K. Plain but exceptionally fine paintwork and mahogany veneers were also used in the new sleepers; then a letter appeared in *The Times*, deploring their starkness.

A lot of work was put in on the problem of articulated carriages. These were never truly liked by the operating department on account of imaginary ill-effects from hot boxes and similar defects and to the feeling that breakdown troubles were potentially greater. But they offered great attractions—cheaper and lighter trains, less train resistance, less track noise; and even marginally better riding, thought Gresley. But Bulleid thought they rode harder and added to the springing by experiments. He powerfully followed up Gresley's work after the lull under Thompson, and in 1921 produced the quintuple set for the King's Cross–Leeds service. This comprised two composites, two diners, and a central kitchen car—five carriages on six bogies. The electric kitchen got in the news: Bulleid designed this after long consultations with specialist suppliers. An interesting point about the bogies was that their axle boxes had the same width of whitemetal bearing strips as conventionally-used bogies carrying only half the weight. At first double width strips were used to give the same unit bearing pressure, but these ran hot. The width was reduced to half, and heating eliminated. The quintuple set ran beautifully on the G.N.R. main line, restored by 1920 to its silken quality after a slight lapse during the war years. I remember going on a trial run as far as Peterborough one Sunday, taken for a treat by my father accompanied by Peppercorn who was then in charge of the Wagon Shops. After gathering speed, glasses filled to the brim were indeed set on the diner tables, and they did not spill until the Grantham stop. The only minor casualty occurred at lunch (taken at the Great Northern Hotel, Peterborough: diner trials never included lunch trials!), when Peppercorn was surprised by the super-strength horseradish sauce. He gasped a warning and laughed, while his cheerful blue eyes swam with tears.

The Midland Railway at this time had the enviable reputation of the best turned out carriages; their handsome Crimson Lake was beautifully cleaned by a material known as Perfectol. Bulleid tried this, and found it admirable but costly: the chief chemist remarked that he could make up some equally good material very much cheaper. In due time, a gallon jar of " Chemists Special " was delivered to the carriage shops, but it had such a revolting smell that Bulleid considered it unfit for use. This was duly reported to the chemist, who said " Oh, that is easily remedied, I'll add an aromatic hydrocarbon." Bulleid was highly impressed, hearing this catchy phrase for the first time, and he was even more impressed when a sample was delivered to his office late the following Friday afternoon; it looked quite good and it had a very reasonable smell. When he entered the office on Monday morning, however, he was alarmed to see the sample had separated out into three distinct layers. He was looking incredulously at it when Gresley entered, caught sight of the expression on his face, and said rather briskly " Don't tell me anything about that—I'll tell you. You tried some special carriage cleaner; you found it too expensive; the chemist said ' I'll make some ' and he produced a sample which you couldn't possibly use; you complained to him about the smell, and he said ' I'll add an aromatic hydrocarbon '—you thanked him, and now he has sent you this sample." They looked at the sample again. " How typical of a chemist," Gresley added.

Amalgamation and its likely effects figured throughout the main rumours of 1922; people in high places were cagey. Then one day in the early autumn, returning home together on the Avenue Road tram, where paradoxically the noise kicked up by the centre-flange wheels facilitated private conversation, Gresley said that he had been appointed C.M.E. of the amalgamated East Coast lines, with offices in London. Bulleid must have shown a decided flash of enthusiasm, because Gresley's response was simply " What, would you like to come?"

In April 1923 Gresley and Bulleid moved into the new London and North Eastern Railway C.M.E.'s offices near the junction of the overbridge and main departure platform No. 10 at King's Cross. They set up a small Drawing Office for scheme, detail, and checking work: after checking, Gresley signed the loco drawings and Bulleid the carriage and wagon drawings. New design was almost entirely done at Doncaster: the other Drawing Offices merely continuing with the usual stream of minor and detail work, standardization, etc. Doncaster had thrown a double-six as far as the new engineering bosses were concerned; and since both Gresley and Bulleid were inclined to be technically arrogant, a trait which tends to flourish in their 40 to 50 age-group, Doncaster methods were in and the other constituents could like them or lump them. The directors poured a little oil on to the fires of unfairness by choosing Great Northern green as the L.N.E.R. passenger loco colour instead of, say, Great Eastern blue. At top level, there was much North Eastern influence: they were the largest constituent company and had the largest loco stock so retained their numbering, while the G.N.R. added 3,000 to existing numbers. Darlington was a large and important Works and in charge there stayed A. C. Stamer, who had been appointed Gresley's Principal Assistant.

Bulleid got a rude shock when he examined the G.E.R. suburban carriages: " They are falling apart," he reported with righteous indignation to Gresley, " Most of the body frames are rotting away." And, in fact, things were so parlous that all the L.N.E.R. money for carriage building had at first to be allocated to this major replacement. If more thought had been given to *why* the G.E.R. had been too short of money to maintain its rolling stock, some unpleasant discoveries of 35 years later would have been usefully anticipated. Everyone thought the new varnished teak carriages looked fine, but there were complaints about their riding. Bulleid, like everyone else, knew all about the crowded suburban trains into Liverpool Street; but only by personal inspection did he grasp that in rush hour traffic the carriages ran with 21 passengers per compartment. Then, as now, this crowding was accepted as part of the railway contribution to civilization. On setting the bogie springs to suit this loading, the riding became tolerable.

This incident, more than any other, impressed on Bulleid the need for accurate reports and the value of continually touring the zones of operation. He developed a theory that railway officers should buy their tickets and travel under precisely the same conditions as the normal passenger, to ensure they saw railway services from the customer's viewpoint. Whilst he did not exactly practice this perfection, he certainly got around all the L.N.E.R. and many of the other companies' Works. He was particularly welcome at Inverurie: here T. E. Heywood of the Great North of Scotland Railway reigned, with responsibilities including permanent way. Heywood could never hit it off with Gresley, so on the rare occasions of a Gresley trip so far from base the presence of Bulleid was soothing and technically advantageous.

The Bulleid failure to recognize that people will not accept something different merely because it is technically better or more ingenious, was illustrated by the reinforced concrete brake van. This bizarre proposal was well executed and even in 1924 would have been an economic proposition in batches of fifty or so. The only serious trouble was condensation when the guard got his stove going, and this was cured by applying an insulating spray. But the new construction was never *sold* to its users, and it became disliked and feared on rumours of what might happen in an accident.

With G.N.R. tradition the L.N.E.R. ran their fitted goods trains fast, and Bulleid was rather concerned that although the rule book demanded a full brake application in emergency, no driver appeared ever to have made a full application on a fitted freight train. Accordingly one night Bulleid set off on a fast down goods, 45 vans and brake, hauled by a 2-6-0 which boasted a Flamman speed recorder. Speed was run up to 60 mph approaching Holme, Bulleid gave the word, and as planned the driver made a full brake application, then shut the regulator, and finally shifted to full forward gear. The engine seemed to stop rapidly, then it was jerked hard forward by the bunching vans, then arrested again as they opened out. The whole train came to rest in 700 yards, amid considerable noise and subsequent adverse comment by the guard. A coupling broke, about halfway along the train: the fireman was able to re-make it from the other coupling and then doubled back to the engine. They gave a crow whistle, got a green light from the guard, and went on their way. Subsequently, "I have had an extremely adverse report about the behaviour of a fitted goods," said Gresley, "Don't do that sort of thing again. You are not in charge of the department." Bulleid moved towards the door, feeling the time was not ripe for a prolonged discussion. "Have you got the Flamman diagram? We want to learn all we can from the results," said Gresley. . . .

In 1924 the triennial meeting of the International Railway Congress Association was held in London. One of the French papers was so badly translated that Bulleid complained during its presentation. The Section President, Sir Henry Fowler, promptly signed him on as a translator. This led to his becoming sub-editor of the English edition of the monthly Bulletin, and he retained his interest in it long after retirement. He always regretted the lack of sympathy in England to railway ideas from the Continent—"Compared with ideas from the Continent, ideas from the Great Western are almost popular," he was heard to remark, probably about the time of the Pacific/Castle exchanges. Either he or Gresley often went to the Monthly Conference of the French Railway C.M.Es., and there compared problems with such friends as Lacoin, Vallentin, and Collin and Lancrenon (respectively P.O., P.L.M. and Nord).

It is rather typical of Gresley and Bulleid that they were too busy to do anything special in the 1926 General Strike. Among a lot of design work—new and improvement—there was still much to do on standardization. Bulleid devoted a lot of effort to finding which was the best of the several types of fusible plug in use. The results were lengthy and rather inconclusive. "But which have we the most of?" asked Gresley. "Well, of course, the North-Eastern type," Bulleid replied. "In that case the North-Eastern type should be adopted," said Gresley.

Occasionally there were operating upsets, as when the civil engineer put a local ban on 0-6-2 tanks after a derailment near North Berwick. Bulleid went to argue the case, which was comparatively easy since these engines had never proved prone to derailment and track conditions around King's Cross, their home territory, were far from ideal. After such minor battles Gresley would stand comfortably with his back to the impressive fire in his office, and discuss form with Bulleid. Humanly, they sometimes discussed their wisdom, and sometimes the stupidity of others. They did not always agree: once Gresley took up his fireside position quite indignantly, wanting to know how it was that none of his assistants ever seemed to come up with any suggestions. "By the way," said Bulleid, casually, "You remember that draughtsman you agreed to see last week"—"Of course I do, the dam' fool." "Well, there you are," said Bulleid, "Do you think he'll ever come back with another suggestion?" Gresley was slightly penitent; each found it easier to see brusqueness in the other than in himself.

Many important engineering advances can be traced to individual engineers having a special interest in some particular technology: in Bulleid's case this was welding. Impressed with its desirability compared with riveting whilst still an apprentice, and impressed by an early large-scale application to a barge whilst Works Manager at Richborough, he raised the idea of welding a carriage underframe with Gresley and met unyielding opposition. He proceeded with sundry welded components, and then decided that a demonstration should be staged, in the carriage shops at York. The riveting flange was cut away from a typical footstep bracket, and the bracket was butt-welded in its usual position on a section of a carriage frame. It was then taken to the Smithy and the toughest striker was shown how to set about breaking the bracket away from the frame. At his next visit Gresley was asked to come and see the test. The striker swung his 14 lb. hammer with tremendous effect and bent the bracket flat against the frame without worrying the weld. " I wouldn't have believed it," said Gresley, as they stood and looked. " I think we could safely weld a carriage underframe," suggested Bulleid. " Of course," said Gresley. Feeling their way, they welded the first frame largely to the existing design, and even allowed the same camber of $1\frac{1}{8}$ in. over the total length, which was known from experience to result in a truly flat frame when loaded with the standard carriage body. But the welded frame, besides being lighter, only settled by $\frac{1}{4}$ in. when the body was fitted—causing interest but embarrassment. The technique was fast pushed ahead by Bulleid and the Works Managers, manipulators soon appearing at Gorton Works when they started welding wagon underframes. Here exploitation of welding was inhibited by the Railway Clearing House standard design. Bulleid had been on the Carriage and Wagon Superintendents Committee of the Clearing House since 1920, and was instrumental in achieving standard wagon details—axle boxes, buffers, springs, etc. In spite of L.M.S. and G.W.R. opposition he also succeeded in having rubber buffer and draw-gear springs adopted as alternative standards.

In 1928 and 1929 Bulleid presented papers to the Institution of Locomotive Engineers; rather surprisingly, both were on subjects which Gresley had personally dealt with—respectively the Booster and the Poppet Valve. Both had tables of figures showing their advantages, both got faint praise from the author, and both (like papers on compounds) marked a decline in the application of the gadget described. The Booster got a brisk discussion: it threw into sharp relief trailing wheels *v.* more coupled wheels and, therefore, wide *v.* narrow fireboxes. J. Clayton pointedly asked why one needed trailing wheels and an extra 12 tons weight, when a " Castle " was as good as a Pacific, as the recent exchange trials had shown. Bulleid's written reply is interesting:

> Mr. Clayton is a more persuasive advocate of the narrow firebox than I of the wide. Mr. Ivatt's small and large Atlantics are convincing examples of the advantage of increased boiler capacity.
>
> The designer should constantly keep before himself the future, and the probability that it will demand greater loads and higher speeds, and that the success of his design will depend upon the engine being able to cope with much increased demands during its useful life. The wide firebox gives him greater latitude in designing the boiler.

At the Poppet Valve paper, given in February 1929 with J. R. Bazin in the chair, Bulleid remarked upon the attraction of the totally-enclosed drive which it permitted. . . .

The amalgamation had the effect of presenting the fewer railways as huge potential customers, and Bulleid was always ready to try reasonable proposals from suppliers. The experiment with cast aluminium panels and doors for a 1st/3rd class composite carriage came about in this way, as a straight cost contest, aluminium *v.* teak. Teak won. This was the sort of experiment he would discuss after meetings of the A.R.L.E., of which he became secretary in 1931, taking over from Sir Henry Fowler. The formal business was rather thin, including such items as tyre profile gauges, steel for laminated springs, shrinkage allowances for tyres. After some work on boiler repair costs this subject was dropped as reliable bases for comparisons seemed too hard to find. But the informal discussions were very valuable, as Ivatt, Churchward and Co. had found years before.

They were all getting keen on welding. But not boilers, of course: so Bulleid thought he really must have a go at a welded boiler, and he approached Babcock and Wilcox. At that time, about the end of 1933, they were exceptionally busy and were not able to co-operate with any novel design and experimental work: but to show willing they offered as samples three all-welded barrels suitable for an ex-N.E.R. class "J" 0-6-0 goods engine. These were duly made up into normal class "J" boilers at Darlington and went into trouble-free service.

Whereas Gresley had worked very much on his own in designing the Yarrow-boilered 4-6-4 No. 10,000, he called considerably on Bulleid when planning a new large express passenger engine for the heavy trains and difficult gradients north of Edinburgh to Aberdeen. There were shades of Bulleid's 2-6-2 essay of 1903 in the 2-8-2 wheel arrangement selected, and he concurred completely with Gresley in all major design features—the largest possible boiler and firebox, large superheater with 220 psi boiler pressure, three 21 by 26 in. cylinders to give 43,460 lb. starting tractive effort with the 6 ft. 2 in. wheels, and Lentz valve gear with 9 in. exhaust valves. There were also some design features based on French practice—the Kylchap double blast-pipe, and double chimney. From Bugatti's experiments came the wedge-shaped cab front. Then there was the intermingled business of partial streamlining, with its good effects in publicity but hampering effects on accessibility and clearing of exhaust: Bulleid and Gresley got themselves rather involved with wind-tunnel tests. The very variety of shapes suggested and the diametrically opposite requirements of stream-*lines* and steam *clearance* relentlessly force one to compliment the Great Western shape of chimney and taper boiler.

Bulleid was highly delighted at the name chosen for the first 2-8-2 passenger loco—*Cock o' the North*—and at its power and performance. In June 1934 it hauled a 650 ton test train over Stoke summit at 56 mph with 30 per cent cut-off. When coasting, it ran freely at 70 mph. So it went up to do its first Scottish stint in July. Meanwhile, a decision had been taken to run a steam-powered high-speed King's Cross to Newcastle train, and Gresley put experiments in hand to select the most suitable combination of train timing, weight, and motive power. A key experiment was held in November 1934 when a train of weight 147 tons stood in the suburban station at King's Cross headed by No. 4472, *Flying Scotsman*, with Bulleid on the footplate. On getting the right away a really lively start was made, and the train cantered into the gas works tunnel with a verve longed-for by all passengers—and with some disregard for the inhibition-forming track between the station and the tunnel. As they made light of the climb to Finsbury Park, Bulleid recalled the slow dreary clanking of so many trains leaving "The Cross," and reflected again upon the irritation that the 0-6-2 tanks which pulled trains *into* the station were not permitted to help by shoving them *out* again; the reason for this prohibition apparently stemmed from a derailment just inside the tunnel in the 1880s, which had been ascribed to over-exuberant banking. Bulleid returned to the more stimulating reality of 83 mph at Hatfield, and found no time to examine his temporary office of 1905 as they shot through Hitchin at close on 95 mph. When Stoke summit was passed at over 80 mph Bulleid could not help reflecting that it was good fun, but could have been done with the same engine ten years earlier: he had always been a strong advocate of hard driving and brisk schedules, and had always deplored long, rambling trains and over-taxed engines. In fact, they took 152 minutes for the 185 miles to Leeds. Then on another test with No. 2750, *Papyrus*, a speed over 100 mph was maintained for 12 miles near Essendine: Gresley pressed on with his "A.4" Pacific design for the *Silver Jubilee* express, resulting in the streamlined *Silver Link*.

Cock o' the North's sister engine, *Earl Marischal*, emerged from Doncaster Works in October 1934—an identical twin except for its Walschaert's valve gear with conjugate lever arrangement for the inside cylinder. Gresley liked to have a control when he did a major experiment with valve gear—a lesson Bulleid never learned. But it was *Cock o' the North* that Gresley sent to Vitry-sur-Seine for trials on the locomotive testing plant. He stayed for some of the trials but Bulleid was there for the full three weeks, made hectic by persistent hot boxes. In despair he arranged a road test at short notice and not only recorded 2,800 horse power on a Tours–Orleans run but did so with ice-cool boxes. The driver was astounded by the performance at speed of this "goods engine," and remarked that if it had to be worked really hard it would be impossible to fire fast enough with this little shovel—pointing to the standard L.N.E.R. shovel. Then, after a one-day exhibition at the Gare du Nord, in company with a Nord engine and the President's saloon, *Cock o' the North* returned to Vitry —and hot boxes. A detail spotted during the succession of hot boxes was that whereas the plate above the box vibrated in normal running, it was always still when a box was running hot. By sheer luck Bulleid happened to notice one of these plates suddenly stop vibrating: he immediately stopped the engine, dropped the wheels, and found that a crown-sized piece of whitemetal had been bodily removed. He felt that this clearly-indicated local oil-film breakdown must be due to a vibration beat on the test plant rollers, with perhaps a large contribution from the frame not being on the centre-line of the bearing, and considered it a valuable lesson. He was satisfied by the consistently good lb.-per-drawbar-horsepower-hour figures except that he felt they could be slightly bettered by improved combustion: he became aware after the first week that, as he approached the plant of a morning, he could tell if *Cock o' the North* was performing by a decided show of smoke: whereas no such smoke was noticed when French engines of similar grate area and power were on trial. He proposed an ash pan and damper alteration to Gresley, but quite failed to get any response.

Back in England Bulleid was preoccupied in getting the finishing touches on the "streamlined" silver coaches for the *Silver Jubilee* train. They involved many a discussion with the design consultants, White Allom, and everyone was duly impressed when the train, with its 4-hour booked time between King's Cross and Newcastle and 70 mph average speed between King's Cross and Darlington, looked and acted the part from its first appearance on 30th September 1935. Nor did Gresley rest on his oars: Bulleid was again on the footplate when *Silver Fox* attained 113 mph in August 1936.

It came as a complete surprise to technically-enwrapped Bulleid when Sir Herbert Walker sent for him out of the blue in May 1937 and said he could have the job of C.M.E. of the Southern Railway if he would apply for it. Gresley, equally surprised, simply remarked "Yes, I think you could do it quite well." Maunsell stayed at hand during September to help the take-over, and on 1st October 1937 Bulleid was installed as Mechanical boss at Waterloo. As on the L.N.E.R., he had no control over Running Shed maintenance except boilers, but he had the loco, carriage and wagon works and design offices, including everything except electrics on electric locos. He inherited an exceptional chief clerk in W. Marsh: and together they quickly produced an accurate and therefore hostile report on the state of the steam loco stock. Modernization of steam stock was viewed glumly at Board level on a railway that had always led the way in electrification, so Bulleid, one eye on keen horse soldier, John Elliot, used his classic Hussar simile: "If you re-equip half a cavalry regiment with armoured cars you do not make the remaining horses any younger." The modernization programme was agreed.

Bulleid felt, and Cobb—the Running Superintendent—agreed, that the first requirement was not a conventional "express passenger engine," but a loco which might be better described as fast mixed traffic. It would have good acceleration, top speed adequate for 75 mph bookings, and availability for mixed passenger and freight workings—including the *Golden Arrow* and the Atlantic Coast expresses. Already sharply aware of the S.R. track loading limitations, he first fancied a 4-8-2, but turn-table problems ruled his out. He then went some way with a 2-8-2 but Ellson, the civil engineer, had a grave and rooted objection to pony trucks, stemming apparently from the Sevenoaks accident. After much argument, including free reference to the successful use of the L.N.E.R. 2-6-2s and 2-8-2s, he agreed to two being built for trial: but since the object of the exercise was quickly to modernize the stock not just to sit watching two experimental locos Bulleid next offered a Pacific, with axle loading 21 tons; and this was accepted.

Using mainly the design team of the Brighton Drawing Office, led by C. S. Cocks, and drawing on all known external sources for best modern practice, Bulleid set about his 4-6-2 design.

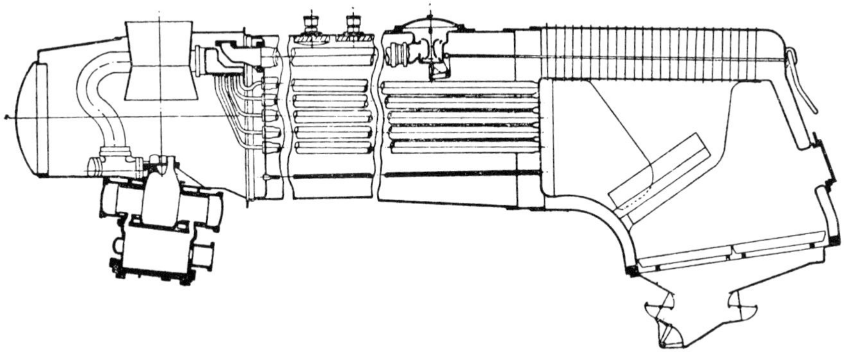

Fig. 18. The " Merchant Navy " boiler—generally recognized as the best of all Pacific boilers.

Boiler

He determined first to ensure that the engine should never be short of steam. He considered a pressure of 30 atmospheres, but thought 20 (280 psi) a better first stage. He also hoped to approach the French superheat limit of 400°C as proposed by Chapelon.

Both the weight limitation and the high pressure ruled out the use of copper for the firebox, and since a suitable mild steel with good welding characteristics was available in this country similar to that used with great success in America, a welded steel firebox was embarked on without trepidation. Besides, Bulleid felt that the burden of maintaining copper fireboxes was really intolerable, as had been found years before in the U.S.A. The welding aspect was further safeguarded by developing the X-ray inspection technique and interpretation of X-ray photographs, in conjunction with Messrs. Babcock and Wilcox. Later, the conventional foundation ring with its unsatisfactory weight and corners, was replaced by U-section steel channel welded in position. Detail improvements were made to the brick arch and to the water feed, and thermic siphons were fitted.

Wheels and Cylinders

Higher pressure allows smaller cylinders and easier balancing: Bulleid took 2,000 ft. per minute as the maximum piston speed and arrived at a 6 ft. 2 in. wheel with 24 in. stroke and hence 18 in. cylinder diameter for a tractive effort of 37,500 lb. He knew that civil engineers generally were

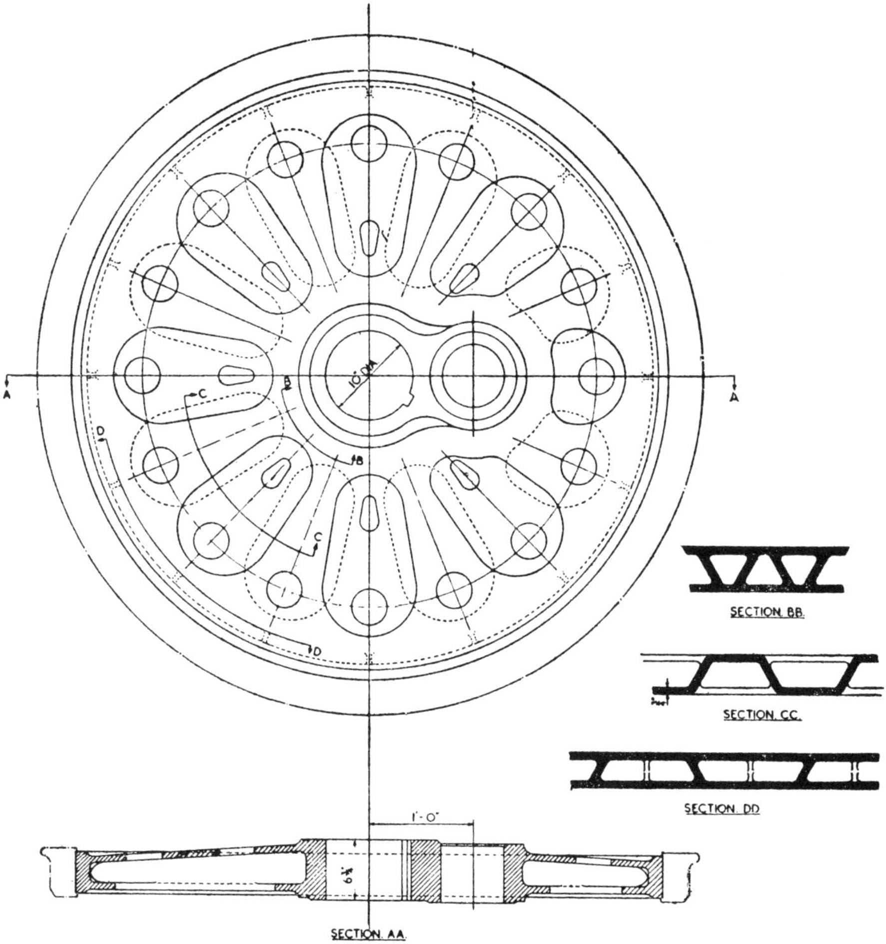

Fig. 19. The B.F.B. wheel. It provides more uniform support to the tyre than a spoked wheel and is 10 per cent lighter.

pressing for limitation of maximum speeds, and although he disagreed with this as a retrograde step even if justified by reduced track maintenance, his reaction was that 100 mph would become the maximum allowable speed. Accordingly, better acceleration was the first target. Like most civil engineers, Ellson was very concerned about hammer blow, and to meet this Bulleid provided three cylinders equally spaced, with equal weights on each crank pin.

Wheels

The B.F.B. type was a design patented in conjunction with Firth Brown. It gave better tyre support and a lip fastening was used to obviate the disadvantages of the Gibson fastening—Bulleid didn't feel quite prepared to move to the American method of relying entirely on friction between tyre and rim. A Delta type trailing truck was designed with the intention of giving as much further improvement to the riding of the engine as the Gresley truck on the first G.N.R. Pacific gave compared with the simple trailing axle on the Ivatt Atlantic.

Frames

Frames were located on the centre line of the axle boxes as a result of experience with *Cock o' the North* at Vitry.

Motion

The wear on motion details caused by grit has to be seen to be believed, and it is not helped by occasional oiling failures, though these may, in turn, be due to numerous factors ranging from poor oil flow to a driver missing an oiling point in dark or difficult conditions. Bulleid therefore decided to make a complete departure from existing practice by totally enclosing the motion in an oil bath between the frames. New motion was designed to suit this extremely desirable objective. Large outside-admission piston valves were chosen.

Axle Boxes

Bronze axle boxes were used on the argument that apart from being the best they are easily made in a railway foundry, and the value of the metal is never lost.

Outer Casing

Bulleid, the debunker of streamlining in 1934, was naturally not going to get involved with streamlining an engine which was not even called an " express passenger engine ": a smooth external casing, however, provided two very great advantages: it permitted easier machine cleaning of the engine, and it concealed all the external pipes about the boiler so they could be run for convenience rather than for appearance.

Sanding

Good sanding is particularly important on an engine with decent reserves of boiler power. Considerable experimental work resulted in an improved steam jet and showed that the G.W.R. practice of calcining the sand was essential to prevent moisture being absorbed and hence to permit a reliable gravity feed.

Cab

Knowing the sensitivity of engine men to design changes, Bulleid made particular efforts to incorporate in the cab and elsewhere features designed to help the men to run their engines. These included the grouping of the controls to suit the driver and fireman, the fitting of superior American type injectors developed by Davies and Metcalf, and steam-operated fire-hole doors. A turbo-generator served the engine, cab, and inspection lights.

Design features which were desired but impracticable, under war conditions, were automatic stokers and T.I.A. water treatment.

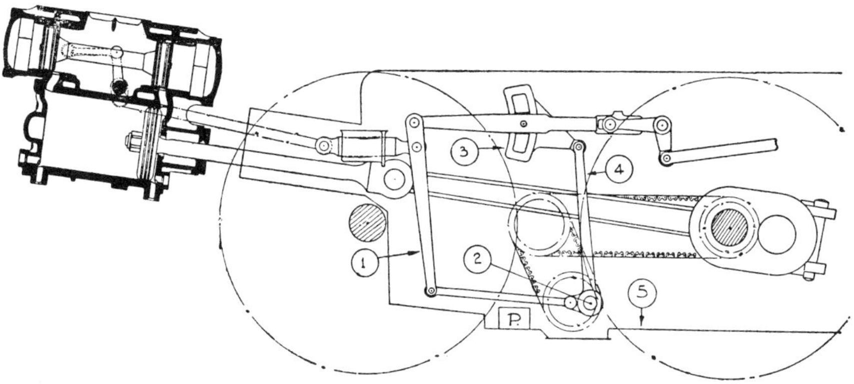

Fig. 20. Bulleid's valve gear. The combination lever 1 is driven in phase with the cross-head from pin 2 on the chain-driven valve gear shaft. The radius rod 3 is driven 90 degrees out-of-phase by placing the eccentric rod 4 at right-angles to its position in Walschaert's gear. 5 indicates the oil bath enclosure, and P is the oil circulating pump.

Details to facilitate Shed Work

Hopper-type ash pan, rocking grate, improved accessibility within the smoke box, and motion not requiring oiling.

Safety

Three large safety-valves; thermic siphons to induce a flood of water over the firebox crown; plug type fusible plugs to act as unhesitating fire-extinguishers; and strengthened firehole doors to reduce risk of a blow-out. Together, these gave the best possible protection to the footplate staff, though on one occasion the safety valves performed a destructive test on Ilfracombe station canopy.

BULLEID PACIFICS COMPARED WITH GRESLEY AND STANIER PACIFICS

		Bulleid		*Gresley* *"A4"*	*Stanier* *"Duchess"*
		"Merchant Navy"	*"West Country"*		
Cylinders	No.	3	3	3	4
,, bore	in.	18	16⅜	18½	16½
,, stroke	in.	24	24	26	28
Coupled wheels	ft. in.	6 2	6 2	6 8	6 9
Bogie wheels	ft. in.	3 1	3 1	3 2	3 0
Trailing wheels	ft. in.	3 7	3 1	3 8	3 9
Coupled wheelbase	ft. in.	15 0	14 9	14 6	14 6
Heating surfaces:					
Tubes and flues	sq. ft.	2176	1869	2345	2577
Firebox	sq. ft.	275	253	231	230
Total evap.	sq. ft.	2451	2122	2576	2807
Superheater	sq. ft.	822	545	750	822
Grate area	sq. ft.	48½	38¼	41¼	50
Working pressure	psi	280	280	250	250
Tractive effort	lb.	37,500	31,000	35,455	40,000
Adhesion weight	tons	63	56¼	66	67
Weight of engine	tons	94¾	86	103	105
Weight of engine & tender	tons	142½	128½	165½	163¼

Seldom can a C.M.E. have designed and produced a new locomotive under conditions more trying than those suffered by Bulleid. Arguing a steam revival and settling the loco type took him almost to the Munich incident; and then the shadow of war loomed over design, and war hampered construction. And there were other duties—the railways in September 1939 came under the control of an Executive Committee (consisting mainly of individual Company Presidents), and Bulleid became a member and later Chairman of the Mechanical and Electrical Sub-Committee for the duration. In December he took over the Presidency of the Institution of Locomotive Engineers—from Sir William Stanier, at the Opening General Meeting of the 1939/40 Session, at the Waldorf Hotel after an Institution lunch. His brief Presidential Address was concerned with the importance of railway operation during the emergency under the Executive Committee. " These are stirring times, and we should rejoice we have our share in them," Bulleid said, recalling his patriotic approach to World War I. He also said " the country cannot be prosperous if the railways are not," recalling his dedicated inability to take a broad view of the country's transport system.

Sir Nigel Gresley's vote of thanks included a calculated *double entendre*: " It would seem he has been made our President, at any rate for the duration of the war, but we hope this doesn't mean in perpetuity."

Early 1940, the " phoney war " period, found Bulleid full in the throes of " Merchant Navy " design problems. Brighton Drawing Office had a lively time interpreting and keeping up with the ideas of their fertile-brained Chief: he would agree a point with them, set off for Eastleigh, have a better idea during the journey, and ring them upon arrival. Sometimes they wished he would travel less. The valve-gear was a particularly happy inspiration: he patented it, but this may have reduced its chances of wide acceptance, as Churchward found. Its compact layout permitted his goal of enclosing it, with the inside big-end, in an oil-bath. The elegance of this proposal was clear to all engineers, though they differed in ability to achieve it.

There were many other matters demanding attention. The *Lord Nelsons* had the reputation amongst Southern drivers of being fast engines but, after footplate trips, Bulleid concluded they were not fast, in the sense of being free-running, compared with L.N.E.R. standards, though they were fine engines and incorporated all the best G.W.R. ideas stemming from Churchward. Accordingly, since they were beginning to require re-cylindering, a lot of design effort was devoted to improving the uniformity of the steam and exhaust passages, reducing bends, and imparting a higher internal surface finish. Then there was the curious incident of the oil feed to the driving axle-boxes. There was no trace of any oil on the Erecting Shop floor under a recently-lifted engine, and yet the oil boxes in the cab were full and the trimmings had been left in place. So there could be *no* oil feed to the boxes. "That was the curious incident," thought Bulleid, recalling a Gresley-Maunsell discussion in which Maunsell had extolled the warm location and how the driver could keep an eye on them—in contrast to the Southern Railway ex-L.B.S.C.R. Atlantics which had Ivatt's oil boxes over the splashers; chilly, inaccessible from the cab, and curiously prone to feed pipe fractures. Gresley was unimpressed, and in Bulleid's experience, these Gresley reactions were generally sound. However, Turbett and Bulleid found that the *Lord Nelson* drivers always gave a good shot of oil into each feed pipe before replacing the trimmings at the start of a journey; it thus seemed to be a simple case of an air-lock and was, in fact, cured by connecting a vent pipe.

There was also a demand from the Running Department for a batch of engines more powerful than the Maunsell "Q" class 0-6-0, and capable of running backwards when necessary without loss in performance. Bulleid decided on a re-designed 0-6-0 with cab-type tender, fitted with a large boiler—in fact, the largest possible using the existing flanging blocks of the *Lord Nelson* boilers. He retained the 19 by 26 cylinder size and the 5 ft. 1 in. wheel size of the Maunsell 0-6-0s but achieved a lot more boiler power within the same total weight of engine-plus-tender:

Feature		*Maunsell Class "Q"*	*Bulleid Class "Q1"*
Boiler pressure	psi	200	230
Boiler max. diameter	feet	5	5¾
Combined heating surfaces	sq. ft.	1432	1860
Grate area	sq. ft.	21.9	27
Total weight in working order, tons	Engine	49½	51¼
	Tender	40½	38

" Q1 " emerged as a full-blooded engine, the most powerful 0-6-0 in the country. Its tractive effort was 30,000 lb. compared with the 26,160 lb. of Maunsell's " Q " class. Of course there was trouble in keeping the weight down to 51 tons, and Bulleid jettisoned the non-essentials—the " austerity " slant. No running board, he suddenly thought, this being an anachronism now that drivers do not have to walk round for oiling whilst running. He

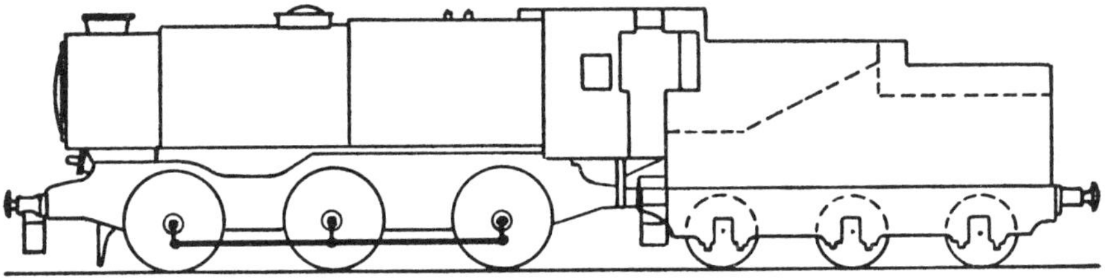

Fig. 21. Q1 "Austerity." Stanier asked Bulleid, "Where's the key?"

also thought he would let the engine's appearance come out naturally—he had already fixed a smoke box shape allowing maximum accessibility, and he was using the large chimney with multiple-jet blast. Pressed, he said that what was functionally correct would come to be seen as artistically correct. Pressed further, he admitted he did not admire the " Q1 " shape, and here he was in excellent company. When Stanier was shown its photograph, he merely remarked " I don't believe it."

The excellent performance of the " Q1 " class dispelled some of the emotional dislikes of the engine crews, but they thought its braking power was inadequate for its tractive capabilities, and they also feared fast reverse running. To scotch this fear, Bulleid staged a demonstration run: he climbed on to the tender and proceeded tender-first from Ashford to Maidstone, covering one stretch at 75 mph. The objection was withdrawn. He disposed of other minor worries at a Mutual Improvement Class at Feltham one Sunday, batting well in a free-for-all question session.

Construction of the new Pacifics progressed well under Turbett at Eastleigh Works, and when the first engine was christened *Channel Packet* in March 1941 Bulleid expressed himself as satisfied that his design intentions had, in fact, been satisfactorily interpreted. Technically, some of the design anxieties were over. The design weights were achieved after some minor adjustments. Tests carried out over Barnes Bridge showed that the target of negligible hammer blow had been achieved.

The reaction of the footplate staff was dramatically favourable. For the first time on the Southern Railway they had been offered an engine which was not only considerably more powerful than existing engines but had such a reserve of boiler power that the engine man's major fear of being short of steam was virtually removed. To this was added an exceptionally well laid out cab, and the best riding qualities ever achieved. Their only complaints were of proneness to slipping and of poor visibility from the cab, partly due to the size of the boiler casing, but mainly due to steam and smoke beating down.

The reaction of the shed maintenance staff was, however, gloomy. This was partly because the thinking behind the design was not properly communicated to them, and partly because they were offered a situation which always infuriates maintenance men, i.e. they were asked to carry out repairs to inaccessible items whose inaccessibility they were told was due to their not requiring repair. This situation persisted in the teething trouble stage. However carefully one carries out pipe runs and component placing, there are inevitably leak-prone situations, and on these Pacifics part of the boiler casing had to be removed in order to get at such leaks. Numerous securing screws had to be removed and, to make matters worse, these were really too small for their duty. Bulleid later recognized that something in the nature of a piano hinge or a device giving the facility of an ever-ready case was an essential accessibility adjunct to the sort of protective casing with which his Pacifics were clad.

More serious were teething troubles connected with the motion, where there was delay in finding the cause of fractures in the cross shaft operating the piston valves. A man with a keenly inventive mind is seldom the best trouble-shooter, and Bulleid was no exception. Nor had his team much experience or equipment in this field, as was shown up by failure theories that would not stand scrutiny. Hares were started—lack of lubrication, inadequate clearances, wrong metal—when the trouble was a misplaced keyway causing a stress-raiser. Then more hares were started—chain drive uncertain, excessive multiplication at the rocking shaft—when the duty was not clearly understood. In fact the motion was so light that it took only 3·8 h.p. to drive a set rigged up in the Erecting Shop at the equivalent of 90 mph. But this was without steam: and finally indicator diagrams showed a pressure difference at the two ends of the piston valves, which was rectified by providing a balancing cavity. Trouble with steam passage areas once again, in fact!

Bulleid got further wind tunnel tests going to improve the engine front so that steam would clear better, and then turned to the major trouble—excessive loss of oil. The only crumb of comfort was that, all being well, a "Merchant Navy" would only use as much oil as the two "King Arthurs" which would otherwise be needed on the boat train: but sometimes all wasn't well, and then the oil consumption was positively staggering. The reciprocating rods to the piston valves were found to pump out the oil, which scoured the sump front quite clean. The design of glands and seals was not up to this boisterous application, and the shed fitters were uncertain how to deal with obvious minor leaks. Moreover, the oil *got* everywhere, including such undesirable places as the track causing slipping and the boiler lagging causing fires. One engine caught fire to such purpose that the crew had to abandon it and the local Fire Brigade was called. An ugly bureaucratic argument then followed as to whose responsibility it was to extinguish blazing steam engines.

No technical advances come without struggles and joltings from the easy life, however: and everyone except the maintenance sections of the Operating Department liked the Bulleid Pacifics. " Well done, they are fine engines," came a personal message from the General Manager, Sir Eustace Missenden, in late 1941. After full debate it was decided unanimously to continue with the type and from this decision came the second batch of ten " Merchant Navy " class engines in late 1944 and the lightweight " West Country " and " Battle of Britain " classes which appeared in April 1945.

There was a period in the middle of the war when Bulleid was working desperately hard for the Executive Committee, in particular on the problem of wagons: in a special note he put the grave situation into hard focus by pointing out that a supply of 40,000 wagons per year would just keep the already run-down stocks from further deterioration, let alone permit an improvement. By taking these extra-mural duties in stints sandwiched between consecutive nights of travel, he found time to attend to his Southern Railway and war material manufacturing duties, which themselves demanded considerable travelling. Not that all trips were of unremitting toil: there was an occasional visit to the Assistant for the Isle of Wight, a rather delightful job in which G. L. Nicholson had charge of everything and accordingly reported to all the bosses. When the C.M.E. came down to look over the carriage paint shop at Newport he was rather surprised to be met at Ryde by Nicholson in his modest motor car. Quarr Abbey lies on the route, a delightful Benedictine Monastery where, curiously, the choirmaster was a grandson of William Dean. " Possibly you might care to pause for a few moments to look round," Nicholson suggested, casually. They entered, received V.I.P. treatment and an excellent lunch from the Prior, and arrived at Ryde very late indeed.

By this time the first 25 " West Country " class Pacifics were on the road: extra popular with their drivers on account of their air of being special to the West Country, and on account of various minor improvements. Bulleid was very pleased with them, and he delighted in their free-running: " They almost seem to gather speed when the regulator is shut off on a down gradient," he remarked affectionately on one occasion.

In 1942 the electrical engineer, Rayworth, had obtained sanction for three electric locos for goods haulage. When the rather sketchy and modest proposal came to Bulleid for the vehicle and wheel design, he reiterated that the thinking must be upon " mixed traffic " lines, won his point after a struggle, and came up with designs for a Co + Co loco. A speciality was the bogie, with no bolster nor centre pivot and four pads carrying the weight and traction. These engines with their English Electric traction motors were a decided success and Rayworth freely acknowledged the value of the mixed traffic approach. This led in due time to his proposal for three diesel-electric locos based on English Electric equipment, an idea anticipated by H. G. Ivatt on the L.M.S.

Diesel thinking on the electric/steam powered Southern Railway early in 1946 was not as odd as it sounds, because there was such a coal-shortage panic that at Government request Bulleid had prepared plans to convert 1,200 engines to oil-burning, and to equip the running sheds to suit. He rejoiced in this order for many reasons: it would permit maximum power, at present restricted by variable coal quality and the limit of sustained manual firing. It would increase loco availability by reducing shed time, and it would remove the dirt horrors—smoke, ash, sparks and cinders. Previous oil conversions had never been *total* at any one shed, so the full labour-saving potential had never been exploited. Nor was it this time, because with all the equipment ordered on priority and therefore quickly delivered, there was a reversal of policy, and the whole plan was cancelled.

The Southern Railway had a lot of so-called exchange duties—important freight workings between South and North London goods termini. These were nobly done by various hard-working and rather attractive 0-6-0 tanks, and when in 1946 more were needed the C.M.E. was duly asked to supply. Bulleid eyed these tanks with distaste, seeing them as fussy and archaic. " You don't really want them," he argued, " Because they are confined to one class of duty. What you need is a substantially more powerful mixed-traffic tank locomotive with full route availability." Such a locomotive would also replace the " M.7 " class 0-4-4 tanks on branch line push-and-pull duties and could work a train from Waterloo to any branch terminal. Again he won his argument, and with particular pleasure because his thoughts were on the next logical development of the general-purpose steam locomotive—a frame carrying a large boiler with driving cab at each end, and mounted on two six-wheel bogies, each powered by a 3-cylinder engine and capable of quick removal and replacement by a spare bogie in the event of wheels, motion or engine requiring repair. There is no doubt that Bulleid cheerfully wrote up a modest request for a few 0-6-0 tanks into his " Leader " engine: he composed a rather idealistic list of desiderata and enthusiastically added that it would work fast passenger trains up to 480 tons and goods trains up to 1,200 tons, with fuel for 200 miles. " And any road," said he, " It's no use thinking of a modern engine with less than 100 per cent adhesive weight." He included a brief description in his Presidential Address to the Institution of Mechanical Engineers on 18th October 1946, adding that sanction had been obtained for the building of five such engines.

The duties of the President, always demanding, were added to by preparations for the Institution's Centenary: and when on 12th June 1947 Bulleid presented a set of four papers by the four C.M.Es. of the main line railways one marvelled at his success in coaxing written work from Ivatt and Peppercorn. Together the four papers gave a good slant on current Railway thinking: Bulleid's paper alone suggested there was room for significant improvement to the conventional steam engine.

Return to peacetime conditions found Bulleid once again restless at slow timings and sketchy use of motive-power: he vigorously pointed

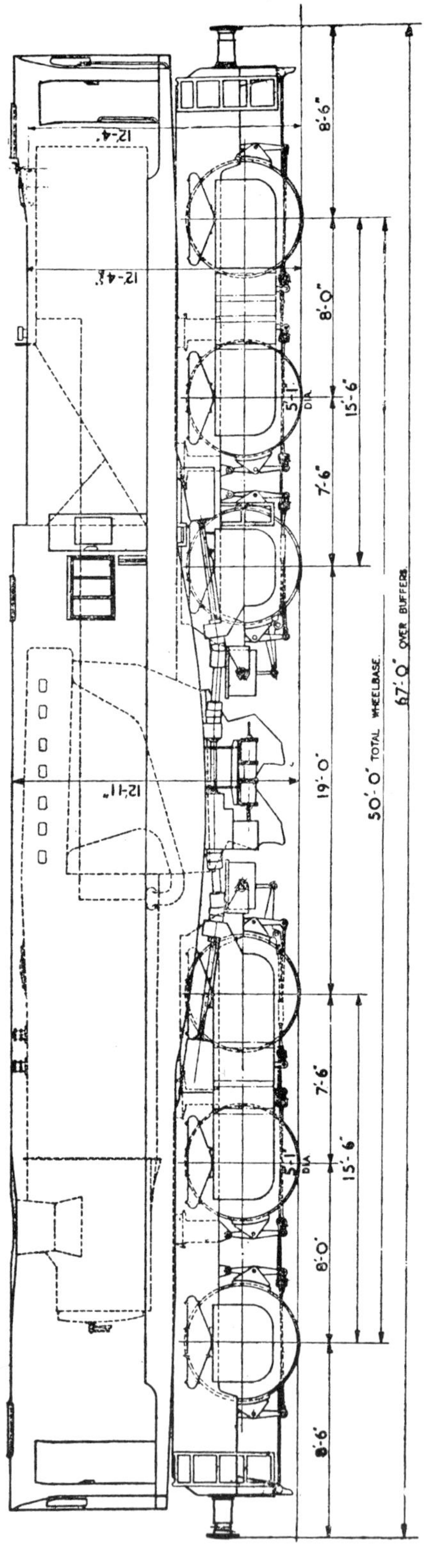

Fig. 22. *The Leader*. A sophisticated Garratt.

out that a " Merchant Navy " could haul the 450-ton *Golden Arrow* over the rather notorious 78 miles from London to Dover in 78 minutes, adding that this was the sort of performance the public expected. A series of six trial runs was agreed, and Bulleid took the unusual step of arranging, with the Motive Power Superintendent, to have a briefing session at Stuarts Lane shed with the three sets of enginemen. Once again he stressed particularly the need to keep the engine in full gear until the speed reached 20 mph. Bulleid said afterwards that the men seemed keen and all set for good performances, with the possible exception of Driver Pick: but it was Pick who first " broke " even timing when he steamed into Dover half a minute early on the fast test schedule. Possibly even more credit was due to his mate, for an extremely arduous hour and a quarter: Bulleid regretted again the lost oil-burning opportunity, and recalled some Great Central experiments with pulverised coal in the 1920s and shuddered at the recollection—" You could write your name everywhere in the dust." He then implemented the plan of 1941, and fitted one " Merchant Navy " with a mechanical stoker. This allowed the use of very low grade fuel, an important aspect of coal economy which was never followed up.

There was nothing insular about Bulleid, and he had seen several unfortunate results of nationalization in the European Railways: these magnified his own rooted objection to the nationalization of our railways, and he watched the approach of the fatal 1st January 1948 with distinct disfavour. He had built up a great regard for the Southern, and was ready to see any directive from the newly-formed Railway Executive as a tiresome and probably incompetent imposition. R. A. Riddles was clearly intending to produce a new range of standard engines with the best conventional modern features, not experimental stuff: he therefore did not favour the " Leader " and only after some pressure did he agree to let the building of one proceed.

On the carriage side, Bulleid cheerfully ignored the rule that all painting was to be to the British Railways standard red when he completed the first Tavern car. He had got this inspiration whilst at the Chequers, Pulborough. There had been grumbles from the catering people that passengers lingered too long over a cup of something, and so he provided attractive straight-backed oak settees, delightful to look at but basically hard after 15 minutes' sitting. As the first car progressed in the Works, the shop humorist chalked " Sorry no beer " on it—a mark of approbation. Forgetting his precept about the strictly functional design looking right, Bulleid had the outside painted to resemble a Tavern. And then the Executive came to inspect, and liked it. " They never even realized it was not to the standard colour scheme," remarked Bulleid, delighted at the excellent reaction. But the delight was short-lived. A multi-signature letter appeared in *The Times*, deploring the whole idea. Other papers, who often deplored stick-in-the-mud railroaders, joined in. Executives who had liked the car a few days before suddenly found they loathed it.

But if the Tavern cars revealed schoolboy Bulleid, fooling with coloured chalks, we are right back into the shrewdest design realms with the double-decker. Ever since the affair of the springs on Liverpool Street suburban coaches Bulleid had been appalled at the numbers of passengers having to stand: and in his mind was the picture of French double-deck carriages and, of course, the reflection that this country is the stud, cradle and incubator of double-deckery on tram and bus. So when Sir Eustace Missenden found that it would cost about £10 million to extend platforms and sidings and provide an additional power station, to carry more passengers per suburban train by increasing their length, Bulleid proposed and obtained sanction to build one double-decker train. Lancing Carriage Drawing Office surpassed itself in carrying out the numerous Bulleid suggestions to conserve every centimetre of space, and the resulting job was quite a triumph of design and layout, achieving 30 per cent more seated passengers for the same carriage length and weight. There was considerable enthusiasm at its first private view in September 1948: amongst those interestedly present was Herbert Morrison and he said to Bulleid " This is wonderful. It is just what my electors want. How many can we have by Christmas? " Even Lancing could not turn out complete trains in 10 weeks from scratch: but in any case there was no follow-up order. The public accepted the one train with no particular emotion either way, but the running people grizzled faintly about the extra numbers discharged simultaneously at termini and about what they would do if it got involved in an accident. Once again, Bulleid had failed to sell an innovation to his opposite numbers who would then, in turn, have sold it better to the passengers. Of course the truth is that, like so many inspired designers, he couldn't be bothered to *sell* his designs. He preferred to get on with his next idea, ruthlessly feeling that if " they " hadn't the sense to appreciate the stuff, that was their look-out. But he did remark at the time that it was " Quite preposterous to build only one train. We should have built 10, and then they would have had to use them and build more."

Design work was proceeding on the " Leader " at Brighton, but the little 3-cylinder engines presented numerous problems. Bulleid felt that sleeve valves were essential, and since lengthy running trials would be advisable for such an innovation he converted one of the Ivatt/Marsh ex-L.B. & S.C.R. Atlantics. The result was a decided success, save that the engine lost power because the cylinder diameter had to be reduced. T.I.A. continuous water treatment was fitted on the " Leader," as on the Pacifics where it gave a wonderful improvement, extending the washout period to two months.

And so came the day when the " Leader " appeared, and teething troubles started in the powered bogies: and though the boiler steamed well the fireman had a fearful hot spot at engine centre whilst the driver was in his cool cab at either end—a worry easily curable by oil-firing. Chapelon had watched the sleeve valve development with great interest and sent over a congratulatory message: this pleased Bulleid almost as much as his C.B.E. in the 1949 New Year Honours List.

But 19th September 1949 was coming into view, Bulleid's 67th birthday. Irritated by Nationalization, slightly cross with himself for not making the "Leader" engines removable *en bloc* from their bogies, and beckoned from Eire for consultation, he resigned from British Railways. He had, meantime, been elected President of the Institute of Welding, and so his term of office was conducted, so to speak, from Dublin. In his Presidential Address on 25th October 1949 he gave an excellent descriptive summary of advances in welding techniques and of the design development therefrom, spanning his lengthy railway experience to date. One sentence in it illuminates the mentality of the truly progressive designer—he described the rejection by the Clearing House Committee of the first welded wagon frame proposal as " an example of the tyranny of standardization."

With Coras Iompair Eireann, first as consultant and later as C.M.E., there was much solid work to do in the provision of diesel power and in improved carriage design and production. But above all came the opportunity to design and build an improved " Leader," in the guise of the turf-burner. The Irish are not unduly disposed to worry about where their fuel will come from in the event of some international incident, and it was bustler Bulleid who first kept up interest in peat-firing by providing over-size tenders to transport the vast bulk needed, and who later designed and built the mixed-traffic turf-burner locomotive. Technically this was important, with its boiler design slanted to suit local manufacture and, above all, with its development of the powered bogie, this time with a simple piston-valve engine designed to be separately removable from the bogie.

So fell the technical curtain for the steam locomotive; and it shows how they might have looked and lasted, if it had come at the end of the second act instead of at the end of the play.

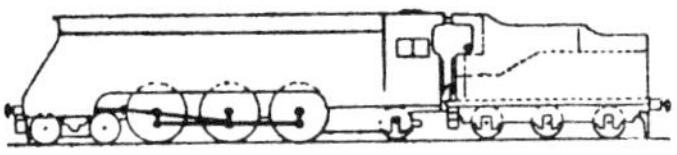

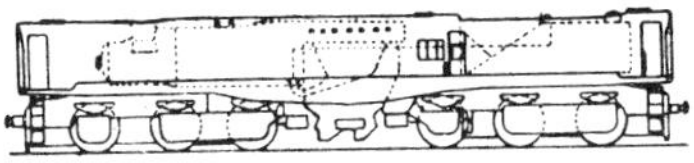

Above: "Newton" class 2-4-0 *Phaeton* built 1872. Ivatt's own caption to this reads: "Photo at Crewe, August 1873.
L. & N.W.R. Engine running express trains between Crewe and Carlisle. Driver D. Naylor. Fireman H. A. Ivatt."

Below: Part of the A.R.L.E. group on their 1892 Summer meeting at Grasmere. In front: Dean, Ivatt, J. Stirling. Behind: Billinton, Johnson, Adams, Manson.

Above: Typical executive passes of the 1890s: G.N.R. in gold; North Eastern; Great Central in silver; and Great Eastern, shaped to wear out any pocket.

Below: Ivatt's condensing suburban 4-4-2 tank, 1899, here seen heading for Potters Bar. Most of them worked for British Rail, later. *Real Photographs*

Above: The first British Atlantic, No. 990, transformed from "workshop coat" of grey to full G.N.R. colours, on 20th May 1898, and later named *Henry Oakley*. *British Rail*

Below: 30th December 1903. Ivatt and Sturrock with "Long Tom" No. 405. The original "Long Tom" was a heavy gun used against Ladysmith and featured in Boer War popular songs. So it was an obvious topical choice for naming this long-boiler-barrelled loco in 1901. *British Rail*

Above: Ivatt's 0-8-2 condensing suburban tank, 1903, with advertising as on buses . . . rejected by the G.N.R. The poster advertises G.N.R. trains to Sheffield, Nottingham and Leeds, and shows No. 990 with six-wheel bogie carriages. *British Rail*

Below: The first big-boilered Atlantic, No. 251, as it first emerged from the Crimpsall with stove-pipe chimney and driving wheel splasher taken horizontally to the firebox casing. *British Rail*

Above: Two super-polished, dust-sheeted engines being carefully taken from Doncaster for the 1909 London Exhibition, under the care of apprentice A. H. Peppercorn and the power of rebuilt Stirling 2-4-0 No 867. *British Rail*

Below: On show at the Imperial International Exhibition, White City, 1909 — the latest G.N.R. Atlantic No. 1442 side-by-side with Stirling's already long famous 8ft "single" No. 1, preserved by Ivatt. *British Rail*

Above: South end of Doncaster station with L. & N.W.R. "Precursor" No. 412 *Marquis* starting a Kings Cross express during the 1909 interchange trials. The Atlantics came out about 5% lighter on coal. *J. R. Bazin*

Below: Though many standard parts came in handy, this was the end of the road for Ivatt's 4-2-2; the scrap road at Doncaster, 1918. *British Rail*

No 990

No 2

Above left: Nos. 990 and 251 at Finsbury Park heading home to Doncaster and celebrating the Plant Works Centenary, September 1953.

Below left: Gresley's first carriage design, 1905, making the car portion of Ivatt's steam railcar for the Louth-Grimsby line.

Above: H. N. Gresley beside his first 3-cylinder engine, May 1918. No. 461 was the pioneer of class "O.2" but with the unsatisfactory rocking-shaft type of 2-to-1 gear. *British Rail*

Below: Looking decidedly more nonchalant than in 1918, Sir Nigel Gresley beside his 100th Pacific. The Chairman presented him with a silver model of the engine. *British Rail*

L N E R
4472

Above left: L.N.E.R. *Flying Scotsman* and R.H.&D.R. *Typhoon* posing for the cameras at Kings Cross to amuse Gresley and his friend Captain Howey. *Fox Photos*

Centre left: Gresley's 1930 2-6-2T design seen here as B.R. 67624 on the Caledonian line passing Haymarket, Edinburgh en route to Fife.

Below left: Up "Silver Jubilee" near Potters Bar on 28th December 1938 — rescued by Ivatt Atlantic No 4446 (slightly hotted up by Gresley)

Above: The Rolls Royce of 2-6-2s, *Bantam Cock*, No. 1700, on a Glasgow to Fort William through freight — near Crianlarich and still climbing. *P. Ransome-Wallis*

Below: Class "K.4" 2-6-0 *Cameron of Lochiel* with 5ft 2in driving wheels for the West Highland line of the North British Railway, here seen leaving Fort William for Mallaig. *E. D. Bruton*

Left: Newsreel shot at Vitry — the sound-track at the left carries the voice of Bulleid explaining the trials, and the considerable noise of No. 2001. *Pathé*

Below: "Merchant Navy" class No. 35028 *Clan Line* on the all-Pullman (plus luggage van) "Golden Arrow" near Chislehurst in 1954. *Brian Morrison*

Right: "Battle of Britain" class No. 34071 *601 Squadron* on the down "Golden Arrow" at Bickley in 1952 — with resting fireman. *J. G. Click*

Below right: "West Country" class cab; left-hand drive, both injectors controlled from the fireman's side, steam-operated firehole doors and turbo-generator lighting. Steam heating. *British Rail*

GOLDEN
ARROW

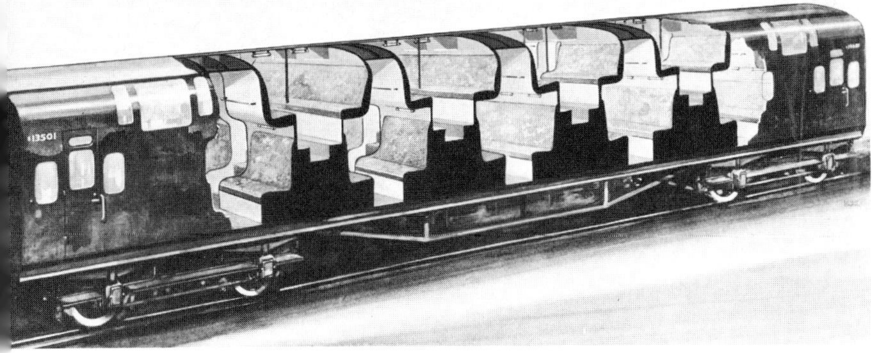

Above left: Class "Q1" 0-6-0 No. 33022 ambling along the Guildford-Horsham line near Bramley with an excursion train to Brighton. *Derek Cross*

Below left: You had to agree, when inside Bulleid's tavern car, that it did look and behave like a mobile tavern. *British Rail*

Above: Double decker carriages. They ran for twenty years during which they provided an extra hundred million seated passenger miles. *British Rail*

Centre right: Ivatt/Marsh L.B.S.C. Atlantic No. 2039 *Hartland Point* fitted with sleeve valves and (shades of 1902) a stove-pipe chimney. *R. Curl*

Right: "Leader" class No. 36001 on one of its limited test runs, 1951.

Above left: Bulleid in the CME's office, Inchicore, August 1950. Previous occupants portrayed included McDonnell, Aspinall, Ivatt, Maunsell, Bazin. *H. A. V. Bulleid*

Below left: The C-C Peat Fuel Locomotive of Coras Iompair Eireann, more generally known as Bulleid's Turf Burner, being hauled from the Inchicore erecting shop by H. A. Ivatt's 2-4-2T No. 42, built 1892. *J. G. Click*

Above: On board the Turf Burner. Bulleid explains some technical delight to Armand, General Manager of the French National Railways, in French. *J. G. Click*

Centre right: Typical South Devon engine during Churchward's apprenticeship — broad gauge 4-4-0 saddle tank No. 2132. "Protection for driver and fireman very scanty," as J. G. Robinson recalled in a letter to Bulleid in 1942. *British Rail*

Right: Churchward's steam railcar, 1905, at Plympton station, hindered by a bogie carriage. The G.W.R. did not want it to look like an engine. "They had ample power and rode well," Stanier recalled. *J. R. Bazin*

Above: With standard boiler, top feed, external steam pipes — "Star" class No. 4043 *Prince Henry* near Dawlish in 1949, hauling L.N.E.R. carriages to Newcastle. *E. D. Bruton*

Below: A tidy load for "County" class 4-4-0 No. 3804 *County Dublin* on down Weymouth express at Sonning, 1926. *M. W. Earley*

Above: Churchward's "County" tank No. 2247 near Reading in 1932 with assorted coaching stock and working hard in defiance of the distant signal.
M. W. Earley

Below: Good G.W.R. publicity in 1909 — showing their huge new engine *The Great Bear* and their ability to swing it around.
British Rail

920

Left: The first British Mogul — Churchward's 2-6-0 No. 6393 on the old S.E.&C.R. line passing Wellington College overbridge near Wokingham with a Hastings-Birmingham train. *M. W. Earley*

Below left: Near Princes Risborough on the G.W. & G.C. joint line in 1951 — class "28XX" 2-8-0 No. 3831 being overtaken by the wind. *J. F. Russell*

Right: Stanier said this was a characteristic portrait of Churchward, taken about 1920. *British Rail*

Below: At Haddenham, Bucks, July 1961 — No. 7036 *Taunton Castle* on an up inter-city express; and Armstrong/Collett 0-6-0T No. 6429 linked for push-pull with carriage *Thrush*. *G. M. Cashmore*

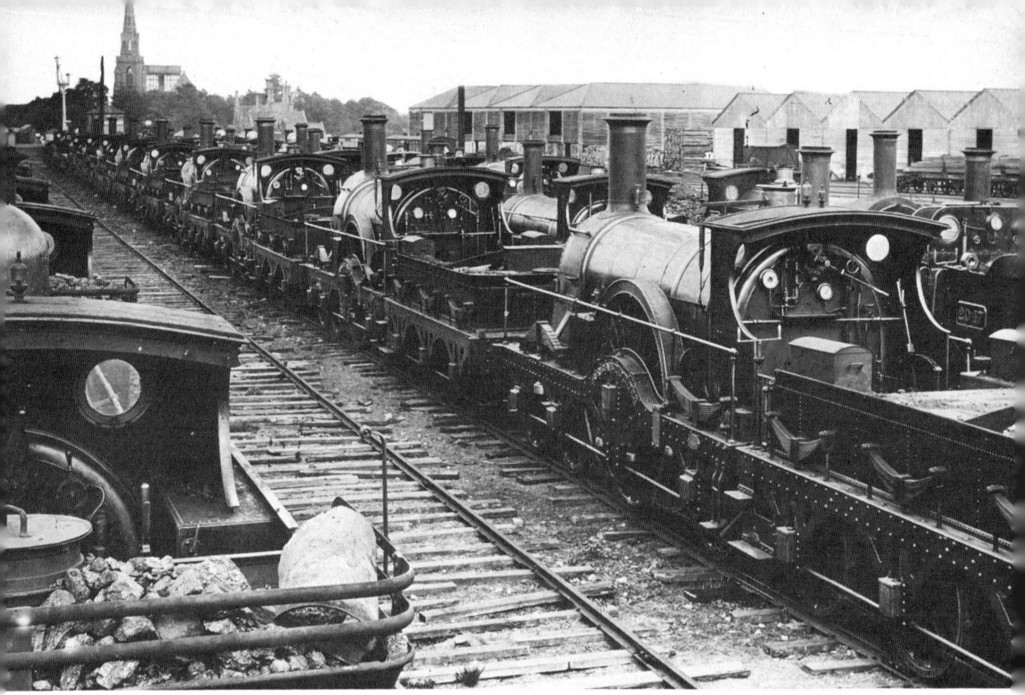

Above: Lines of obsolete broad gauge engines at Swindon as seen by apprentice Stanier in June 1882. *British Rail*

Below: At the Festival of the Iron Horse, Baltimore, 1927. All-American Britannia flanked by Stanier and driver Young of Old Oak.

Above: Stanier's first engine, the 2-6-0 mixed traffic. Here is No. 42970 toying with a slow passenger train from Leeds at Manchester Exchange in 1960. *J. R. Carter*

Below: The first two L.M.S. Pacifics, class "8P", *The Princess Royal* and *Princess Elizabeth*, on shed at Carlisle Kingmoor in July 1962. *Paul Claxton*

Left: L.M.S. Pacific cab. When I asked Sir William if the huge manifold for the auxiliaries was really necessary he said "Your uncle would have had a bit of string for the whistle, like on the North Western". *British Rail*

Right: The all-purpose go-anywhere "Black Stanier" — No. 45084 climbing towards Oban on the old Caledonian line with a sizeable goods train. *W. A. V. Anderson*

Below: Known as *Gracie Fields* because it sang as it went, the 1935 Turbomotive, a success by the design teams led by Stanier and by H. L. Guy of Metropolitan Vickers. *Popular Science Educator*

48265
45675

Left: "Coronation" Pacific No. 6222 *Queen Mary* in March 1939 passing Tamworth at 80mph with well-cleared exhaust promising 1500 draw-bar horsepower.

Right: W. A. Stanier en route to India on Col. Mount's Pacific Committee, 1938. *Universal Pictorial Press*

Left: Night time at York Motive Power Depot — or, as we used to say, Shed. Left to right, "Black Stanier" No. 45005, 2-8-0 No. 48265, "Jubilee" No. 45675. *M. S. Burns*

Right: On Fowler/Stanier rebuilt "Royal Scot" No. 46118 *Royal Welch Fusiliers* in 1958 approaching Shap summit from the north. *J. G. Click*

46256

NORTH STAFFORDSHIRE RAILWAY COMPANY
H G IVATT
FREE
PASS
No 117
FOR SERVICE
NATIONAL
EMERGENCY
MAY

Left: One of the last two L.M.S. Pacifics, No. 46256, *Sir William A. Stanier, F.R.S.*, built with sundry improvements including Delta trailing truck, seen here with banking assistance.

Right: "Precursor" cab showing the original 6-spoke reversing wheel. For notching-up data, see page 165. *British Rail*

Left: H. G. Ivatt's North Staffordshire free pass, and his 1926 bronze medallion awarded for "having a good time, driving engines".

Right: Ivatt's arrangement of a central geared drive to the two Caprotti cam boxes on class "5MT" 4-6-0s Nos. 44738 to 44757. The control linkage from the driver's cab is between the sand-box fillers and the smokebox saddle. *British Rail*

Above: Ivatt 2-6-2 class "2P" tank in action with plenty of steam leaving Horsted Keynes in April, 1955.
S. C. Nash

Below: Two Ivatt 2-6-0s class "2F" on a modest passenger train entitled "The Lakes Express", and both blowing off steam up the 1 in 62 bank near Troutbeck, 1959. *R. Leslie*

Above: Ivatt 2-6-0 class "4F" on light passenger duty leaving Ryhope East for West Hartlepool, May 1958.
I. S. Carr

Below: "Black Stanier" No. 44767, mercifully relieved of its double chimney, fitted with outside Stephenson valve gear. Drivers rated it a "strong" engine.
C. E. Weston

Above: No. 10,000 right away from St. Pancras on 15th January 1948. Ivatt is reluctantly climbing off and Stanier (in bowler) walks clear. *Topical Press Agency*

Left: Steam retreats, diesel advances — Ivatt's prophetic 1947 Christmas card designed in the loco drawing office, Derby, by F. G. Carrier. *F. G. Carrier*

Above right: J. F. Harrison (extreme left), the Mayor of Doncaster, and H. G. Ivatt after naming Peppercorn Pacific No. 60123 *H. A. Ivatt* in 1948. *Doncaster Gazette*

Right: This complicated track-spreading locomotive was designed and built at Derby, using standard parts of No. 10,000, an Ivatt 2-6-0, and an Ivatt war-time tank. It pulled a truck with Crewe Outdoor Machinery Department impedimenta of the 1910 period, and was among the presents handed to H. G. Ivatt on his retirement. *British Rail*

H. A. IVATT

H.G.IVATT
10000
L
L M S
L N W
CREWE O.D.

CHAPTER 4

G. J. Churchward and G.W.R. developments

The Churchward family had already been at Stoke Gabriel quite some time when a Squire Churchward built Hill House in 1485. So when George Jackson Churchward was born there on 31st January 1857 he was indeed a true son of Devon. As might be expected from this lineage, he enjoyed the country and fishing and shooting; but he was a studious boy, and showed a marked ability in mathematics and a marked interest in mechanical devices. In 1873 therefore, when he was 16, young Churchward became a pupil of John Wright, the Locomotive, Carriage and Wagon Superintendent of the South Devon, Cornwall, and West Cornwall Railways. This was a typical Squire's choice, convenient and parochial: the Works were a mere ten miles away, at Newton Abbot.

Three desiderata of a successful apprenticeship or pupillage are learning to get along with mates and bosses, under easy and difficult circumstances: realizing that everything done in a Works can be done better: and a gimmick. Churchward grasped these respectively by his family upbringing, his mechanical flair, and the making of a steam motor-car in collaboration with a fellow pupil, R. N. Grenville, in 1875. They designed and built this tiller-steered steam-engined three-wheeler completely save for the boiler, taken from a small fire-engine. It is preserved in Bristol Museum.

When the Great Western Railway absorbed the South Devon and Cornwall Railways in 1876 Churchward went to Swindon to complete his pupillage: and in 1877 he entered the drawing office in the locomotive works. In those days there were several separate drawing offices—in the loco works, the carriage works, and for signals, surveying, construction, planning. Churchward got around these offices, and was soon engaged on design work for the Severn Tunnel pumping station at Sudbrook, and the installation echoed the Cornish pumping engines he must often have seen when on the Cornwall Railways.

Interest in an automatic brake took a decisive turn in the 1875 brake trials on the Midland railway—joined by several companies, but excluding the G.W.R. The result was a stronger move towards the vacuum brake, though for sheer performance the Westinghouse proved the better. George Westinghouse was making great efforts to sell his brake and he naturally visited Joseph Armstrong, the Locomotive, Carriage and Wagon Superintendent of the Great Western. Armstrong merely said he would see about it, which he did by handing the job over to his son, Joe, and delegating Churchward to assist: he clearly saw the two as a promising pair. Then Joseph Armstrong died unexpectedly in 1877, and was succeeded by William Dean, who took the decision to design an improved automatic vacuum brake for the G.W.R., and gave the necessary support to " young Joe " and to Churchward, who was entrusted chiefly with the carriage side. Dean also had an eye on Churchward, and after a short spell as Inspecting Engineer for materials, he was appointed Assistant Carriage Works Manager, reporting to James Holden who looked after the Carriage and Wagon side for Dean. And then in 1885 Holden went to the Great Eastern Railway and Churchward succeeded him as Carriage Works Manager.

Meanwhile the Great Western's vacuum brake, with its crosshead vacuum pump and high vacuum (25 in.) and brake cylinder of 22 in. diameter for coaching stock, was successfully developed and in extended use when " young Joe " died in an accident in 1887. He had shone as an inventor but not as a recorder: no patent covered the work, but the fact that its success was due mainly to his efforts was reiterated by Churchward on several occasions.

Churchward was soon amongst trouble with axleboxes running hot, and he noted that in their reports his inspectors always gave dirt in the bearings as the cause. He had studied the work of Osborne Reynolds, and was clear in his own mind that a hot box was due to a local failure of the oil film, hence metal-to-metal contact, heat, metal pick-up, damage. Thus he saw the two essentials in an axlebox to be an adequate bearing surface free from high spots, and a well-maintained oil film. He then developed the O.K. axleboxes for carriages, with a large pad below the journal to feed the oil film and with proper metallic contact between the brass and the box to conduct away the heat generated by the normal friction losses while running. He also carried out a telling demonstration that the ingress of an abrasive will not cause a hot box if the lubrication is correct: he took a brake van and fitted it with a funnel and pipe giving direct to one of the axleboxes. This van was attached to a Swindon to London train, and during the journey he fed flour emery down the pipe. The inspectors who met him in at Paddington were astonished to find this box as cool as the other three: the journal had undergone a cool lapping operation and when examined was of fine finish but of shape approaching an hour-glass.

Now that " young Joe " Armstrong was dead there was no obvious successor to William Dean, the competent but ageing autocrat, who had been Chief Superintendent of the Locomotive and Carriage Department since 1877. This fact was probably brought home to the Board when it was realized that the Locomotive Works Manager, Samuel Carlton, was due to retire in 1895. Churchward was therefore appointed Assistant Works Manager early in 1895 and took over when Carlton retired at the year end.

Here the Squire factor in the Churchward upbringing helped again: it provided the determination to obtain for Swindon Works the best plant and facilities obtainable. This went well with the technical competence to choose, and the undoubted Churchward flair for selecting good,

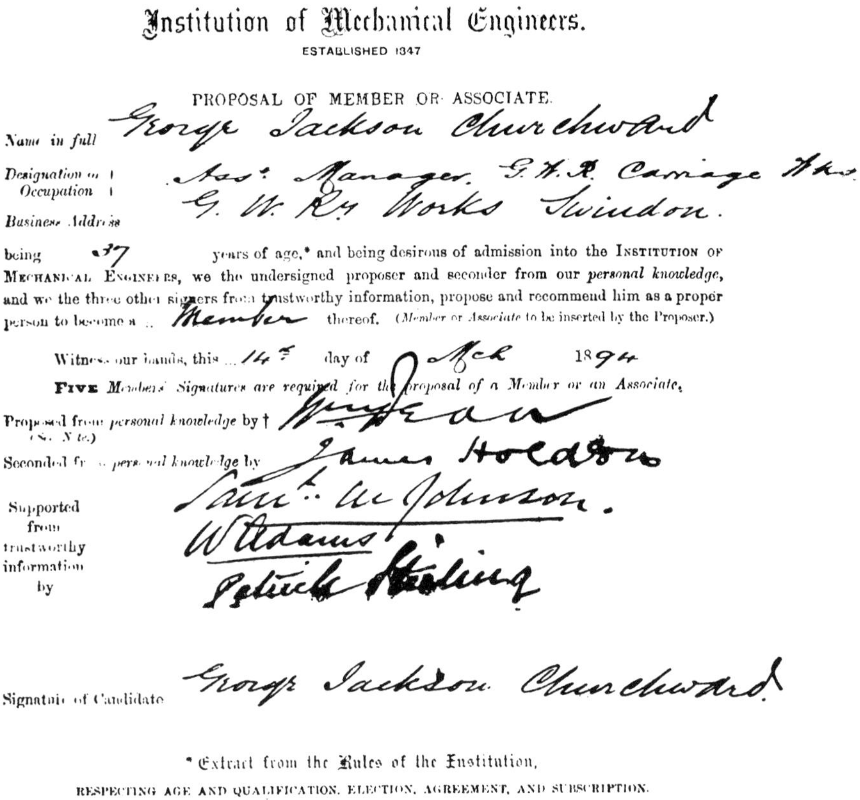

Institution of Mechanical Engineers.

ESTABLISHED 1847

PROPOSAL OF MEMBER OR ASSOCIATE.

Name in full George Jackson Churchward

Designation or Occupation Asst Manager. G.W.R. Carriage Wks

Business Address G. W. Ry Works Swindon.

being 37 years of age,* and being desirous of admission into the INSTITUTION OF MECHANICAL ENGINEERS, we the undersigned proposer and seconder from our *personal knowledge*, and we the three other signers from trustworthy information, propose and recommend him as a proper person to become a Member thereof. (*Member or Associate to be inserted by the Proposer.*)

Witness our hands, this 14th day of March 1894

FIVE *Members' Signatures are required for the proposal of a Member or an Associate.*

Proposed from *personal knowledge* by † (*See Note.*) Wm Dean

Seconded from *personal knowledge* by James Holden

Supported from trustworthy information by
Saml. W. Johnson.
W Adams
Patrick Stirling

Signature of Candidate George Jackson Churchward

* Extract from the Rules of the Institution,

RESPECTING AGE AND QUALIFICATION, ELECTION, AGREEMENT, AND SUBSCRIPTION.

Fig. 23. Dean, Holden, Johnson, Adams, and Patrick Stirling support Churchward's application for Membership of the Institution of Mechanical Engineers, 1894.

if slightly solid, engineering things. He began at once to re-equip the works with the most modern British and American machine tools, generally larger and able fully to exploit the improved tool steels which were becoming available. One such machine was a very large open-sided American planer. A few of these machines had individual electric motor drives, but most were belt-driven at that time, and Churchward also started installing 30 h.p. electric motors to drive each section of the line-shafting.

In 1895 also, Dean introduced the " Duke " class 4-4-0 for work west of Newton Abbot, and this was the forerunner of a series of engines all of which had the same design of cylinders, valve gear, double frames, axle-boxes, rods, etc. The " Dukes " had 5 ft. 8 in. driving wheels, the " Badmintons " 6 ft. 8 in. wheels, for faster passenger trains, and later the " Aberdares " had 4 ft. 7½ in. wheels, for heavy goods trains. Whilst sticking to these engine and frame and wheel arrangements, Dean tried several boiler and smokebox developments: and of course the whole pattern of experiments was carried out by Churchward as Swindon Locomotive Works Manager. Already dedicated to standardization, he was an enthusiastic supporter of the Dean policy and of his experimentation to find suitable standards; and he was duly appointed Chief Assistant to Dean in 1898. This appointment virtually named him as Dean's successor: and a good Chief leans to the ideas of his successor towards the end of his tenure of office, in order to smooth the transition and give scope to his swelling enthusiasm. Dean was aided in this by a spell of poor health at the turn of the century, and Churchward first attended the G.W.R. Locomotive, Carriage, and Stores Committee on 20th December 1899. The minutes show Churchward getting sharply off the mark.

> G. J. Churchward attended the Committee in the absence of Mr. Dean who is taking a short holiday for the benefit of his health.
>
> Mr. Churchward represented the necessity for providing 20 additional passenger engines and tenders, the cost of construction of which at Swindon Works he estimated at £51,000.

It was agreed to recommend this expenditure to the Board; and the 1900 price of about £2,500 for a Swindon 4-4-0 is interesting.

In 1900 the Churchward influence spread far wider than the locomotive works. In March he published details over his name of a new G.W.R. 20 ton all-steel coal wagon, with tare weight 8 tons 6 cwt. Sharing Dean's dislike for the current type of wagon brake, then operable from one side only, he collaborated with Dean on the design of the " either side " brake, which they duly patented. This turned out to be a highly educational example of an improvement turning round and swiping the improver; the " either side " brake was always applied when a rake of wagons needed braking, whereas with the other wagons it was even chances, depending which way round they happened to be. Therefore G.W.R. wagon brake blocks wore out twice as fast and wasted G.W.R. money.

In the drawing office, by this time centralized, Churchward was taking particular interest in boiler design. He worked closely with Dean in fitting two types of larger Belpaire boilers to the last five " Duke " class engines, and his influence was seen again when the " Atbara " class 4-4-0s succeeded the " Dukes " with large, domeless Belpaire boilers and straight top frames.

Still further Churchward signs appeared in 1902 when Swindon turned out the large 4-6-0 No. 100. This repeated the domeless Belpaire boiler, but departed from Dean practice in two notable particulars: first, it had a stark appearance, with angular lines, exposed wheels, and outside connecting rods, all in contrast to the wrapped-up appearance of a Dean design. Secondly, it had a piston stroke of 30 in., compared with the common 26 in. Churchward knew that high cylinder efficiency stems from a high expansion ratio, and to achieve this high ratio he took the steps of paring down the clearance volume and increasing the stroke in relation to cylinder diameter.

It was during the early months of 1902 that Churchward's dissatisfaction with the current boilers and valve events grew more marked; so he sat down and worked out how he would set about improving the engine and boiler designs, and how he would provide for experimental work to furnish the necessary design data.

Aged 45, and a mature, thoughtful, autocratic man, Churchward succeeded Dean as Superintendent of the Locomotive and Carriage Department on 1st June 1902. He became responsible for 12,000 employees at Swindon and 15,000 elsewhere on the line: and the only organizational change compared with the Dean era was that Signals became a separate department. With the job went the house, *Newburn:* but whereas Dean had taken all the premiums from eight pupils at £150 and from about 50 apprentices at £20, it was resolved that in future pupils be limited to six and that one-third of their premiums and all apprenticeship premiums should be paid to the Works.

June 1902 was a most eventful month for Churchward, and in the various actions he took one can see portents of his future successes.

Consequent upon his own promotion he made H. C. King Locomotive Works Manager and brought C. B. Collett from the drawing office to be Assistant Works Manager. Under Collett he formed a team of two junior assistants to carry out experimental and development work, and to these posts he appointed G. H. Pearson and J. W. Cross. Time proved that he had a gift for selecting young men who were not only able, but were willing to carry out his ideas in practice.

Also on the subject of Staff he felt that the draughtsmen and the inspectors should be elevated from weekly to annual staff, and he put this up at his first fully-fledged attendance at the Locomotive Committee, at the meeting on 11th June 1902. It was disallowed, but he returned to the attack in October with the draughtsmen only, won the point, and thereby placed on annual staff, among others, G. H. Burrows.

Ably supported by the drawing office under Burrows, he proceeded immediately to design and build in the works a small stationary steam engine. It incorporated his thinking on locomotive valve events, and had a much longer valve travel and greater steam lap than hitherto. He satisfied himself that in this way he achieved a much fuller opening to exhaust when the engine was notched up.

On 13th June 1902, proposed by Wainwright and seconded by Holden, Churchward was elected to the Association of Railway Locomotive Engineers, and thereupon attended his first meeting—held at Lyndhurst, with lunch and carriages by courtesy of the L. & S.W.R. S. W. Johnson was in the Chair, and those present also included H. A. Ivatt from Doncaster and D. Drummond on his home ground. On the agenda was a proposal emanating from the Engineering Standards Committee that the Association might give some guidance on the matter of standard specifications. Sure enough, the following motion was proposed by H. A. Ivatt and seconded by T. Hurry Riches, and carried unanimously:

> "That each Member fill in particulars on the Form which will be sent by Mr. Churchward, who has kindly undertaken to tabulate the same, with a view to arriving at a Standard Specification for Materials, to be used in the construction of Locomotives, Carriages and Wagons."

This firmly linked Churchward's name with standards and specifications.

Pearson and Cross were making excellent progress at Swindon on solving some of the boiler circulation problems. They modified a washout plug to carry a small spindle, with a water vane to operate in the boiler water spaces and an indicator on the outside. Churchward took the greatest interest in the subsequent circulation experiments, and was impatient for data. One day only a few weeks after taking office he found that the Chief Clerk, following the normal procedure of "protecting" his Chief from interruptions, had sent Pearson and Cross away. So on returning from the Works he approached his office through the Chief Clerk's office, pointed to his door, and said "That's *my* door. If my people want to see me, *I'll* tell them when I don't want them." This was an order as autocratic as many of Dean's, but more popularly aimed. It represented a marked change in approach, because previously the Chief Clerk had been as tough as a stage door-keeper and it was rare to get in to see Dean. The alteration was extremely well received, particularly as Churchward, though autocratic, did in fact both listen to suggestions and remain approachable. Furthermore, he made sure his staff got around: between 1902 and 1905 he sent five of them to the U.S.A.

It became clear after a series of Pearson and Cross experiments that the boiler water circulation left much to be desired: the water was not flowing freely into the barrel, and full advantage was not being taken of the hottest regions around the firebox and firebox tubeplate. To improve the flow between the water legs of the firebox and the barrel, Churchward increased the barrel diameter at the firebox end, from 5 ft. to 5 ft. 6 in., the lower portion remaining horizontal. So came the taper boiler.

Instead of the usual square firebox, Churchward painstakingly developed curved side plates and crown to allow free circulation and also to permit expansion of the firebox and casing with minimum stay stresses. Simultaneously the drawing office was laying out a standard valve gear for outside-cylinder engines, using Stephenson link motion to give a valve travel of 6¼ in. with a steam lap of 1¾ in. With this gear Churchward, determined to have free passage of steam and exhaust, decided upon piston valves of diameter 10 in. He also arranged short and straight passages between steam chest, cylinder, and exhaust.

This energetic design work, first exploited in engine No. 98, left Churchward scant time for other jobs. At the A.R.L.E. meeting on 28th November 1902 he admitted he had not done the promised tabulation, and he reported that a joint Committee of the Civil and Mechanical Engineers were charged with practically the same task. McIntosh said that this Committee was held up by lack of information, whereat Ivatt adroitly proposed that, since Mr. Churchward had received this very information, he might kindly compile a Test Specification acceptable to the Members. Mr. Churchward kindly agreed.

Ivatt then called attention to the work being performed by the 4-cylinder de Glehn compounds of the Nord railway in France—adding in his deadpan way that they were, of course, Atlantics. S. W. Johnson said he thought they were very good engines—they were, of course, compounds. Wilson Worsdell pointed out that the Americans had hitherto gone in strongly for Compounds but were now giving them up. Then Churchward rather scooped the discussion by remarking that he had ordered one of these French Compound Atlantics, in order to compare its working with the working of engines on the Great Western Railway.

The French engine had a boiler pressure of 227 psi, and so it is not surprising to find Churchward adopting for the G.W.R. a standard boiler pressure of 225 psi. This he first applied in his second 4-6-0, No. 171, *Albion*, which differed from No. 98 in this respect only. Both engines appeared in 1903, and by this time Churchward had in fact established his basic designs for boiler, cylinders, and valve gear.

More—he had so well established himself that in May 1903 the Board formally acknowledged the valuable work he was doing.

He had also established the concept of a 4-6-0, with ample speed and great reserves of power, as being a forward-looking standard to adopt for passenger working. Not that he was dogmatic about this: he was extremely impressed both by Ivatt's large-boilered Atlantics and by the French compound Atlantics. At a paper on "American Locomotive Practice" before the Institution of Civil Engineers on 31st March 1903, Churchward opened the discussion and said:

On boilers:

"Probably, to English locomotive-engineers, the part of the paper which deals with boilers is the most interesting; especially the reasonably wide firebox which the author has described. An express engine with a similar box has just been put on the Great Northern Railway by Mr. Ivatt, and I trust it will have a good trial in England. I think English locomotive-engineers are within measurable distance of adopting it, and I am sorry that the French 'Atlantic' engine, which is to be put on the Great Western Railway, is not fitted with it—but I am taking this engine as it stands.

"The author has omitted to mention that the sloping top to the firebox is practically a necessity in such long boilers as are used with 4-4-2 or 4-6-0 engines, and especially with the 2-6-2. A boiler is now obtained with a 15 ft. or 16 ft. barrel, and perhaps a 9 ft. box. When the brake is applied, the water in these long boilers runs to the front end to such an extent that the back of the roof-sheet is quite uncovered; and by dropping the back of the roof of the box 3 in., the benefit of 3 in. of water is obtained when the brake is applied."

On standardizing locomotives:

"Much has been heard recently about standardizing locomotives, and Englishmen have sometimes been told that it is largely done in America. This sounds curious to any one who carefully watches American practice; because if there is one striking feature about this practice it is that every batch of engines turned out differs considerably from those built previously. In fact, American locomotive-builders have allowed no idea of standardization, or of anything else, to stand in the way of bringing the power of their locomotives up to the highest possible point."

On piston valves:

"From what I have gathered on the subject—and the author's observations seem to bear it out—trouble has been experienced in America with piston-valves, but American Engineers mean to overcome it. On the Great Western Railway piston-valves have been tried and have given considerable trouble; they are undoubtedly one of the most troublesome pieces of mechanism with which anyone can have to deal. I have set before me the task of curing the defects, if possible; feeling quite sure that engineers will never have a chance of utilizing to the utmost the power of the locomotive, and bringing it, in economy, within anything like reach of the compound, without the use of piston-valves. Seeing the success attained through a long series of years with plain snap rings upon pistons 18 ins. to 20 ins. in diameter, running at high speeds, I do not think there is any reason to despair of getting a tight piston-valve before long. Piston-valves are supposed to use much more steam than the flat valves, and this belief is held not only widely, but strongly on the Great Western Railway. Against it, however, I wish to set the experience of at least one piston-valve engine, weighing about 68 tons 10 cwt. This engine, on its first 4,000 miles, working the heaviest express between Bristol and Exeter, has consumed only 33.5 lb. of coal per mile. While piston-valves remain tight their economy is, if anything, superior to that of the ordinary flat valve."

On cylinders and frames:

"In designing outside cylinders with piston-valves on the Great Western Railway, it has been necessary to come down nearly to the bar frame at the front end, in order to get a reasonable arrangement of the piston-valve. Up to the present, no trouble has been experienced with it; and although it may be a little more expensive to build in this way, it makes a better arrangement of valves and ports than is possible with the slab frame."

These remarks show his determination and his progress in design improvements, and his desire to acquire further information. From his carriage side experience he had acquired a great belief in large bearing surfaces to minimize hot boxes, and all his standard engines had large journals, with a running clearance each side of the bearing, in which a healthy oil film was maintained by large wool and horsehair pads. Even allowing for the fact that they were large enough not to have to be thrashed, the Churchward engines were remarkably free from hot boxes.

Two more prototypes were built in 1903, incorporating the standards so far adopted, *i.e.*, boilers, cylinders, and 10 in. long-travel piston valves. One was a 2-6-2 tank, and the other a 2-8-0 freight engine—the first in this country.

Each month at the Loco Committee meetings Churchward obtained sanction for a batch of new, or sometimes second-hand, machine tools, to keep up a steady flow of improvements in Swindon Works. In July 1903 he recommended proceeding with the scheme for a new running shed and facilities at Old Oak Common, and this was agreed, at a cost of £110,000. Dean had first put forward this scheme in 1899 at an estimated cost of £70,000. Occasionally Churchward's proposals were curtailed: his recommendation in March 1904 to fit seven new dining cars with electric lighting, at an extra cost of £201 each, was agreed for four cars only!

The steam rail-car boom had started, and Traffic were demanding 30 more cars of the type Churchward had recently designed, after a rather abortive experiment with a car borrowed from the L.S.W.R. At Churchward's recommendation, the Loco Committee in October 1904 agreed to purchase these to competitive tender from outside contractors, manufacture to be in accordance with Swindon drawings. With them were also wanted 14 trailers, and this was a pointer to what finally pipped these rail cars—a love of tacking on trailer cars and vans and horse-boxes, which overtaxed the little engines. Other branch-line services were operated shuttle-fashion with an 0-6-0 tank engine in the middle of four carriages. Someone disliked the array, and Swindon drawing office designed a coach-simulating cover to fit over the engine. This cover caused frightful inconvenience and irritation in the running shed, and curiously enough it soon became damaged in an unfortunate shed mishap, and disappeared from use.

The dynamometer car built by Gooch was still in use in 1902, but Churchward, in checking the calibration of the spring which recorded draw-bar pull, found hysteresis errors. Pearson, whose duties included running the car, designed a new laminated spring with rollers between the ground plates: this performed so well that it was used in the new G.W.R. dynamometer car Churchward had built in 1903. But road testing, with its numerous variables, is tantalizing to the meticulous experimenter: and, after reading the work by Professor Goss on loco testing in America, Churchward designed and built in 1904 a stationary testing plant at Swindon. Though this was limited to 400 h.p. output from the loco on test, it permitted many useful tests to be carried out and later confirmed and extended on the road with the dynamometer car. During one test the engine draw-bar broke, and the engine went through the doors of the shed—which were closed at the time. After that they generally put a tank engine with its brakes on in front of the engine under test.

The French Atlantic, *La France*, reached Poplar Docks in 13 packing cases on 19th October 1903, and Churchward was justifiably pleased when Swindon erected it, hitched on a standard tender, and had it rostered on regular duty by Thursday, November 12th. It carried G.W.R. No. 102, taking similar turns of work with No. 171, *Albion*. Churchward insisted on the proper discipline of strictly comparing like with like in experimental work, and therefore converted *Albion* into an Atlantic. The results of the comparative trials showed *Albion* to be a match for *La France* in performance and coal consumption, and cheaper to build and maintain. But the French engine rode better, on account of the better balancing in a 4-cylinder engine; and there were some design features which Churchward relished and adopted—among them the inside big end, and the bogie arrangements. This bogie, with its double compression spring control and supporting pads close to the wheels, was always referred to by Churchward as " the de Glehn bogie " and it became standard, in turn, on the G.W.R., L.M.S., and British Railways.

In April 1904, discussing Sauvage's paper on " Compound Locomotives in France," Churchward said:

> "A steady pull on the drawbar at the back of the tender of 2 tons at 70 mph on a 6 ft. 6 in. wheel takes, if I may use a colloquialism, a great deal of getting; and when we have it, it takes a great deal of keeping up. The G.W.R. has two or three engines running today which will do this, and *La France* is one of them.
>
> " It seems no doubt ambitious to expect such power as is developed at 55 per cent and 65 per cent cut off by the compound locomotive out of a cylinder in a simple engine cutting off at 20 to 25 per cent; but I am pleased to say that, with the assistance of an efficient staff, a good deal of very hard work, and a determination to see what can be done with the valve gear, I believe such improvements have been made in the steam distribution that a satisfactory result can be ensured from as high a cut off as 15 to 20 per cent."

Churchward backed up this unequivocal and historic claim by re-stating that the 2-ton drawbar pull at 70 mph had been measured on *La France* with the high pressure cut off at 55 per cent and the low pressure at 54 per cent, and adding that the same performance had been measured on a G.W.R. simple engine with 18 by 30 cylinders and boiler pressure 200 psi at 25 per cent cut off. Not only were all these figures taken most carefully with the new G.W.R. dynamometer car, painstakingly calibrated, but to reduce road-testing variables and their attendant uncertainty the favourite *locale* was the long stretch of level track on the Somerset flats between Bristol and Bridgwater. The sustained 70 mph was ample support for the Churchward family motto " swift as the bird flys."

Swindon was certainly getting results, and the publicity boys at Paddington were not asleep. A G.W.R. hand-out was usual, in the Technical Monthlies. The technique of foretelling, reporting, and confirming was adopted—three separate announcements of one item—a technique not unknown today. A typical instance was the Paddington–Plymouth non-stop service inaugurated on 1st July 1904—246 miles in 4 hrs. 25 min., average 56 mph. Tough, practical engineers on the other railways allowed themselves to become irritated by this publicity, and an emotional barrier hindered the quick acceptance of Churchward's progressive designs.

The year 1905 was notable for the extension of the French compound trials, and for the fixing by Churchward of his standard boiler and most of its design details. In that year he had two more, larger Atlantics delivered from France, and built a dozen more Atlantics, to permit extended trials of 4-4-2s against 4-6-0s. And in due course the Churchward hunch of 1902 was vindicated when the Running Sheds voted for the 4-6-0s, particularly favouring the greater adhesion and hence greater reliability on the more steeply graded sections of the G.W.R. system.

Churchward Standard Boilers

Standard boiler No.		1903/4				1921
		1	2	4	5	7
Grate area	sq. ft.	27.1	20.4	20.6	16.6	30.3
Total heating surface	sq. ft.	1842	1267	1479	1114	2232
Superheater	sq. ft.	262	82	192	78	290
Barrel dia. max.	ft. ins.	5–6	5–0	5–6	4–9	6–0
Barrel dia. min.	ft. ins.	4–11	4–5	4–11	4–2	5–6
Working pressure	psi	225	200	200	200	225

The standard boilers had taken up a very great amount of design effort. Externally their appearance was altered by the taper extending from the throat-plate right to the front end and by top-feed pipes encircling the boiler at the "dome" position where Churchward placed his safety valves and top-feed clack-boxes. Inside, the feed-water was distributed by trays towards the front of the boiler, being warmed in the steam-space and giving up dissolved oxygen and so reducing corrosion troubles. The steam collection was from the high top corners over the throat-plate by means of a branched pipe: Churchward specified a steam space 2 ft. deep at this point. The regulator was a flat valve with small pilot opening, in the smokebox. The fact that the firebox casing tapered towards the cab meant that the back plate was about the same width as the smokebox tube-plate, and there were direct longitudinal stays between these plates.

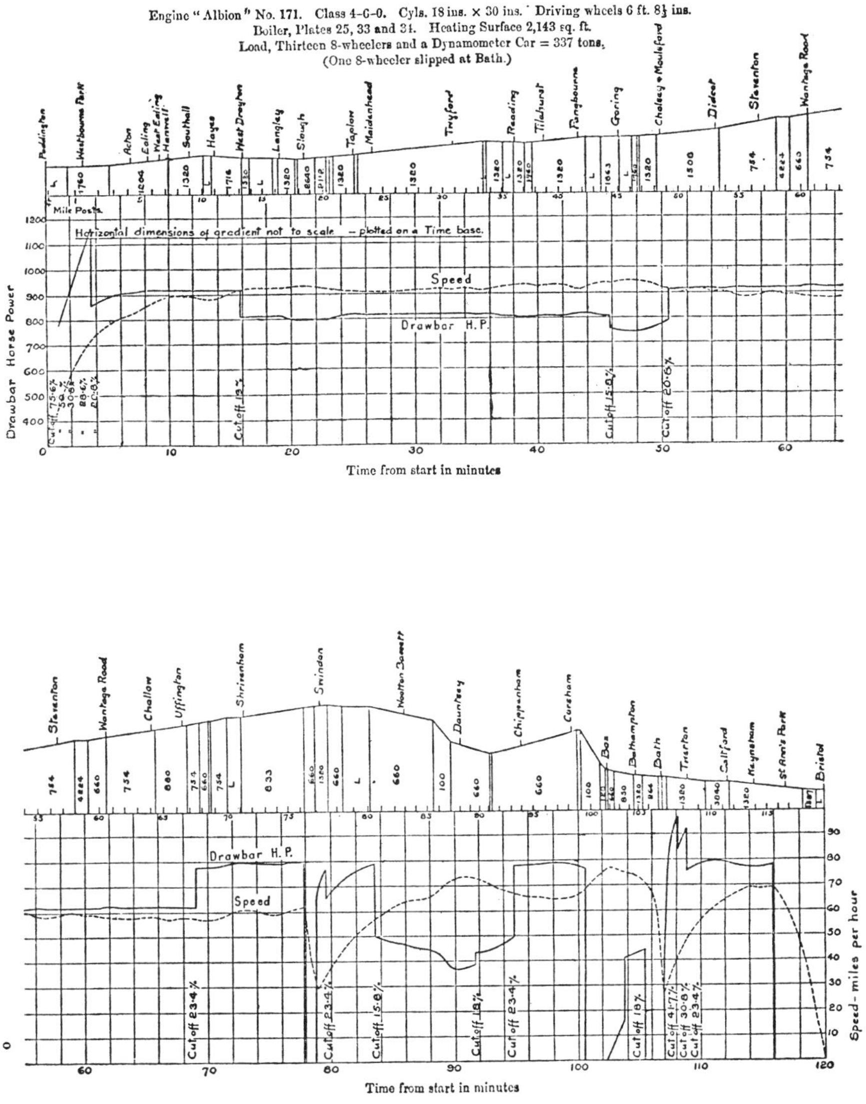

Fig. 24. Power and speed curves for No. 171, *Albion*, as 4-6-0 hauling thirteen 8-wheelers and dynamometer car =337 tons behind tender, from Paddington to Bristol. Regulator full open throughout.

No sling stays were used, after Churchward had satisfied himself by trials that they were unnecessary. The firebox casing taper also permitted wider cab windows, with improved look-out.

As design progressed Churchward spent a lot of time in the drawing office with Burrows the Chief Draughtsman and the appropriate Section Leader, discussing each problem at the board of the draughtsman concerned—accompanied sometimes by Pearson or Cross, or if a manufacturing aspect was involved by H. C. King the Works Manager, or his assistant, Collett. Churchward was a real design leader in the three important aspects that he personally supplied sound ideas, he equally encouraged the ideas of his staff, and he kept the whole team eager to solve problems together. He also freely used his Swindon Record Office to turn up current foreign practice as published in the technical press. Particularly in the case of the boiler he felt that the more ideas they considered the better: and so he wrote a short description of his own design findings to date (2,500 words and eight drawings) together with current data on large British, French and American boilers (23 drawings and a table of dimensions) and presented it under the title *Large Locomotive Boilers* at a meeting of the Institution of Mechanical Engineers in February 1906, attended by 200 members and 100 visitors. The main points he raised were wide *v.* narrow fireboxes, growing importance of water circulation as boilers grew larger, causes of tube and stay troubles, tube diameter to length ratio, his experiment which showed that steam collected from the top of a flat firebox casing gave less priming than collection from the dome, and his forthcoming trial of a Schmidt superheater in the Great Western Railway standard No. 1 Boiler, as fitted to No. 171, *Albion.* He concluded with speed and horse-power diagrams of a Paddington–Bristol run by *Albion* hauling 337 tons.

This paper provoked an excellent discussion, continued at a subsequent meeting in March, 250 attending. Churchward was again very well supported by his own staff, both King and Wright taking part in the discussion. Churchward's replies confirmed many of his design fixes:

On water softening:

" Mr. Hughes, of the Lancashire and Yorkshire Railway, started by touching the crucial spot in the whole of our dealings with the modern large locomotive boiler, namely, softened water. That is, in my opinion, the secret of using the modern high-pressure high-capacity boiler. It is perfectly hopeless to try to cure boiler troubles when the scale-forming ingredients are present in the boiler; they must be taken out before the water is fed into the boiler. My own Company is softening water pretty generally, and our experience is that tube troubles with the higher pressures between 200 and 225 lb. have been so moderated by the softening of the water, that, in effect, we do not get more trouble than we previously had with hard water and lower pressures."

On the G.W.R. French Compounds:

" The French compound will pull two tons at seventy miles an hour on the draw-bar, and it takes a remarkably good locomotive to do that."

On alleged disadvantages of the long, narrow firebox:

" This I believe is a difficulty, or an assumed difficulty, against which a great many people have run their heads quite unnecessarily. It has been found on the Great Western, that both in the French engines and in our own engines, with a proper slope of the boxes, a 9 or 10 ft. box can be fired without any difficulty whatever. As a matter of fact, some of the 9 and 10 ft. boxes that are running at present are more easily fired and easier to work on the foot-plate than a number of the old 6 and 8 ft. boxes cut on the straight. If you will keep in your mind's eye for a moment the short flat portion that goes over the trailing axle in the ordinary long box and then the considerable bit of slope that runs down, you will find that 75 per cent, I should say, of the coal is put on to the flat part of the box and the rest fed down. There is really no trouble whatever in this respect, and the difficulty of firing is no argument to my mind against the long boxes at all."

On valve travel:

" I was glad to hear Mr. Pendred defending a long lap on the valves. The Great Western uses a very long lap, but we have got over the difficulty he quoted, of the engine being apt to ' go blind ' and stick on the centre, by increasing the travel of the valve. The usual valve opening can be obtained, namely, that we are able to cut off as long as 75 per cent."

On the appearance of Churchward engines (James Stirling, retired Loco Engineer of the South Eastern Railway had said " they are novel in shape and expensive in construction: they may be good but they are certainly not ' bonnie,' to use a Scotch expression"):

" I know that I have been accused of spoiling the appearance of the British locomotive as much as any man in the country, but I take exception to the statement. In my opinion, there is no canon of art in regard to the appearance of a locomotive or a machine, except that which an engineer has set up for himself, by observing from time to time types of engines which he has been led from his nursery days upwards to admire. For instance, people like to see a long boiler, with an immense driving-wheel about 8 ft. in diameter, just like the old Great Western broad-gauge engines. Engineers must admit that the time has gone by for studying appearances in the construction of the locomotive boiler at any rate."

After this rather weak argument it is not surprising that Churchward told Burrows to think about improving the appearance of the engines: in due course the job was given to Holcroft and he evolved the simple curves at the cylinder and cab ends of the running-boards which became a characteristic G.W.R. feature. But this seems to have been Churchward's sole deflection into aesthetics, and for the most part 1906 found him deep in further design explorations. He had read up the work done by Professor Goss in America, and the extensive report on the Pennsylvania Railroad locomotive tests at St. Louis in 1904, and these led to a series of experiments on the Swindon testing plant and on the road, from which were evolved the standard smokebox arrangements, with a formula connecting blast-pipe tip, chimney height, and throat diameter. Then there was an outbreak of trouble when engines on heavy banking duties at Cockett were worked for lengthy periods at full regulator in full gear, and the blast was so fierce that severe blow-pipe action burned away some firebox stay heads. Seeking a simple means of limiting the blast, Churchward designed the jumper-top blast-pipe in which a heavy top ring moved upwards and thereby increased the orifice, when the exhaust pressure exceeded a certain value. In some ways this device is out of character with Churchward, as it both complicates and adds a moving part: he must have clearly perceived the obvious alternative of standardizing a larger, fixed blast pipe orifice but feared this would reduce the free-steaming characteristics of his boilers.

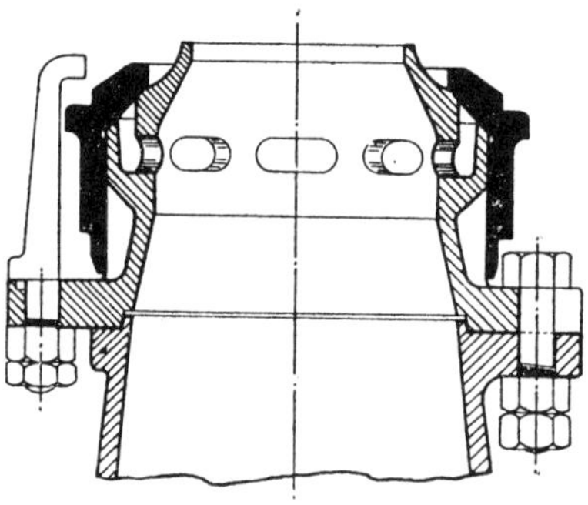

Fig. 25. Churchward's jumper-top blastpipe.

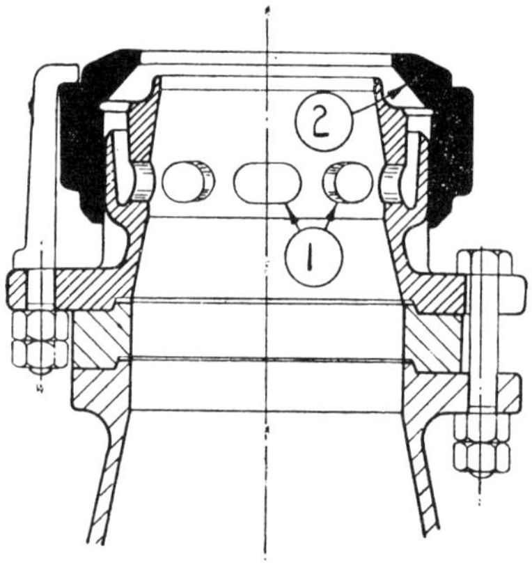

Fig. 26. The jumper-top blastpipe as applied on the L.M.S. Exhaust steam acts through the orifices 1 on the jumper-top 2 causing it to lift and thereby increase the blastpipe opening, thus preventing a further rise in exhaust pressure.

The G.W.R.'s pioneering Automatic Train Control equipment involved a simple plunger striking a fixed ramp between the rails, and the resulting blow caused maintenance troubles in the early trials. This caused W. A. Stanier to propose an improvement involving a more complicated lever system, and Williams asked him to take his idea direct to Churchward. After studying it with characteristic care, Churchward merely said " Have you seen the specification for the ' gilderfluke ' engine?" This was a complex engine which included every refinement and complication, even a device for transforming the exhaust into new coal on the tender. Burrows duly had the Stanier idea set out, by Jimmy Milne who was then a draughtsman, but it came to nought.

Trouble with piston valves persisted, and when Churchward saw in the technical press reports of the American semi-plug type he bought the rights to make and use them in this country. Their principle delighted his sense of making the steam pressure perform adjustments for him, as in his jumper blast-pipe; the semi-plug piston valve rings are forced into and locked in their operating steam-tight position when steam enters the steam-chest. With the regulator closed, however, the rings are no longer in contact with the walls of the steam chest so that when drifting there is practically no wear and, incidentally, a very free-running engine. Just as Churchward inspired a closely co-operating design team, so he received unusual co-operation in the case of difficult manufacturing operations: but in spite of this Swindon found it hell's own delight to get those damned rings tight and when at last they succeeded by progressively refining the machining tolerances and cutting out the tricky hand-scraping operations, it remained a Works job and was never done at any of the Running Sheds. W. A. Stanier saw all this going on, from the perspective of his job as Divisional Locomotive Superintendent, Swindon. He experienced the tribulations, and appreciated the triumph, when Great Western patience was duly rewarded and the semi-plug valves gave extremely good results.

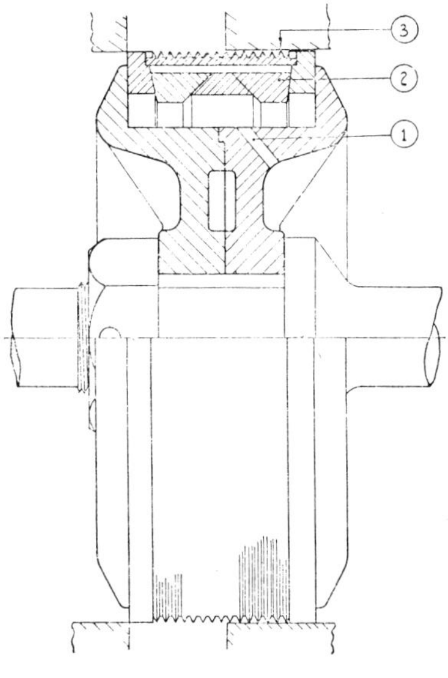

Fig. 27. Churchward's semi-plug piston valve, 1906. When the regulator is open, steam passes through the holes 1 to the ring assembly 2 and causes it to seal against the steam-chest wall 3.

Also in 1906 Churchward fitted the first superheater on a British locomotive. This was a Schmidt type, and after experimenting with another type, from America, he designed his own Swindon superheater, differing from the others in having smaller diameter tubes, to obviate a core of non-superheated steam, and in permitting easier withdrawal. He aimed at dry steam to avoid condensation, rather than a high degree of superheat.

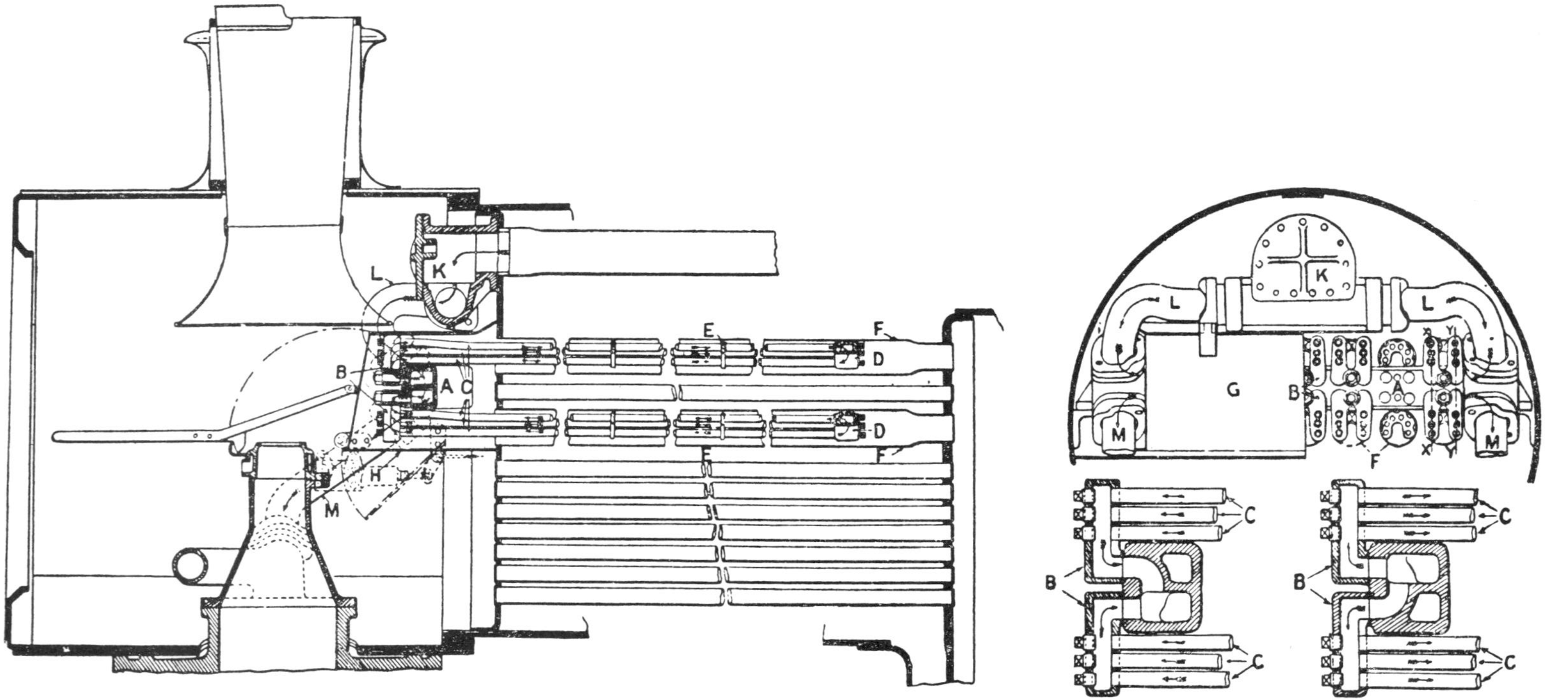

Fig. 28. The Swindon Superheater, 1912. Main header A connects with fingers B carrying tubes C whose ends are coupled in pairs to bends D. Plates E support the tubes C in the large flues F. Hinged plate G encloses the header in the smokebox, and the lower flap H is a damper, automatically opened when the regulator K is opened. Steam then passes along L to the top chamber of header A, to one finger B, through tubes C and back via second finger B to the lower chamber of header A, thence through pipe M to the cylinders.

With his own and the French 4-4-2s running satisfactorily Churchward perceived there was one missing comparative factor—namely, that his were all 2-cylinder engines whereas the French trio had 4-cylinders. Refreshingly clear in his mind, probably inspired by Ivatt, that compounding was not worthwhile, he built a 4-cylinder 4-4-2, *North Star*. The presence of two inside big-ends switched his thoughts from Stephenson to Walschaert's valve gear, and in laying it out he saw that he could dispense altogether with eccentrics by having the left inside crosshead drive the right expansion link, and vice versa. Simultaneously and independently Deeley of the Midland used the same idea on his large 4-4-0s for the Carlisle run, and patented it: so Churchward never extended its use. It was attractive in saving two eccentrics, and difficult only in the queer-shaped cross-over links attached to the backs of the crossheads in addition to the connecting links attached to their fronts. All this gear was contained between the frames, the valves for the outside cylinders being driven by rocking shafts from the inside. Churchward valiantly stuck to his principles in this 4-cylinder design. With the same 6 ft. 8½ in. driving wheels, and wanting the same tractive effort, he fitted cylinders 14¼ in. diameter by 26 in. stroke and equal length connecting rods for virtually perfect balancing. Here he scored slightly over the compounds as their different cylinder sizes for low and high pressures involved some counter-balancing. With his insistence that the cylinder axis should be horizontal, he obtained an arrangement rather similar to that of the compounds, the inside cylinders being well forward and the outside cylinders in line with the rear bogie wheels. The engine performed excellently, but soon after its appearance came the decision that the 4-6-0 arrangement was preferable: and so the famous " Star " class was born.

The first " Star," 4-cylinder 4-6-0 No. 4001, *Dog Star*, appeared in 1907, leading a litter of ten; and apart from the wheel arrangement it differed from the 4-4-2 *North Star* only in its valve gear. This, probably on account both of the Deeley patent and the fact that any failure affecting an inside connecting rod put the entire engine out of action, had conventional inside Walschaert's valve gear with expansion links operated by two eccentrics on the leading coupled axle. From the word go these " Stars " were fine performers, very free-running, capable of high speeds and heavy duties. They ran the non-stop Paddington–Plymouth trains, and the 2-hour services to Bristol and Birmingham. But one mystery surrounds them: why did the essentially practical Churchward fit internal Walschaert's gear? Its inaccessibility was obvious on the drawing-board, and notorious in Works and Sheds. Approach from above was baulked by the cross-members stiffening the frames in line with the outside cylinders, and the inside cross-head slide-bars were sandwiched between the smokebox and the framing carrying the bogie pin. There certainly was a strong prejudice at the time against exposed valve gear, but such prejudices did not deter Churchward, as he had himself pointed out. It is far more probable that he never fully realized the serious and costly

1. Jumper-top blast-pipe
2. Blower-ring
3. Spark plate
4. Distributor for cylinder oil
5. Regulator valve
6. Superheater header
7. Front tube-plate
8. Tray for feed water
9. Safety valves
10. Delivery nozzle for feed-water
11. Steam-collecting mouth
12. Longitudinal boiler-stays
13. Fire-hole deflector-plate

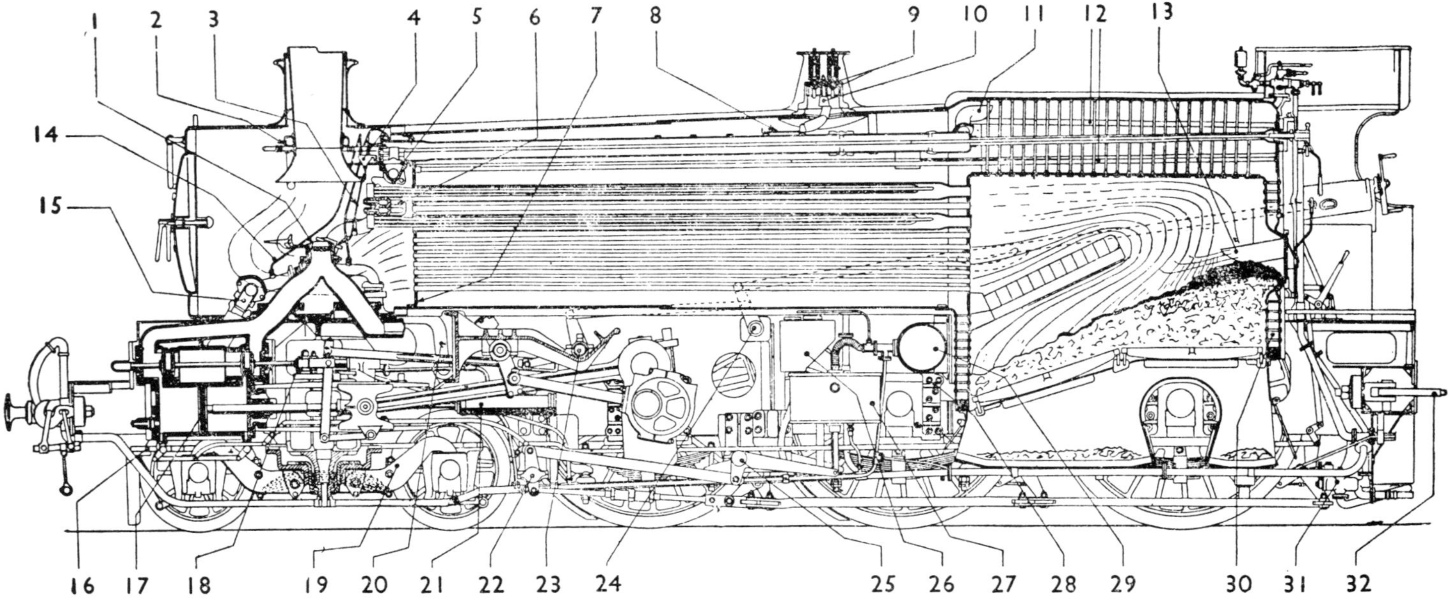

LONGITUDINAL SECTION OF "STAR" CLASS FOUR-CYLINDER 4-6-0

14. **Oil pipe discharging into steam pipe feeding inside cylinder**
15. **Steam pipe to inside cylinder**
16. **Top member of bogie frame**
17. **Piston**
18. Rocking lever connecting inside and outside valve-spindles
19. Equalising beam for bogie axle loading
20. Steam-pipe to outside cylinder
21. Air pump for maintaining vacuum in brake system
22. Brake-shaft
23. Reversing shaft
24. Intermediate reversing shaft
25. Intermediate brake-shaft
26. Sand-box
27. Brake-cylinder
28. Horncheek
29. Vacuum brake reservoir
30. Fire-box water-space
31. Injector
32. Draw-bar between engine and tender

effects of poor accessibility, because he lacked Running Shed experience; his deserved reputation was such that the overall wisdom of his design would go unchallenged.

Compared with the 20 2-cylinder " Saint " class 4-6-0s, the " Stars " were reckoned by the Running Department to be " one coach stronger ", though both engines had the same No. 1 standard boiler. The difference may have been imaginary, but may be partly accounted for by the better valve events from the Walschaert's gear on the " Stars."

Churchward clearly saw that both the " Saints " and the " Stars " left him some room for an increase in power, though they were quite man enough, or rather engine enough, for their present duties. But he had had a constant struggle to keep down weight on all his large engines, because his vision of power requirements was in fact ahead of accepted track loadings. So possibly he saw the building of a really large locomotive as a good broad hint at permanent way limitations. Anyway, at first request in January 1907, he obtained Loco Committee permission to build one 4-6-2 at an estimated cost of £4,400.

When *The Great Bear* appeared in 1908 it caused a justifiable sensation. The first British Pacific, it weighed 97½ tons and, with its 8-wheel 46-ton tender, its overall length was 71 ft. By comparison, a " Merchant Navy " was 95 tons, and 70 ft. overall length. The 20 ton loading on each driving axle limited its use to the Paddington–Bristol run. In appearance it was marred by the comparatively small Churchward cab but, interestingly, Churchward did provide a " matching " tender, although it was unnecessary for the rostered duties.

Churchward designed the front end of *The Great Bear* just like the " Stars " but with 15 in. cylinders. Only the boiler was a departure from his preferred practice; he provided 42 sq. ft. of grate area but in a firebox of curtailed volume; and the tubes were 23 ft. long, compared with 15 ft. in the " Stars." Though adequate for all it was called upon to do, this boiler was a comparatively poor steamer and the experimental work necessary to improve it was not considered by Churchward to be worthwhile. The fact that incidental trouble arose from the trailing truck owing to the axleboxes overheating merely confirmed Churchward's dislike of trailing wheels and the placing of wide, shallow fireboxes over them.

Many and varied were the duties of a Locomotive, Carriage and Wagon Superintendent in the early days of the twentieth century. Material specifications were decidedly sketchy, and this alarmed those responsible for the ever-increasing sizes and weights of engines and trains. Churchward was dedicated to setting realistic standards, and a notable success came when his proposed Standard Materials Test Specifications were adopted by the Association of Railway Locomotive Engineers at their November 1903 meeting. The Standards Committee of the B.S.I. asked the A.R.L.E. to appoint two representatives, and Churchward said that he had better be excluded, because he and Whale were already members of it, representing the Railway Association on behalf of the G.W.R. and the L.N.W.R.

respectively. Members accordingly agreed not to vote for Churchward: but this was agreed in mellow summer meeting surroundings at Bowness; and sure enough, they forgot all about it when they came to vote, and it was found at the November meeting that they had elected Churchward and Holden as their representatives. Then some of the manufacturers came back with complaints about the stringency of the specification covering tyres, axles, and springs, and the sub-committee appointed to deal with this naturally included Churchward and Holden. Churchward's proposed standard profiles for loco, carriage and wagon tyres were in due course accepted. So were his proposals, based on returns from 27 railways, for drivers' retiring ages: annual medical examinations after 60, age limit 65 on long-distance non-stop trains, retirement at 70. In collaboration with Hughes and Marsh he drew up a common procedure for the reporting of accidents. With these sundry jobs for the A.R.L.E., and through work on other committees, including the Council of the Institution of Mechanical Engineers to which he was elected in 1905, he was in continuous close touch with many of his opposite numbers on the other railways. But the G.W.R. and Swindon always had first call on his time, and in fact he was unable to get to any A.R.L.E. meetings between November 1907 and November 1913. During this spell he kept up his efforts on standards by written communications, and his proposal to standardize on 4 ft. 5½ in. between the backs of tyre flanges was virtually accepted in June 1913 when the range 4 ft. 5½ in. to 4 ft. 5⅝ in. was conceded.

It was rather typical of Churchward that he did not take on more than he could cope with: thus when traffic had demanded a batch of ten 4-4-0s in 1903 he built to the Dean "Atbara" design but fitted one of the new standard taper boilers and de Glehn bogies. These engines were known as the "City" class, and *City of Truro* is preserved. Then a further 20 4-4-0s were needed, for duties including the Newport–Hereford–Shrewsbury runs where the track would not take the new 4-6-0s. For these Churchward built a synthesised loco, almost entirely from the range of new standard parts. The result was the old "County" class, a notoriously rough-riding engine. They were cleared out when the track was improved to take the 4-6-0s, and of course all salvaged components, being standard, were used on other engines.

It is not surprising that Churchward pioneered the 2-6-0 "mixed traffic" engine. Like all good design leaders he kept the broad picture in mind, and he registered clues as they were presented. It was his practice to hold 3-monthly meetings with all the chief Works and Running staffs: at a typical 1910 meeting there would be Wright and King from the local Works; Marrilier from C. & W.; the Running Supt. Waister, and his Assistant Williams; and the eight Divisional Superintendents, Swindon being represented by W. A. Stanier. It became apparent that the old barrier between passenger and goods working was vanishing, and that, then as now, the Running people wanted above all a general purpose engine, powerful enough for goods traffic but with sufficient turn of speed and accleration to maintain light passenger bookings. This was an important clue to working secondary services.

Modern, inside-frame versions of the ageing "Barnum" 2-4-0s and "Aberdare" 2-6-0s with 4 ft. 7½ in. wheels were also being asked for: and Churchward had these examined in the drawing office where Holcroft found it impracticable to fit cylinders with 10 in. piston valves between the bogie and the smokebox saddle, so an entirely new design would be necessary.

Then there was the clue of the successful 4-6-0s running freely at high speeds. Technical news from overseas showed the growing popularity of Moguls: Holcroft had been impressed by them on his trip to Canada, and had duly reported to Burrows. And so with some hindsight we can understand Churchward's clarity of purpose when he walked up with Burrows to Holcroft's board and inaugurated the mixed traffic engine with one of his simplest and most successful directives, "Very well, then; get me out a 2-6-0 with 5 ft. 8 in. coupled wheels, outside cylinders, and the No. 4 boiler—and bring in all the standard parts you can."

The forces acting during the design stage to defeat the inclusion of standard parts have to be experienced to be believed: but by keeping his eye strictly on the ball and persevering with standards generally and his range of standard engines in particular, Churchward largely completed his major design work with most of its refinements during 1910. The G.W.R. stock of his standard engines at the end of 1911 was as follows:

Type	*Class*	*Qty. built by* 1911	*Qty. built by* 1921	*Driving wheel dia.* *ft.*	*ins.*	*Cylinders*	*Boiler No.*
4-4-0	"County"	35	40	6	8½	18 × 30	4
4-6-0	"Saint"	45	72	6	8½	18½ × 30	1
4-6-0	"Star"	40	60	6	8½	15 × 26	1
2-6-0	"4301"	20	290	5	8	18½ × 30	4
2-8-0	97	35	84	4	7½	18½ × 30	1
	"4700"			5	8	19 × 30	7
4-4-2T	"County Tank"	20	41	6	8½	18 × 30	2
2-6-2T		115	130	4	1½	17 × 24	5
				4	7½	17 × 24	5
				5	8	18 × 30	2
				5	8	18½ × 30	4
2-8-0T	"4200"	1	95	4	7½	18½ × 30	4
Total at year end		311	812				

Further batches of all these engines, except the 4-coupled types, were built between 1911 and 1923.

Churchward spoke again on design and design philosophy on 17th March 1910, when he opened the discussion at the Institution of Mechanical Engineers on George Hughes's paper on "Compounding and Superheating." After expressing doubts as to whether like had always been compared with like, he went on to say:

On piston speeds and cut-offs:

"I think the author is quite right in the statement he makes that the fast piston-speeds give an advantage in the reduction of the condensation or the effects thereof; but I suggest that, in designing an engine specially for the competitive trial it would have been quite easy to put up the piston-speed of the simple engine. This has been done on the Great Western Railway, where a 30-in. stroke on a 55-in. wheel is used, which gives very much higher piston-speeds than the author contemplates for his engines. I quite appreciate what is said in the Paper as to the ill effects of having to shut up the exhaust-valve so early, only I will go further and say that it is nearly equally damaging to the simple engine as it is to the compound. I think every effort should be made to prolong the closure of the exhaust as far as it is practicable. The Great Western Railway has succeeded in getting it to nearly 72 per cent at 25 per cent cut-off, which I think will be a considerably later point than the author has in mind."

On clearances:

"The clearances, although not large in regard to common practice, are at the same time greater than can be obtained with careful and special design. It is practicable to get a $5\frac{3}{4}$ per cent clearance at any rate in a simple cylinder for a locomotive, which will give it a considerable advantage naturally over a cylinder having 7·4 clearance as mentioned in the Paper."

(A member said $5\frac{3}{4}$ per cent clearance was very interesting and novel; would Mr. Churchward state the distance left between piston and cylinder cover? Mr. Churchward said it was between $\frac{3}{16}$ and $\frac{1}{4}$ in.)

On superheating and lubrication:

"With superheating, which is rather more interesting to me than the compound question, no doubt the lubrication is the important point which has to

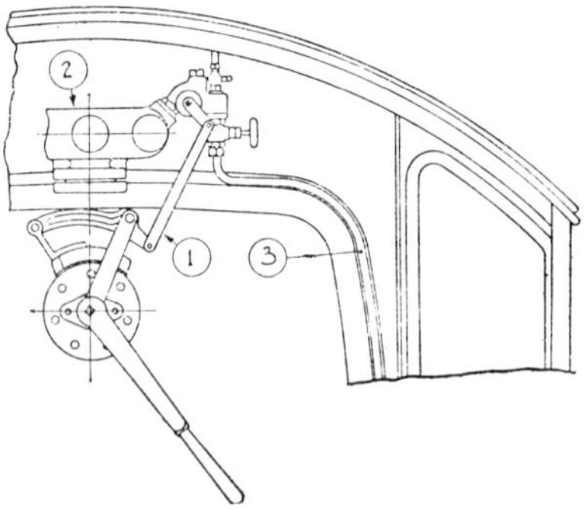

Fig. 30. Churchward's automatic valve, actuated by the regulator. Opening the regulator causes the linkage system 1 to open the steam valve on the manifold 2 and pass steam along pipe 3 to the sight-feed lubricator and thence to the cylinders.

be considered. It has been found on the Great Western Railway, in the course of a considerable amount of work with superheating, that the question of lubrication must be specially attended to, and unless the lubrication is not only effective and sufficient, but also continuous, there is certain to be trouble from high superheat. The continuous character of the lubrication is, I think, quite as important as any other factor. The tendency of men to drift with an engine, having no lubrication applied to the pistons and to the valves, is destructive to a degree in a superheated engine. The Great Western Railway has found it necessary to make special arrangements for the lubrication, and have therefore applied an automatic valve actuated by the regulator by which a small amount of steam, such as would pass through ½ in. pipe, is admitted to the engine while drifting, under practically all conditions. It is so arranged that the driver cannot open the jockey-valve of his regulator without first opening the lubricating pipe. By this means we have ensured the engine getting lubrication, with a small amount of steam to distribute it, under all conditions of work."

On insistent demands by Traffic Depts.:

"As the efficiency of the locomotive is increased, more work can be done on trains, either passenger or goods, and if the author's experience on the Lancashire and Yorkshire Railway agrees—as I expect it does—with mine on the Great Western Railway, he will find that every pound of efficiency that is put into the locomotive is immediately absorbed by the traffic department in giving the engine extra work by means of which the efficiency is swallowed up. Up to the present, even having the 'Great Bear' in mind, on the Great Western Railway at any rate we have not arrived at the limit of the capacity of the traffic department in this particular respect."

In 1912 Churchward found that his work at Swindon on standards was ever-increasing, and so he took H. C. King to be his Assistant on special duties. King was no respecter of persons and, knowing of old the teamwork involved in setting standards, Churchward admonished him when he took up his new post "Be careful you wear velvet gloves, and be damned careful whom you step on." Consequent moves came early in 1913 with the appointment of Collett as Loco Works Manager, and Stanier as his Assistant. Churchward was justifiably pleased with the Works, which he and his staff had energetically kept up to date and extended as necessary; and with the usual human mixture of pride and helpfulness he was ready to show anything to his opposite numbers. H. N. Gresley took up such an offer during 1913, some 18 months after he succeeded H. A. Ivatt. True to form, and wishing to give detail answers to any questions that might be put, Churchward got Collett and Stanier to accompany Gresley and himself on the Works tour. In fact, as the hosts well knew, there were numerous items at Swindon waiting to be applied on the other railways and to pay dividends. Gresley undoubtedly took enormously useful mental notes but, outwardly, he managed to convey that a lot of what he saw was of doubtful value; at which Churchward was veteran enough to smile to himself, and Collett and Stanier were young enough to be hopping mad but polite enough not to argue.

Aged 56, a commanding figure with an even and tactful temperament, Churchward had inherited from his father something of a country squire appearance, including a liking for the appropriate tweedy suits. He could and did afford to smile to himself when various theoretically approached and practically proven Swindon ideas were ignored elsewhere—often with painful results. His dissemination of all that he and his staff had learned and applied was beyond reproach. Each new engine had received the usual display in the technical press, with drawings and data. New slants were put over in papers and in discussions on papers. Staff obtained good posts on the other railways. Visits to Swindon were offered. Questions asked and chores dished out by the A.R.L.E. and other bodies were dealt with fully and studiously. No. 4005 *Polar Star* was lent to the L.N.W.R. in 1909 and a full set of drawings supplied to the Crewe Drawing Office, though of course they may never have been unrolled. Besides, you could go to Paddington and see most of the Churchward features, excepting of course the inside motion, without even having to buy a platform ticket. And for the same price per mile as on any other railway you could go for a ride and see that in fact the G.W.R. performances were probably the best in England. Publicity issued from Paddington continued to make corresponding superiority claims, and their frequent moments of truth continued to build up a decided anti-Swindon reaction. Probably this reaction was felt even more keenly at Board level than by the Locomotive Superintendents. In an imperfect world, with human Boards, engineering failures can look like incompetence and successes like extravagance. Sometimes they are. Churchward himself had to combat criticisms that his engines cost far more than Crewe engines.

In contrast to his squire-like appearance Churchward was an exceptional craftsman. He never lost this pleasure, which he had first felt so keenly in pupil days on the car project at Newton Abbot. Unmarried, he had practically no domestic deflections from his excellently equipped workshop at *Newburn*, the Chief's house at Swindon. He maintained and improved his car, and enjoyed an occasional discussion of car troubles whilst in the Works. Once he complained to Stanier about trouble with the low-tension ignition on his Weigel, and Stanier had some short ends of tungsten tool steel drawn down to $\frac{3}{8}$ ins. diameter: from these he himself made and fitted new contacts.

Churchward next attended an A.R.L.E. meeting on 28th November 1913, and at once moved into action by proposing Henry Fowler as Hon. Secretary to follow Wainwright of the S.E. & C.R. who had just retired. Then started another marathon discussion about tyre profiles; the standards for thick flanges had been accepted at the June meeting and now a decision had to be made on thin flanges. Churchward said again that they must all consult their engineers: the G.W.R. engineer, Grierson, objected most strongly to the distance between the backs of the tyres being increased. " If we think we are going to get a lot of extra freedom by thinning the tyre, when we are passing round curves with crossings in them, then we deceive ourselves," Churchward added. Gresley said that a greater distance between flanges would help on curves without check-rails, and Billinton and Malcolm both said that by increasing the distance they had reduced the frequency of fractured crank-axles. Churchward again urged them to consult their engineers, but there was some reluctance—" they will form all sorts of opinions." " Why cannot they co-operate with their engineers," thought Churchward, puffing at his pipe which was giving some combustion trouble. He took from his waistcoat pocket his silver matchbox with its attached hardwood plug, and tamped the temperamental tobacco with deliberation and precision. After further puffing confirmed that the operation had succeeded, he looked round the meeting and said " I propose we send our suggested thin tyre sections to our respective Engineers, and ask them if they will agree to them." Pickersgill seconded, everyone agreed, and they moved off to lunch where they were joined by Ivatt, Worsdell and other honorary members.

War clouded the 1914 winter meeting of the A.R.L.E. and a letter of condolence was sent to the Locomotive Superintendents of France and Belgium. The technical business included approval of a proposed A.R.L.E. standard method of calculating locomotive heating surfaces. Churchward added that several similar standard methods were needed, including one for calculating tractive effort. Ivatt again joined them for lunch, and there was talk of the effects of the war. Ivatt was helping to train young commissioned officers in the handling of a revolver: not yet 65, he remained quick on the draw. Hannington was serving in France—running English

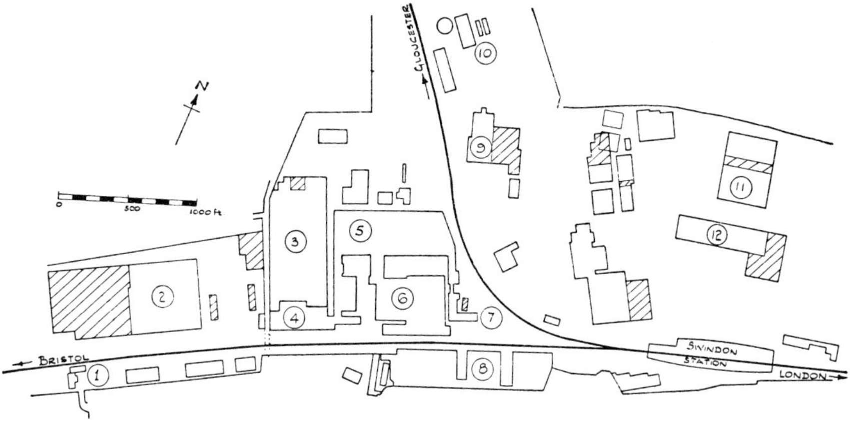

Fig. 31. Swindon Works, G.W.R., 1920. Shaded areas added by Churchward.

1 Newburn.
2 Machine and erecting shops.
3 Boiler shop.
4 Iron foundry.
5 Rolling mill.
6 Machine and erecting shops.
7 Offices.
8 Carriage shops.
9 Running shed.
10 Gas works.
11 Carriage lifting shop.
12 Wagon lifting shop.

locos and finding how difficult it was to repair them with local metric tools. His S.O.S. to Stanier for a supply of Swindon tools provoked an immediate and sympathetic response from Churchward, " We are all in the Government now, Stanier, send him what he wants." There were growing calls on the Railway Works for munitions, staff was being depleted and traffic increasing, and it was rumoured that some high-up would be called to the Munitions Department in Whitehall.

Henry Fowler was duly called. Among his techniques to get the Railways making munitions, one was to place on the table, nonchalantly, a sample item made by the Midland at Derby. This happened once when 2-in. fuses were sorely needed, and Churchward hurried back to Swindon after the meeting, sent for Stanier and said " Why aren't we turning out fuses? " Stanier was rather nettled by this and argued, " Well, it's like this, sir, do you want one fuse or do you want 3,000 a week? We can make you one next week in the tool room, the same as Fowler has done. If you want 3,000 we've got to organize for it and get the machines going." Churchward agreed to turning over part of the cylinder shop, and they duly made 3,000 a week. Fowler was knighted before the end of the war, and earned it.

Way back, engineers were either Civil or Military. In peacetime, you could drop the " Civil " and they were just Engineers. On all the Railways, " The Engineer " fully described the civil engineer in charge of track, bridges, buildings. At the turn of the century the title " Superintendent" for the Engineer's opposite number on the mechanical side began to look inferior or even derogatory, so it gradually changed to " Chief Mechanical Engineer." Churchward adopted this title in 1916.

Copper was in short supply in 1916 and at the A.R.L.E. meeting in November a committee of four was set up to enquire into the steel specifications, plate sizes and radii, etc., suitable for steel fireboxes. Hill, Bowen Cooke, Churchward and Hughes were the four. Churchward commented that he used steel stays up to the top of the brick arch, and that he had found steel satisfactory for the tube plate, leaving the rest of the box copper. Both Hill (Great Eastern) and Hughes had some engines running with steel fireboxes.

Churchward was President of the A.R.L.E. for 1917. At the June meeting, 80 per cent of boiler pressure was tentatively accepted as the figure to take in calculating tractive efforts, though Churchward said he took 90 per cent because in tests at slow speeds he had obtained 93 per cent. At the same meeting came the first thoughts of engines, carriages and wagons to be built after the cessation of hostilities. Hughes emerged as the Convener of a committee of carriage side representatives, and Churchward as the Convener of a committee consisting of the Locomotive Engineers of Companies represented on the Railway Executive Committee.

At the November meeting, Hughes lengthily reported progress on the standard wagons. On the loco side, Churchward said that on the previous evening the committee had decided to proceed with two standard locomotives, a 2-6-0 and a 2-8-0. A sub-committee under Maunsell would look after the proposals, and Messrs. Maunsell and Fowler would do preliminary designs for the 2-6-0 and 2-8-0 respectively. The type of superheater was in doubt: so a vote was taken in which 14 to 5 favoured the Robinson Superheater.

Excellent progress was competitively made by Maunsell and Fowler; and at the next meeting, on 28th June 1918, Churchwood tabled full details of the two engines. "The main parts," he explained, "such as cylinders, piston valves, motion, valve gear, etc., will be interchangeable, and the weight will not exceed that which can be accepted by certain of the Companies. The boiler pressure will be 180 lb. per sq. in., but the boilers have been designed so that a pressure of 200 lb. can be used if desired." In the ensuing discussion the designs were generally agreed, except for a difference of opinion about the brake: wisely it was decided that the more fundamental decision of a standard brake must be settled first.

Some leading dimensions of the two standard engines are given on p. 52.

At the same meeting, Hughes reported good progress on the standard wagons, except that whereas a length of 20 ft. was desired some companies were known to favour a limit of 17 ft. Churchward therefore proposed, with the aim of getting ahead with standard *components* for the wagons, a *choice* of standard length, 17 or 20 ft. Gresley seconded this brilliant impasse-clearer which was agreed.

But it was all rather in vain. Loading gauge differences proved intractable, voters abstained, prior interest was taken in standardizing interchangeable details, enthusiasm dwindled, and action never started on a common design, which was apparently seen as a potential blow to everyone's pride.

Meanwhile Churchward, fortified by the award of a C.B.E., which in his quiet way he had richly earned, was involved in his own new 2-8-0 design at Swindon. The *Great Bear* had been in the habit of hurrying to Bristol by day with passengers, and hurrying back by night with fitted freight. Churchward rather disliked its bulk and its trailing wheels: but since with 6 ft. 8½ in. driving wheels it ran freely at 80 mph, as did the "Stars," he could see no reason why a 2-8-0 with 5 ft. 8 in. wheels should not run equally freely at 68 mph. Moreover he knew there was considerable "fat" in his designs, and he wanted to exploit some of it. And so in April 1919 there emerged from Swindon No. 4700, using the No. 1 boiler as on the "Stars" and incorporating mainly standard parts. Sure enough, it was soon being timed at 66 mph on the Goring stretch with a passenger train. Unlike the Pacific, it could travel over all the main lines. Churchward saw he had moved forward another step, and he must have realized that if pressed he could have turned out a pretty inspiring 4-8-0: but why worry, all the existing engines could handle the traffic, he was due to retire in a couple of years, and young Collett knew exactly how to make a bigger " Star," when required. So he pressed on with other work and other interests, including the elusive quest for a chisel-pointed " dry-as-it-writes " stylo pen. One day he chanced to walk into his Chief Draughtsman's office just as Burrows was examining a recording accelerometer which O. V. Bulleid had brought down to show him. In the lid was a packet of spare wires for the recording pens. " Without a ' by your leave or with your leave ' " as Bulleid later said rather crossly to Burrows, Churchward helped himself freely to the spare wires and withdrew. On the way back to his office he met Stanier and triumphantly confided, " I've been looking for these all over London."

In 1920, again true to form, Churchward took C. B. Collett to be his full time Assistant, in order to facilitate the succession. They worked closely together on such jobs as the fitting of a larger boiler on the 2-8-0 No. 4700. They also had preliminary discussions on the extent and manner of enlarging the " Stars " and Collett later brought out the design of the resulting " Castle " class, in 1923, with *Caerphilly Castle*, which is preserved. Churchward kept up his Committee work, making contributions to A.R.L.E. meetings up to January 1921. He also kept up his love of fishing, unbroken from Stoke Gabriel days. So, when pressed by the Works to say what he would like for a presentation when he retired at the end of 1921, he asked for a fishing rod.

The presentation took place at a mass meeting in the Mechanics Institute. On the platform were various section heads, and also the Works Committee, whose Chairman gave a very eulogistic account of how the men appreciated their Chief, and dramatically wound up by hoping that every hair on his head would be a candle to light him to glory. Churchward, noted to the end for his direct manner of speech, and his bald head, turned to the Chairman and said, " There won't be many of them, Watkins!" With the extensive surplus cash after buying the fishing rod, Churchward arranged a trust fund to provide annual Apprentice prizes.

After retirement he became unhappily afflicted by deafness and impaired sight, and these led to his tragic death in December 1933. He was looking closely at the ballasting of the main line alongside his garden at a time normally free of traffic, when he was run down and killed by a South Wales express, running late. Local respect for " the old man " was unquenchable, and he was deeply mourned.

His listed achievements made impressive obituary tributes; and at the Institution of Locomotive Engineers in 1936, in his vote of thanks for Stanier's Presidential Address, Sir Nigel Gresley said:—" I was pleased to hear Mr. Stanier refer to his old Chief, Mr. Churchward, because I have always thought, and still think, that locomotive engineers in this country owe more to the ingenuity, inventiveness and foresight of Churchward than to any other chief mechanical engineer. I know that his influence on the locomotives of this Country still exists in a very marked way. Look

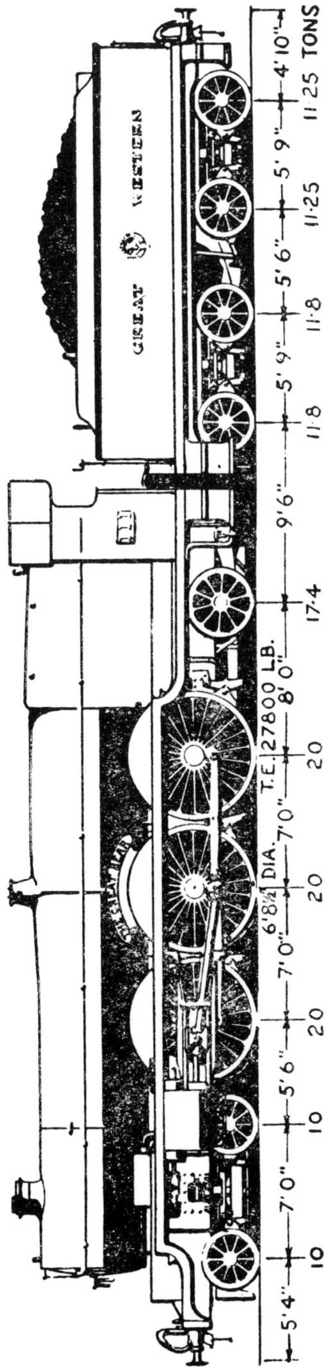

Fig. 32. Churchward's Pacific, *The Great Bear*, 1908.

[*A. J. Creswell*

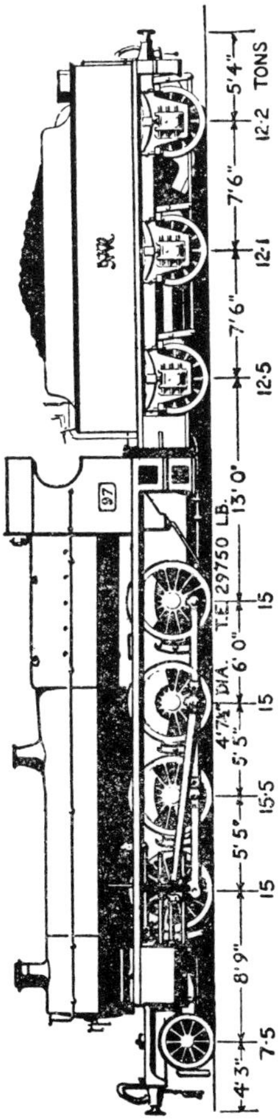

Fig. 33. Churchward's 2-8-0 No. 97, 1903.

[*A. J. Creswell*

at the latest locomotives of the Great Western, of the Southern, of the L.M.S., obviously, and also of the L.N.E. There is a great deal of Churchward's work which I was only too glad to incorporate on the engines of the London and North Eastern."

If actions speak louder than words, the best Churchward tribute of all came from W. A. Stanier.

CHAPTER 5

W. A. Stanier's mighty re-stocking of the L.M.S.

William Arthur Stanier was born on 27th May 1876 at Swindon and made up his mind to be a mechanic of some sort when he was five. About this time he ran into domestic trouble by pinching meat skewers and heating them in the fire to bore holes in wood: this form of improvisation was not liked by his parents, but even so five more years passed before he acquired his first set of real tools. He went away to school at Wycliffe College, Stonehouse, Glos., where he was a middle-of-the-road performer: but he was able to live at home again when he started work at Swindon in January 1892.

Stanier's father had followed William Dean from Wolverhampton to Swindon in 1871 and being a versatile man carried out many duties in addition to being Dean's chief clerk: he inaugurated mechanical and chemical tests on incoming material, and he started technical education at the Mechanics Institute for the Swindon apprentices. He was therefore able to encourage his eldest son's work at night classes: but as a point of interest he was not in a position to affect his son's apprenticeship course, which was run rather casually by one of the Works Manager's clerks and undoubtedly coloured by the likes and dislikes of the individual foremen. Dean himself only knew his few pupils—and that vaguely.

Young Stanier started as an office boy, and his earliest recollections include the last 7 ft. gauge train going through Swindon, and the dramatic week-end early in May 1892 when the broad gauge was converted. The last of the old broad gauge locos came up to Swindon and were put in sidings where the present erecting shops were later built. The carriages and wagons were parked in extensive sidings at the Carriage and Wagon works. That very month, on his 16th birthday, Stanier started his formal apprenticeship, and had a brief encounter with the formidable William Dean. He had been sent to fetch foreman Ellis from one of the machine shops and had paused to look at a new drilling machine when he became aware that things had become quieter and one or two people nearby had melted away. Then a high door in a partition opened and an important looking figure emerged and fixed the lad, whilst the following simple conversation took place:

"What special work are you on here, boy?"
"I was sent to get Mr. Ellis, sir."
"Why don't you do it."

2-4-0 tanks for the Metropolitan service were being built at Swindon about this time, but when Stanier got into the erecting shop he worked right through on the re-building of Dean's 7 ft. 4-4-0 No. 14, *Charles Saunders*, and subsequently on a new batch of 4-2-2s which were being built simultaneously with the conversion to this wheel arrangement of the "3001" class 2-2-2s, after the Box Tunnel derailment showed a leading bogie to be necessary. One of the apprentices' few perks, in an era of long hours and close discipline, was to accompany an engine on its first trial run after general repair; and so Stanier enjoyed his first footplate ride.

After completing his five years' apprenticeship he stayed on for six months in the pattern shop, accepting (after some argument with the foreman about his competence) a weekly rate of 22s. against the full patternmaker's starting rate of 24s. Then he began his Drawing Office experience with a year in the Carriage and Wagon section, and a further year spread over the loco, experimental, and structure sections. His jobs included the design of the underframe for a new G.W.R. dynamometer car, in which was incorporated a special transmission spring having an excellent characteristic free from hysteresis due to rollers placed between the leaves—a G. H. Pearson design.

In December 1899 Stanier was appointed Inspector of Materials—a job in which the name probably still carried some weight! His father had been promoted to Stores Superintendent in 1892 but saw Dean about the works from time to time: at one such casual meeting Dean suddenly asked "What's your boy doing, Stanier?" "Well, he's inspecting incoming materials at the moment." "Oh," said Dean, "I'm going to send him down to the shed as a mechanical inspector. But it will be a 6 o'clock job, mind!" This did not worry young Stanier, nor, fortunately, his mother who had to cope with the early morning start once again: and so off he went down to the shed, to do the very job upon which he had to rely for shed data in future L.M.S. days.

As mechanical inspector under the Divisional Locomotive Superintendent, W. H. Williams, Stanier worked very closely with Williams's assistant and was practically a second assistant: but he had more to do with the mechanical maintenance of the engines and was much involved with the leading fitters and boilermakers. At that time Swindon shed housed about 40 passenger and 60 goods engines, and its responsibility included control of the sheds at Gloucester, Severn & Wye, Oxford, Reading, Trowbridge and Weymouth. At some of these sheds Stanier did brief spells as relief foreman. Smoking on duty was forbidden, and when 3rd class engineman J. H. Thomas broke this rule twice in rapid succession Stanier rebuked him for setting a particularly bad example, seeing that he was one of the men's leaders.

Another promotion came quite quickly, and with it annual staff status, when in February 1903 Stanier was installed as Assistant Divisional Superintendent at Westbourne Park. This was a key period in G.W.R history: though Churchward took over formally as Locomotive, Carriage and Wagon Superintendent in June 1902 he had been Works Manager since 1895 and thus, traditionally and practically, first assistant to Dean.

Moreover Dean had handed over more and more of the work to Churchward since 1899. So, after preparations during the period 1901 to 1905, the great programme was launched for re-equipping the G.W.R. with a range of standard locomotives based on standard components. These preparations included many running trials, which were seen at first hand by Stanier at Westbourne Park. Prominent amongst these were the trials of *La France*, the de Glehn compound Atlantic, to match whose boiler pressure of 227 psi Churchward built a 4-6-0 No. 171 *Albion* and then for experimental parity converted it into a matching 4-4-2. Later the trials were extended by Churchward building a further batch of Atlantics, but in contrast with 171 these were very poor steamers. One day in 1905 when Churchward was at Paddington he sent for Stanier and asked him what was wrong with the Atlantics. " Well, they don't steam," Stanier replied, " We have done everything we can, trying alterations to the blast-pipe and smokebox, but still they won't steam." " Then what's the matter with them?" " The only difference I can see compared with 171 is that 171 had a hump across the centre of its ash-pan with a damper on each side. But the other 4-4-2s were built with a flat-bottom ash-pan and only the front and back dampers. I don't think they are getting enough air under the grate." " Dammit, Stanier," Churchward exclaimed, " I believe you're right." The engines were altered and the trouble eliminated.

If these engine trials added to the work of the Shed, they also added interest and knowledge. Stanier still found time to address the footplate staff, at their Mutual Improvement Classes, on valve gears, particularly comparing Stephensons with the recently-introduced Walschaerts. He also taught the evening class for drivers and firemen at Willesden Technical School during 1904 and 1905. Nor did he lose touch with Swindon: always a keen swimmer, he played for the Swindon water polo team and, early in 1905, he became engaged to a Swindon girl. And so he was not sorry when, in April 1906, just after he had completed the transfer of the Westbourne Park shed to Old Oak Common, he was moved back to Swindon as Assistant to H. C. King, the Loco Works Manager. King's Assistant Works Manager was C. B. Collett. This turned out to be a six-month assignment, and pleasantly interrupted by his marriage on July 4th. His main job, which took him right back to machine tool interests, was to double the productivity of the wheel lathe for bogie and tender wheels, by increasing the power and depth of cut.

And so in October 1906, aged 30 and just married, bags of solid experience already gained, and salary advanced to £500, Stanier was appointed Divisional Locomotive Superintendent of the Swindon Division.

It was quite something to be Head of the running department at Swindon. The trials enginemen ran all the new engines as they came off the Works, and were able to point out anything needing attention: and then the working of the engines was followed up by the mechanical inspectors. Stanier therefore saw a good deal at first hand of the Churchward standard engines as they came out in the period 1906–1912. He drove some himself: they went through Works trials then running-in trials: and then after acceptance by the Running Department at Swindon they had to be put on local services to get the journals run in. At that time machining techniques were far less well developed and the running-in period was very important. So an engine might run for three weeks on local trains, and after that the Shed to which it was allocated would run it for a further three weeks on locals till they were satisfied they could put it in its appropriate link. By this date working hours had been shortened and engine working became more intensive, with most engines run on two shifts compared with the one-team-one-engine situation when Stanier first went to Westbourne Park; and this again emphasized the importance of running in.

Another notable trial of the period was the inauguration of Automatic Train Control equipment on the Oxford to Fairford single line. The thinking behind the G.W.R. system of A.T.C. was admirable, including the twin basic philosophies of fail-safe and the fact that the signals remained the driver's instruction, the A.T.C. equipment serving solely as an aid in reading them. Stanier saw the system fully proven and decisions taken to extend it: and then he found himself viewing it from the Works aspect when, in 1913, he was appointed Assistant Works Manager, Swindon.

Cross-postings between the design/manufacturing/operating sides of an organization are now an accepted facet of staff progression with enlightened management: Stanier found the change particularly rewarding because of the great interest always taken by Churchward in seeing that the equipment and techniques in the Works were the best available at the time. And so, supported by his Works Manager, Collett, he kept these improvements going and began the conversion of belt-driven machine tools to individual drives. He also fed into the Drawing Office minor improvements seen possible in the Works with the eyes of a loco running man: for example he arranged different-shaped knobs on damper control levers so that firemen could operate these by feel in the dark—ergonomics, 1913.

In December 1914, spurred by the G.W.R. installation of A.T.C. between London and Reading, interest in "Audible and other Cab Signals" ran high, and the Institution of Mechanical Engineers arranged a symposium of five papers on the subject. Vincent Raven gave that for the North Eastern Railway, and Stanier for the G.W.R. After describing the system, Stanier quoted from the report of a visiting U.S.A. Commission, "Only the G.W.R. system seems worthy of further consideration." In the lengthy discussions on the five papers, speaking of the London–Reading installation, Stanier said "to the astonishment of everyone at Paddington several of the trains arrived to time during a fog." To a suggestion that the G.W.R. system was not suitable for a driver to repair on the road in an emergency he replied " On the Great Western, at any rate, the drivers would not have time to do so: the traffic people would want them out of the way." Thus at his maiden appearance as a contributor to a Learned Institution, he showed himself decidedly practical, well able to bat briskly in discussion, and not averse to plugging the G.W.R. image.

Then the first war hotted up; and Stanier, at 38 too old for the first overseas drafts, got deeply involved in re-tooling Swindon for munitions. And in 1920, with things only just back to normal, he was appointed Works Manager.

C. B. Collett followed Churchward as C.M.E. in January 1922, and in 1923 he took Stanier as his Principal Assistant. Collett was an extremely competent man but not easy to work with: he did not like his staff visiting other loco works, and he found it abnormally difficult to place full and relaxed reliance upon the work and reports of his assistants. He had suffered the blow of his wife's death in 1923 and he withdrew more and more into metaphysics and psychical research for his interest outside his professional work. But Stanier had worked for him from 1913 till 1920, and they resumed working together again with great harmony in 1923. Fate comes into these relationships, and it was a trick of fate that Stanier found himself only five years younger than his Chief, so that at best he could only hope for a five-year span as Chief himself. Unlike the pre-grouping days, chances of a move to be C.M.E. of another railway were dim. Everybody had at least one ex-C.M.E. as a colleague.

Of course Collett and Stanier had in common a dedication generally to the G.W.R. and particularly to promulgating the Churchward standards: this they did triumphantly with the " Castle " Class, 1923.

Then Collett secured permission for a 22 ton axle loading with the balance possible on a 4-cylinder engine, and in July 1927 the " King " class appeared, keeping the G.W.R. ahead of the L.M.S. when the *Royal Scot* appeared a few weeks later. In the same autumn Stanier accompanied *King George V* to America for the centenary celebrations of the Baltimore & Ohio Railroad. Immediately on arrival he received a cable from Collett not to let the engine work. There had been a derailment, and Collett found that the short bearing springs of the bogie wheels had insufficient travel to maintain weight on the wheel when there was slack in the rail. He had a piece cut out of the rail on a weighbridge and he found that the weight on the wheel was zero when the wheel had dropped only 1½ in. So he arranged for coil springs to be fitted under the spring hangers: and, supplied with the necessary drawings, Stanier got the Baltimore & Ohio to make him the springs, lengthen the hangers and alter the brackets, and *King George V* did her stuff. Americans all thought she " is more like an automobile than a locomotive, and is made like a watch." Stanier rode on the engine hauling a dynamometer car and six Pullmans = 530 tons on a Baltimore–Washington–Philadelphia trip, max. gradient 1/75. The engine behaved admirably, though there was a minor panic when they were running at 75 mph and got a phone message from the dynamometer car that they were approaching a curve with 30 mph speed restriction. This was because the pilotman was preoccupied, in fact needlessly, about the apparatus on the engine for controlling the Westinghouse brake on the train. Stanier described his U.S.A. experiences in his Chairman's address to the Western Branch of the Institution of Mechanical Engineers on 8th December 1927.

I think Collett and Stanier liked being the only C.M.E. and Assistant not resident in London. After all, if you live in Mecca you do not have to go far on a pilgrimage. The Works was very handy for such tasks as the inspection of new carriages and their fittings. Equally, experimental work was quickly done—as when Stanier made up a wooden full-scale model of a connecting-rod and cross-head, to evolve a built-in oil reservoir and feeder for little-end lubrication. One could also keep a close eye on Works equipment and management—though here was a temptation

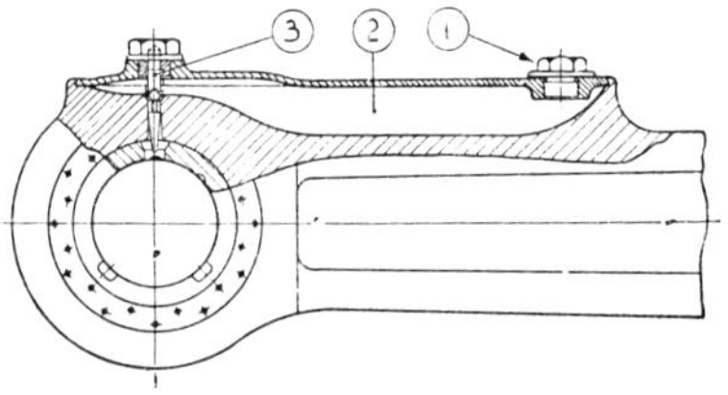

Fig. 34. Stanier's little-end lubricator. Filling-plug 1 gives access to the oil cup 2 formed in the connecting rod. The reciprocating motion throws the oil towards the needle 3 and a flat on this needle regulates the feed to the bearing.

which Collett was wise enough to recognize, and on one occasion he dropped Stanier a hint to let the Works Manager stand on his own feet. Another source of particular interest was the development of carriage bogies, together with the setting of maintenance standards to ensure preservation of good riding qualities and freedom from hunting.

The next new engine was the " Hall " class standard 2-cylinder 4-6-0, a general purpose larger locomotive to take over from many of the earlier 4-4-0 classes. Based closely on the Churchward "Saint" class, it had the same 18 in. dia. cylinders but 6 ft. dia. wheels. Then in 1929 appeared the " 5700 " class pannier tanks, the first 50 being built by the North British Locomotive Co. Stanier was engrossed in improving the motive power stock position of the G.W.R.

The locomotive situation on the four main line railways at the middle of 1931 was decidedly contrasty.

The L.N.E.R. had Gresley in charge and Bulleid as chief assistant: this pair had been largely acceptable to the constituent Companies since the amalgamation, had gained team strength since, and were in fact all set for their finest phase.

The Southern had also emerged comparatively painlessly from the amalgamation. Supported by Pearson and others from Swindon, Maunsell was the unquestioned figurehead on the mechanical side. His office at

Waterloo, complete with gimmick of S.E. & C.R. vice and set of tools, was the rendezvous for periodic visits from Gresley, Collett and Fowler.

The G.W.R. had heard about the amalgamation, but were not frightfully interested. Almost all the small railways in the Welsh valleys had stories about how their locos were replaced by G.W.R. locos which couldn't do the job, but these, progressively funnier as one travelled from Newport towards Swansea, were apocryphal. They certainly caused no loss of sleep to the excellently-established chief, Collett, nor his principal assistant, Stanier.

In sharp contrast to these harmonious scenes, where there were established leaders and a continuously-evolving motive power stud, the situation on the L.M.S. was dark and foreboding. A year before the amalgamation the Lancashire and Yorkshire Railway had been absorbed by the L.N.W.R., a perfectly sensible take-over in very many respects but unhappy in the locomotive department because, though Hughes of the L. and Y. was undoubtedly the correct choice for C.M.E., there were two very unfortunate side-effects. First, the older and larger Crewe became subservient to Horwich. Second, Beames of the L.N.W.R. had the misfortune to be relegated to chief assistant only a year after he had succeeded Bowen Cooke as C.M.E.

Then at the amalgamation Hughes became C.M.E. of the whole L.M.S.R. Again this was the best choice, and moreover Hughes had been a C.M.E. since 1904 compared with Fowler who had taken over when Deeley unhappily left the Midland in 1909. But it was not all that easy for Hughes because the Midland turned out to be the personality partner in the L.M.S. He was near retirement, and apart from the admirable " Land Crabs " he was content to carry out trials to see which of the existing engine types were the most economical performers and could be accepted as standard types. This approach may have been coloured by the Midland " small-engine " slant, and of course the " Compounds " emerged economically victorious. So 100 new " Compounds " were built in 1925/6 in addition to the 40 turned out by Derby in 1924, though everyone outside Derby thought they were too small for the period.

Then in 1926 Hughes retired and there must have been some head-scratching as to whether Beames or Fowler should succeed. The decision was probably coloured by the deplorable railway habit of letting seniority of claim settle such cases, and Sir Henry Fowler got the job. He had achieved considerable success and a measure of fame in ancillary activities such as 1914–18 munitions and the International Railway Congress Association, but his total loco design experience lay in comparatively minor modifications to existing types, and he was essentially a small-engine, Derby-tradition man, excepting the S. & D.J.R. 2-8-0s and the 0-10-0 banker for the Lickey incline—significantly, only seven large engines, and all pre-1920.

The 1913 " Claughtons " were still the leading L.M.S. loco, and though everyone grumbled at their serious fall-off in performance as they approached shopping time nothing was really done about it. In contrast, on the other railways the " Castle " class had proved itself both at home and in the L.N.E.R. interchange; the Gresley Pacifics had since undergone improvement; and Maunsell had scored with the *Lord Nelson.* A high-level decision was therefore taken that a large new L.M.S. express engine was wanted at once: and design was partly based on a full set of S.R. " Lord Nelson " drawings, partly entrusted to North British Locomotive Co., the builders. The resulting *Royal Scot* was a success, the more so as fifty were built without prototype trials; but did nothing to enhance the Fowler reputation.

And so, at the end of 1930, Sir Henry drifted out of the picture. Vice-President E. J. H. Lemon took over as C.M.E. for one year, and search was made for a new C.M.E. Somebody was wanted who would get cracking on the task that should have been started at least four years, if not ten years, before—the provision of a standard range of modern L.M.S. locomotives.

One day in October 1931 Lemon and Sir Harold Hartley* asked Stanier to lunch at the Athenaeum and talked about water-softening: Stanier's contribution was merely that they must know how well they were managing with Loch Katrine water in the Glasgow area, and surely this proved the importance of water treatment. Shortly after, Hartley again asked Stanier to lunch, this time at the Traveller's Club, more appropriately. Stanier told Collett about these cloak-and-daggerish invitations, received the green light, duly lunched, and was definitely asked if he would be prepared to take over as C.M.E. of the L.M.S. Railway. He expressed surprise that this approach had not first been made by Sir Josiah Stamp to Sir James Milne. Formalities were duly exchanged, and the upshot was a chat with Stamp who expressed concern at the number of different locomotive types on the L.M.S. and emphasized the need for a standard range of generally more powerful engines. Stamp then hesitated somewhat, and Stanier, though a sturdy 55-year-old, tactfully suggested that a medical examination might be *de rigueur.* This modest last hurdle cleared, Stanier took over as C.M.E. of the L.M.S. on January 1st 1932.

On the whole Stanier received a warm welcome from his new colleagues and staff at the L.M.S. In particular, a thoughtful welcoming note from H. P. M. Beames included the sentence " You will understand how disappointed I am, but I may say that there is no one I would rather work under than you." But the scene was strange to a Great Western man: not only was the scale larger, but there were four entirely separate large Works compared with the single King-pin of Swindon. Moreover, the

* Sir Harold Hartley reported "After looking over the possible field when Lemon became a Vice-President, I decided that Stanier was the man to get our locomotive programme straightened out. The number of different types we had inherited was appalling. I had no second string, and so I went ahead on my own with Stamp's blessing. I knew something of the Churchward tradition."

running side was not responsible to the C.M.E., so that, compared with G.W.R. practice, there was a departmental barrier against objective performance reports and the control of Shed maintenance practices. Theoretically the running side was responsible to the Motive Power Dept. for operation and to the C.M.E. for maintenance, but the latter was the weaker link. Stanier and Jimmy Anderson, the Chief Motive Power Superintendent, took to each other at once: but they did not always speak identical language. In assessing new motive power requirements, Anderson would express his needs as " so many engines of a certain (existing) type." Stanier took the first of such notes and placed it firmly in his " pending " drawer. Later he received a personal reminder that he had not replied. " No and I don't propose to," he explained, " I am trying to decide what range of new locomotives you need, and I can only do this if you will specify the numbers required and the duties they are to perform." Here he was echoing the heart-cry of all engineering designers trying to get at the *facts*, while the client, with most helpful intentions, persists in fogging them with opinions and masking them by omissions. But Anderson co-operated, and Stanier was soon able to start preparing outline diagrams of proposed engine types.

On the Works side there was much to impress: Crewe boiler-making came as a surprise to Stanier, who had not fully appreciated the stalwart performances put up by the standard range of L.N.W.R. boilers, on such classes as the " Precursors " and " Experiments." These boilers were decidedly on the small side for the engine duties, and the L.N.W.R. footplate teams were expected to, and did, thrash them to keep time with heavy trains. They made a rather invigorating noise, and at night looked highly pyrotechnic. But these boilers did not require excessive maintenance and had long lives; and when it came to steam-raising capacity a " Precursor " class boiler topped 20,000 lb./hr. on test. Stanier obtained some of his boiler data at first hand, and was seen following foreman Tizard through the fire hole of a " Prince of Wales " class boiler in Crewe boiler shop: as a result he confirmed his opinion that the better circulation in a Great Western type of boiler was a great advantage. But incidentally he found Crewe boiler-making of Swindon quality but cheaper, and he must have recollected the occasion when Churchward was challenged by his General Manager as to why two of his engines cost as much as three of Crewe's. Churchward replied " Because one of mine could pull two of their b—— things backwards."

Another good Works feature was the shopping system for loco repairs started by Fowler and H. G. Ivatt at Derby: but Stanier got a bit testy about minor shortcomings. He urged F. A. Lemon at Crewe to carry out a heroic collection and re-conditioning of shop tools and to start a central tool stores: three wagon-loads were collected. He urged shadow-boards for tools at Horwich, and changed the urge to an instruction when nothing happened: four months later he found it done but opinion divided as to the value. " If you spend money to tidy up the shop, you need spend less money to keep it tidy," remarked Stanier, who apart from detail was well aware that he had some excellent Works. He also succeeded, though with difficulty, in getting them to machine axleboxes to running size: the size stemming from his 1903–11 experience when a rule-of-thumb clearance of 14 thousandths on an 8 in. journal was found to promote the necessary oil film. Simultaneously he imported the process evolved by the Swindon wheel shop foreman in 1929 for finishing the journals and crank-pins: they were slowly rotated whilst being worked on by a loose-fitting annular pad impregnated with fine emery, which was rotated at polishing speed by belt drive from an electric motor. For the crank-pins, the motors slid up and down an incline to maintain constant centre distance and tension. This gave a beautiful, close, oil-film-sustaining, matt surface, of the type much publicised in the mid 1940s as "superfinishing." The resulting control of box and journal was first applied to the "Royal Scots," and gave results far superior to the costly hand-fitting and scraping which it replaced.

Less happy was the state of the Drawing Offices. There was really no glimmer of any integrated L.M.S. design and, 10 years after amalgamation, Crewe, Derby and Horwich remained resolutely insular.

Stanier looked round and took a deep breath. He then started on his plan to introduce the proven basic Churchward design features as far as practicable in this new arena, and he resolved by way of a dress rehearsal to apply them first to a small batch of 2-6-0s which were immediately required. These could have been the popular "Land Crabs" but Stanier was obviously wise to take the earliest opportunity of familiarizing both Works and Drawing Offices with ideas very new to them, on a small batch of engines.

Seen in the perspective of thirty-years-after, most of these ideas were sound and well-applied. There was the straight-forward, outside Walschaert's valve gear with long valve travel and cylinders near horizontal. Large piston valves with six rings—Stanier decided on these instead of the rather more elegant G.W.R. plug type, which coasts with reduced friction when steam is shut off, because the latter had proved very arduous to develop to adequate manufacturing and maintenance standards, even under the G.W.R. one-Works set-up. Then there were several routine Churchward details, such as the big-end bearings, axleboxes, and smooth-swept exhaust passages leading to jumper-top blast pipe. Finally there was the boiler, incorporating the Churchward tenets of large circulation space at the firebox front corners, top of barrel tapered to allow a 2-ft. steam space without dome, top feed over trays towards the front end to reduce the oxygen content of the feed-water, and low superheat. It was to the boiler that Stanier paid closest attention: to ensure the placing of the firebox stays truly normal to the critical curved regions at the front corners, he had them positioned in the boiler shop at Crewe before drilling and then copied the resulting dimensions on to the drawings—using the fullsize hardware as a model, in fact. An unfortunate error was made in the tube-plate drawings; Stanier had discussed the arrangement and length of tubes as compared with the large parallel-boilered 2-6-0s but he forgot to specify their diameter. The drawing was duly issued calling for 2 in. dia. tubes, as on the " Crabs," which would have given too small a ratio of length to bore. Stanier liked this ratio to be more than 80:1 and preferably near 100:1. Accordingly he had to go cap-in-hand and get sanction for the extra expense of scrapping and replacing the first batch of tube-plates. No C.M.E. can have been fortunate enough to avoid such tribulations which, as Stanier was heard to admit, are often their own fault for assuming that someone is rightly guessing their unspoken thoughts: but accidents provide clues for safeguards. Beames had been signing all these new drawings to get them away to the shops without delay in Stanier's absence, and so he received a brief note, marked personal, "Are you signing these drawings as Chief Draughtsman or on my behalf, if the latter please sign FOR me. W.A.S." All Chiefs have occasionally to remind people about these axioms of technical discipline, and the more you respect a colleague the straighter you can tell him.

The Chief Draughtsman was Herbert Chambers, an excellent and experienced designer, noted for his heroic and successful effort in co-ordinating (against time) the design work between Derby Loco Drawing Office and the North British Locomotive Co. on the *Royal Scot*, but a dyed-in-the-wool Midland man. He argued with Stanier about all those innovations which he could not readily accept. At one point during these difficult weeks, rather lonely among Midland doubts, Stanier tried to get S. O. Ell from the G.W.R. to come as an Assistant on experimental work; but Collet refused to release him. A good Chief and a good Assistant both know that a nice balance between querying orders and blindly following them is essential, but Stanier and Chambers were unable to find this balance with Chambers as Chief Draughtsman. Stanier, therefore, switched him to be Technical Assistant at Euston and appointed Tom Coleman to be Chief Draughtsman in charge of both Derby and Crewe Loco Drawing Offices, resident at Derby. Coleman came from Horwich, where the air was distinctly less parochial, and had previously worked with H. G. Ivatt at Stoke. He was a hard worker and shared Stanier's dislike of frills. Stanier got along excellently with him, considered him eminently sound and practical rather than theoretical, ready to incorporate all the new ideas, and not too ready to query points differing from previous practice. Chambers may incidentally have done quite a bit of softening-up: Derby had some first-class design techniques and these did not always require modification by what was sometimes rudely referred to as " Wiltshire wisdom." Coleman also had a decided artistic bent which Stanier admired and which contributed to the apparently effortlessly balanced appearance of the many Stanier locomotive types. Paradoxically Horwich Drawing Office had no share in these designs.

After limbering-up on the 2-6-0s and getting straight with his design team and construction problems, Stanier proceeded to the traditional and expected task of a new C.M.E.—the design of a new and more powerful express passenger engine. It may be a salutary reminder that this engine, the first L.M.S. Pacific, No. 6200, appeared in June 1933—only 17 months after Stanier took office. The Pacific is the inevitable step larger than the 4-6-0, and a hefty boiler with wide firebox was provided, again incorporating the Churchward dicta. Stanier decided upon a 4-cylinder arrangement because he was used to it and because it gave a better balanced engine: it permitted him to build a Pacific with 22½ ton axle loads. When he first put forward this proposed design, the Chief Civil Engineer refused to consider it—rather tiresomely, because it was only 5 per cent more than the axle-loading of the 3-cylinder " Royal Scots " and the advantage of 4-cylinder balancing must have been clearly argued and recorded 20 years before, when Bowen Cooke produced the 4-cylinder " Claughton " with 19¾ ton axle loads. However, Stanier went and explained how the arrangement practically eliminated hammer-blow so that the maximum live weight on the wheels would be considerably less than that of some of the existing 2-cylinder engines which had lower static axle loadings. The objection was duly withdrawn.

But weight remained a problem, and in scratching round to reduce it Coleman persuaded Stanier to permit fluted coupling-rods. In contrast to H. A. Ivatt, and of course benefiting from alloy steels and improved balancing techniques, Stanier did not object to considerable mass and throw in his coupling-rods, and he positively preferred a plain, rectangular, thin section, deeper at the centre. This was to allow a little flexibility under shock, a requirement of Churchward in the early days of the " City " class, when there was an epidemic of these engines throwing their coupling-rods. The first remedy tried was stiffening the rods and increasing the bearings, but this was ineffective because when a severe shock occurred it was transmitted to the crank pin and bent it, after which the process of the bent pin throwing its end of the coupling-rod is easily visualized. Whip was therefore allowed by making the rods thin but deep, and Stanier experienced the benefits of this cure whilst at Westbourne Park. Best digested of all are those lessons learned under operating or Works conditions.

Stanier also decided upon four separate sets of Walschaert's gear for his first Pacific, after having several ideas set out on the drawing-board for rocking-levers to operate the inside valves from the outside motion, and failing to evolve a design he liked. After all, this did not appreciably affect accessibility compared with any inside-gear engine, and he was not particularly sensitive to the increased reciprocating masses. Besides he did not wish to run into the troubles encountered by other attempts to save sets of valve gear, as on the " Claughtons " and the Gresley Pacifics.

So building of the engine proceeded at Crewe and soon Stanier was asked along to give it his final blessing before unveiling. This he at first refused, finding the engine decidedly rusty here and there, several fittings left in an aggressively " as cast " condition, and other minor blemishes.

These he rather testily blamed on Crewe's lack of finesse, and provocatively asked whether they would not rather turn a job out to Swindon standards: but to be fair it was a symptom of Crewe economy pushed over by the cheese-paring Stamp regime. Two weeks later the engine, now looking resplendent and rather expensive, was driven to Euston for a red-carpet inspection by the Board. It was not yet named, permission being awaited from the Princess Royal. Mrs. Stanier strolled down the platform to have a dutiful look at it, and remarked to the driver that she was sorry it was without a name. " Well," he said, " we call it the Baby Austin."

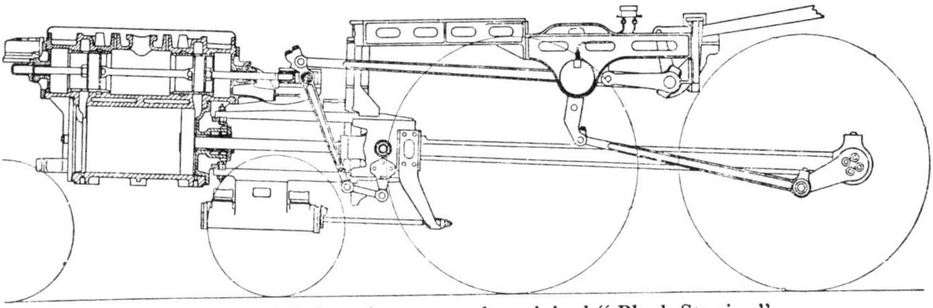

Fig. 35. Walschaert's gear on the original " Black Stanier."

Meantime design was well advanced on the next two loco types, the 4-6-0s. In their early days they were known in the Sheds as the " Red " ones (3-cylinder, Class 5XP) and the " Black " ones (2-cylinder, Class 5MT). The latter name has stuck to this day, though it is now usually expanded to " Black Staniers," but the red ones became less obvious when painted green, and they later assumed their official name of " Jubilees." By this time, Autumn 1933, Stanier had established both his general design requirements and also his intentions about standardization. He was confident that he was near enough to correct design to permit building in quantity without incurring excessive later modifications. In particular he aimed at many identical components covering several classes of engine. Of course there is nothing novel in this obviously desirable aim: the difficulty is to get it carried out, against all the massed forces that perpetually militate against standardization.

The taper boiler was not at first aesthetically acceptable to L.M.S. personnel, who were accustomed to blunt fronts in the " Claughton"/*Cardean*/" Land Crab " style, capped by the original *Royal Scot*: but the proportions of the Stanier engines were liked from the word go, and most people grew to like their appearance more and more—as happens when a major change in motor car cladding shape occurs. Moreover, the functional parts were in a nicely balanced arrangement, and component layout was thoughtful. A minor but common criticism at the time was the comparatively heavy appearance of the motion: the coupling-rod contribution to this has already been explained, but there were also the massive cross-head guides and the longer stroke, both looking heavy compared with, say, a Gresley Pacific.

Whilst the 2-6-0s and the black 4-6-0s were good engines " straight from the drawing board and the Shops," the first red 3-cylinder 4-6-0s were perfect stinkers. They simply would not steam. One of the best Inspectors at Derby, who was additionally very robust and something of a humourist, staggered disconsolately off the first one that came to Derby for a trial run. He had done most of the firing himself and had lost time with a modest train. There was a discussion about " red carpet " trials, and someone suggested that the least that should be done would be to whitewash the coal on the tender, in order to enhance the general appearance and show consideration for V.I.P. footplate riders: to which this Inspector replied that a bit of whitewash on the coal would extinguish the fire. And in fact the malaise did appear to be two-fold: the fire was lifeless however the dampers were manipulated, and the engine appeared to be draped in dank steam.

So began the teething troubles stage, and with two handicaps to Stanier: he was more remote from the running side than in his previous experience, and Jimmy Anderson had retired. His place was taken by D. C. Urie, promoted from Divisional Mechanical Engineer, Scotland, who was a design-trained man, had suffered demotion from C.M.E. when the Highland Railway amalgamated into the L.M.S., and did not particularly like novelties from the G.W.R. This is not a good background for helping with the teething troubles of a load of new engines designed by an imported C.M.E.—specially when the Running man reports to the Operating side (except for maintenance) and all the difficulties affect his own showing of efficiency. There were some difficult scenes, as when the " Jubilees " were formally stated by Urie to be incapable of working the Birmingham 2-hour job. Teething troubles bring modifications, and modifications to blast pipe and chimney and to tube plates for additional superheaters are fairly easy in the drawing office but murder in the Works. They delay the batch of engines you are building, and each engine can carry a different set of modifications. Lemon and Bond at Crewe shuddered as these modified drawings seemed to pour in from Derby, continually upsetting progress in the Works.

For the Running Shed maintenance slant, Stanier had to depend on his mechanical and boiler inspectors. Their experience is wide and unemotional, and they keep an eye, for the C.M.E., on the technical aspects of Shed maintenance on those railways where the Sheds do not report executively to the C.M.E. They had to enforce routine instructions, such as the superseding of the popular existing tapered boiler-tube expanders by the parallel type. Ultimately the former had to be tracked down in boiler makers' tool boxes and confiscated.

Stanier very seldom rode on the footplate of his engines other than taking one ride on an early model of each class. He always held that there was far more to learn from an hour's discussion with a good Inspector who was continually so riding, than from a day's riding himself.

Teething troubles always present these two difficulties: that many of the clues are very subjective, and that the " Confidence Trick " applies. By the latter I mean when a certain factor is exonerated as trouble-free based on a sound premise, and everyone therefore looks elsewhere for the trouble: whereas in fact the premise is NOT sound and the exonerated factor is guilty. In Stanier's case this factor was low superheat. So convinced was he that a low degree of superheat was adequate that the important change to increased superheater area was delayed far longer than necessary. There were some very sound men in the Experimental Section of the Derby Loco Drawing Office at that time, but they were young and they looked rather " Midland " to Stanier and their voice was only dimly heard. Some of their quite painstaking superheater test results were disbelieved. On the Pacifics, however, Stanier spotted (from low steam-chest pressures) that the total area of the steam passage through the superheater was less than the area through the regulator and steam pipes, and it was this fact which first led to the change from 16 to 32 superheater elements. This change was a marked success and Stanier at once told Collett for the " Kings " but the tip was not taken. Hawksworth did it twelve years later.

Far quicker action was taken to improve the ghastly steaming of the first 3-cylinder 4-6-0s. Stanier had fitted jumper blast-pipes, which increase the effective orifice diameter and thus reduce the blast while an engine is being worked in full gear. R. A. Riddles spotted that, far from ever requiring reduction, the blast was never adequate: accordingly the orifice diameter was reduced, and successively the blast-pipe was lowered and the chimney petticoat diameter reduced, and steaming markedly improved. Stanier acquired a fixed belief that 3-cylinder engines are more temperamental than 2- or 4-cylinder designs, as far as blast-pipe and smokebox design is concerned, though in fairness to all concerned one recalls that the " Royal Scots " steamed excellently as designed.

The smokebox regulator was also a trouble spot, though in this case not to drivers but to the Shed maintenance staff. Lubrication was difficult, access deep within the smokebox behind the chimney petticoat was poor, warping of the combined casting gave trouble, and of course there was the ageless complaint—" Why change, when dome regulators were trouble-free? " Here is a detail addition to the " Standard Examination of Engines and Tenders " issued as a circular by D. C. Urie on 5th December 1934:

Item	*Parts to be examined*	*Remarks*	*Engines*	*Period or Mileage basis*
30F	Regulator lubricators	To be examined	All engines fitted with taper boilers	5–6,000 mls.

However, serious work was going ahead to combat the teething troubles, and Stanier undoubtedly inspired confidence and led the combat to success because he was convinced his engines would turn up trumps. Besides, the red ones were not doing at all badly, and the black ones were gaining quite a remarkable popularity, which was specially significant as it contained no element of regional bias. It seemed that there really *was* quite a bit of wisdom from Wiltshire, and the 1934 score-card read something like this:—

	Feature	*Typical 1934 L.M.S. Comment*	*Ultimate Fate*
1.	Churchward Firebox	Excellent	Became standard
2.	Taper Barrel	" Is this really necessary?"	Became standard
3.	Top Feed	Good	Became standard
4.	Smokebox Regulator and elimination of dome	Inferior to L.M.S.	Discontinued
5.	Jumper Blastpipe	Often stuck, or bolted down!	Ultimately discontinued
6.	Parallel Fusible Plugs	Probable overall advantage	Became standard
7.	Low Degree Superheat	The classic error	Corrected
8.	Reduction in heating surface of small tubes	Intended to facilitate repairs	Successive batches of boilers had more heating surface
9.	Deflector plates in Smokebox	Reduce spark throwing, but affect steaming	Chucked out
10.	Coupling and connecting rod lubrication	Very good, except brasses weakened by elongated pads	Further improvements made
11.	Phosphor bronze replacing case-hardened steel valve gear bushes and die blocks	Wear increased, but occasional seizure avoided	Became standard
12.	Steel axleboxes with press-in brasses	Very big improvement on L.M.S. boxes	Became standard
13.	Little-end lubrication of connecting-rod	Admirable arrangement	Became standard
14.	Bogies and Pony Trucks with side bolsters	Good (" Churchward-de Glehn ")	Became standard
15.	" Mechanical Trickle " Sanding Gear	Unsatisfactory	Reverted to steam sanding
16.	28-inch stroke	No trouble	Became standard

When a Chief is confident his team is winning and can be relied upon, it is a good technique for him to disappear for a bit and then emerge with some longer-term development task. Stanier nipped over to Sweden to see a Ljungstrom turbine loco of non-condensing type which had been running for a year or so with some success: the result was a sister for his two Pacifics, in the shape of the Turbomotive No. 6202, whose turbine equipment was supplied by Metropolitan Vickers. As is shown in a comparative table later in this chapter, the Turbomotive justified itself on performance figures: but though Stanier persevered nobly with this experimental engine teething troubles were protracted, and were intensified when the loco was put into normal link working with twenty sets of men working it. It was ultimately withdrawn and rebuilt to a standard type Pacific about 1952, when it finally became clear that the advantages fell short of what was necessary to justify further development of an essentially unconventional machine.

Meanwhile the first two Pacifics had proved themselves, and 10 more were built in 1935. The only changes made were the increase of superheater area from 370 to 598 sq. ft., and the addition of a combustion chamber which increased the firebox heating area from 190 to 217 sq. ft., but took 1 ft. 6 ins. off the tube length. A larger tender with curved side sheets was also provided.

If jobs are divided into chapters, then a chapter of Stanier's era as C.M.E. of the L.M.S.R. ended with the year 1935, after he had collected his resources and led his team positively into the gigantic task of re-stocking the L.M.S. with larger standard locomotives. He had designed all the types required, taken them through most of their teething troubles, cured himself of one or two technical lacunae, and placed massive orders for new engines, both within the Railway and with outside contractors.

Type	*Quantities built each year*							*Total*
	1933	1934	1935	1936	1937	1938	1939	
2-6-0	15	25	—	—	—	—	—	40
4-6-2	2	—	11	—	5	10	5	33
3-cylinder 4-6-0	—	82	48	61	—	—	—	191
2-cylinder 4-6-0	—	20	205	100	100	47	—	472
2-8-0	—	—	12	42	42	2	28	126
3-cylinder 2-6-4T	—	37	—	—	—	—	—	37
2-cylinder 2-6-4T	—	—	8	116	27	34	1	186
2-6-2T	—	—	74	—	27	38	—	139
Total	17	164	358	319	201	131	34	1224

The total of over 500 new engines in 8 new types, all in service and behaving themselves satisfactorily, by the end of 1935, is pretty formidable by any standards; and at that time also most of the further 300 delivered in 1936 were on order.

. . . *and behaving themselves satisfactorily* . . . Looking back at the tail end of 1935 from the vantage point of 1963, one clearly recalls that by this time all the Stanier engines were popular. The Pacifics gave a fine power increase, and the black 4-6-0s were excellent engines by any standards. The red 4-6-0s, which were not at all bad after their blastpipe modifications, must be seen in relation to such engines as the Midland " Compound," because it was from such engines as these that they took over. Now the " Compounds " were never popular with ex-L.N.W.R. drivers, and even a marginal improvement would have pleased them: they got more and were distinctly pleased, though it was only after 1936 that one could say the Stanier "Jubilees" were as good as the "Patriots" or "Baby Scots" as these re-built "Claughtons" were usually called. Ex-Midland drivers never had the "Patriots" but they got "Jubilees" on trains which definitely stretched the "Compounds"—for instance the 9.25 Derby–London, returning 2.25 from St. Pancras. This was a three-day job in Derby's top passenger link. At their worst the red 4-6-0s were almost as good as an average "Compound" on this job, and by the end of 1935 their worst was well over, and a "Compound" was liable to lose time with the increasing loadings. After all, the Class "5X" was a much more powerful loco than the "Compound," and yet it had a firebox only 5 in. longer than the "Compound's" 9 ft.; most firemen came to agree that perhaps it was slightly easier to fire. And of course the ex-Midland drivers at Trafford Park were getting up to Peak Forest like the bats out of hell with the black ones.

As for the 2-8-0s, I well remember visiting Toton shed after they had the first few at work, and they were enthusiastically welcomed: but here again the stage was set slightly in their favour, because the "Garratts" were never liked, and the Fowler 0-8-0s never fully shook off their teething troubles.

All the tank engines were popular with their Stanier boilers, though as a matter of interest the 3-cylinder 2-6-4s for the Tilbury section were the only ones which did not closely follow the Fowler designs.

So as 1936 waxed, everyone connected with Railways came to realize that the mighty re-stocking of L.M.S. motive power, so deftly put in hand, was going to be a resounding success. Stanier was well supported by his staff at Euston: R. A. Riddles had come from Crewe to join him as Principal Assistant, and his deputy was C. E. Fairburn, who had joined the L.M.S. from English Electric as Chief Electrical Engineer. This job was later made responsible to the C.M.E., and it was characteristic of Stanier's insistence on doing the right thing that Fairburn's official title was "Deputy Chief Mechanical Engineer, and Electrical Engineer."

One of the few remaining annoyances was the Research Department. This did some excellent work on the metallurgical side, giving constant help to the works, and from time to time it came up trumps with research detail, such as tracing tyre failures to coarse machining marks so that a change to a fine cut with tipped tools gave a dramatic improvement. Sir Harold Hartley had built up the Research Organization from scratch; it had to serve all L.M.S. engineering interests. It interpreted tasks and priorities through a Research Committee, on which sat the C.M.E. and other Chief Engineers and various distinguished scientists. But just as any individual Works often dislikes advice from a central Research organization, so Stanier found the L.M.S. Research Department distant and ponderous. He had been brought up in the genuine Swindon experimental team spirit fostered by Churchward, and did not realize that with the

LEADING DIMENSIONS OF STANIER ENGINES

Class	Type	Date	Cylinders dia. × stroke in. in.	Coupled Wheel dia. ft. in.	Boiler Pressure lb./sq. in.	Total Heating Surfaces sq. ft.	Super-heater sq. ft.	Grate Area sq. ft.	Tractive Effort lb.	Weight of Engine in Working Order Tons
5F	2-6-0	1933	2 18 × 28	5 6	225	1633	244	28	26,288	69
5	4-6-0	1934	2 18½ × 28	6 0	225	1650	365	28½	25,455	72¼
5XP	4-6-0	1934	3 17 × 26	6 9	225	1641	313	31	26,610	79
7P	4-6-2	1933	4 16¼ × 28	6 6	250	2516	586	45	40,300	104½
7P	4-6-2	1937	4 16½ × 28	6 9	250	2807	822	50	40,000	105¼
8F	2-8-0	1935	2 18½ × 28	4 8½	225	1649	241	28½	32,438	70¼
3P	2-6-2T	1935	2 17½ × 26	5 3	200	1046	74	19	21,486	71¼
4P	2-6-4T	1935	2 19⅝ × 26	5 9	200	1369	240	27	24,670	87¾
4P	2-6-4T	1934	3 16 × 26	5 9	200	1172	209	25	24,600	92¼

complexities of a large organization it is imperative to formalize and define the steps:

7 production model manufacture
6 production model design
5 development of prototype
4 experimental manufacture
3 experimental design
2 applied research
1 basic research

I hope Research people will forgive me for putting the goal at the top of the ladder. Stanier failed to convince his Vice-President that the Research outfit must include design engineers for step 3 and an experimental workshop for steps 4 and 5. Design engineers in the manufacturing drawing office on step 6 would then accept a genuine prototype design from their colleages on step 3, who in turn could get their experimental hardware made without calling on the production shops where it only achieved second priority and interest compared with production work. Moreover the L.M.S. Research staff tended to think they were superior to the Design staff, because their reporting line to a Vice-President was shorter. They dodged some practical work on smokebox dimensions which Stanier wanted done, and were inclined to become theoretical. One of them was once heard to remark that the solid big-end was so satisfactory for outside motion that he couldn't imagine why it was not also used for the inside. Stanier got slightly cross with Research and was not in consequence as lively as he should have been in cross-posting young engineers between the C.M.E. and Research Departments. He was, however, genuinely interested in Apprentice training—an educational interest perhaps inherited from his father. He wrote up a comprehensive note on improvements in the Apprentice training schemes, which were already very good, particularly at Derby and Crewe, and suffered the annoyance of having this placed in a bottom drawer and forgotten by his Vice-President.

There were also some extra-mural activities at this time, notably the Wedgwood Committee, on which Stanier went to India and contributed some terse wisdom. One item of trouble on the agenda was hot boxes, and in fact a useful contribution was made by a positive rather than a fatalistic approach, as Stanier was heard to remark, in particular putting right bad lubrication practices and improving devices to exclude dust.

Stanier was elected President of the Institution of Locomotive Engineers in 1936, and gave his Presidential address on September 30th. The subject was a world-wide survey of loco types. Sir Nigel Gresley's vote of thanks is part-quoted on page 130. Of course the C.M.Es. met one another quite often, but they seem to have avoided talking about the one subject much in the public eye at this time—*speed*. For instance, at the Association of Railway Locomotive Engineers meeting on 19th June 1936 in King's Cross Hotel, the subjects discussed were forging allowances for axles; piston rings; spring links; metal for brake blocks; and tube expanders. Yet those present included Gresley (President), Maunsell, Stanier, Hawksworth, Thompson, Peppercorn, Ivatt, Bulleid, Urie. In fact speed was again on the secret list, and in particular Gresley was thinking about beating his 112 mph record of September 1935, whilst Stanier had almost completed design work on his streamlined " Coronation " class Pacifics.

The L.M.S. had decided to launch a high-speed " Coronation Scot " train between Euston and Glasgow, and also to toe the line as regards the current craze for streamlining. The Great British Public was rather bored by technical phrases such as " air smoothed," and by technical reasons why streamlining was not necessary or practicable: it simply wanted all allegedly fast things to be streamlined. " Right," said Coleman when Stanier told him to make a layout of a suitable streamlined casing: and he produced what was later seen on No. 6220, *Coronation,* in light blue with white bands. Sir Harold Hartley naturally took a strong interest in the whole project, and told Stanier to be sure to have wind-tunnel tests made at Derby to ensure the best streamlined shape. The manufacturing drawings had already been issued to Crewe Works by this time, but wind-tunnel tests went ahead on the Coleman and various other shapes. Coleman's turned out to be as good as the best of the others, so Stanier chuckled to himself and duly passed on the good news. Then doubt was expressed at Board level as to whether the streamlining was really necessary. " Why argue," thought Stanier, " rather please a fool than tease "; so Coleman drew the engine again, but without the streamlined casing. Thoughtfully he inscribed the name plate *Lady Godiva,* and the Vice-Presidents decided not to have the streamline clothing removed.

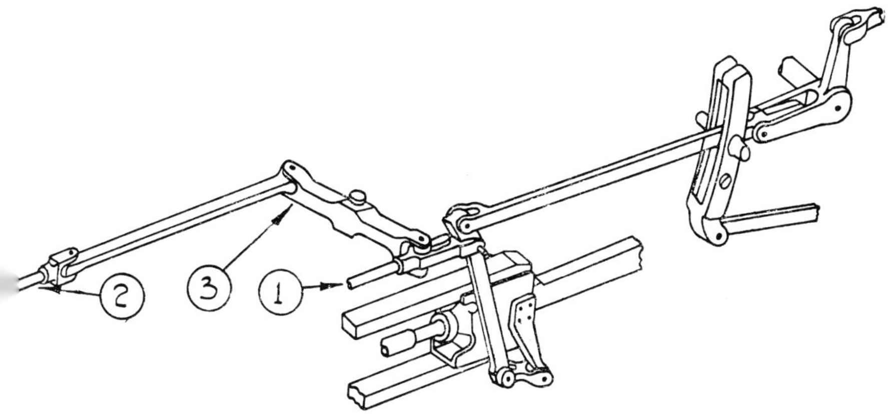

Fig. 36. The outside valve gear on the Coronation Pacifics drives the outside valve spindle 1 directly and the inside spindle 2 through the rocking lever 3. Valve spindle extensions are avoided.

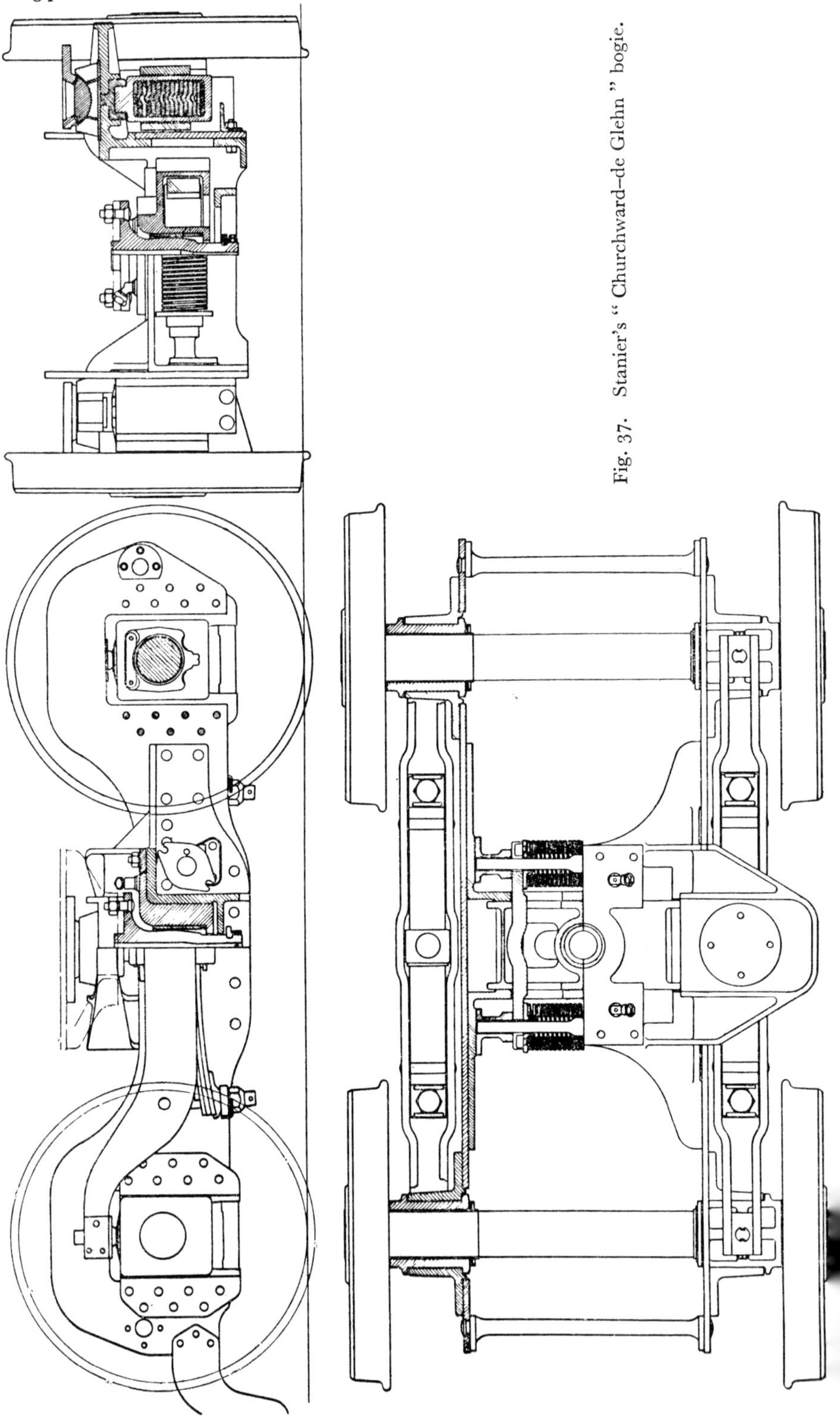

Fig. 37. Stanier's "Churchward-de Glehn" bogie.

Coleman had also produced a satisfactory arrangement of rocking levers to drive the inside valves from the outside motion, so the " Coronation " Pacifics had only two sets of valve gear. The wheels were increased to 6 ft. 9 in. dia., and the cylinders to 16½ in. dia. The boiler was improved, with larger diameter at the firebox end, superheater area 856 sq. ft., and firebox and total heating surfaces considerably increased. The tender carried 10 tons of coal with a steam-operated coal-pusher.

The engine duly reached 113 mph in a trial on 29th June 1937. F. A. Lemon, sitting opposite Stanier, put his legs on the seat as a precaution against what he thought was an inevitable derailment. When Stanier stepped on the platform at Crewe after their breathless arrival, he found among the waiting officials C. R. Byrom, who rather testily said " How foolish to come in so fast." " How foolish to turn a high-speed test train into a reverse curve merely to bring it alongside a platform," retorted Stanier briskly—and thinking, but not saying, that they would probably have been derailed but for the de Glehn bogie. The speeded-up service was inaugurated on July 5th.

This was only one of many speeded-up services in 1937, and both the red and the black 4-6-0s were considerably and successfully involved. Mainly the red ones, of course; but we had the black ones on the Derby–Manchester and I remember in particular No. 5050 being continually reported by a succession of drivers as " riding rough." The mechanical inspectors on the Shed continually reported her O.K. So we gave her an extra special look-over, found everything O.K., and I went on the next trip. In fact, by that unusual workout of tolerances which often makes one machine in a batch differ from the rest, 5050 *was* rougher than normal, but nothing to write home about, nor even to report. Besides, the Derby–Manchester is a boisterous route, with plenty of reverse curves, many bounded by precipices. 5050 had a sand-gun, one of the few gadgets tried by Stanier: it certainly provided a good showing of soot when operated with full regulator and about 40 per cent cut-off whilst approaching the summit. The return stretch from Ambergate to Derby is fairly straight and with slight falling gradients: with full regulator (and a little persuasion) we notched up from the normal minimum of 15 per cent to 10 per cent, then to 5 per cent, and then after another mile or so to just on mid gear. Only after 5 per cent could one really describe the knocking as objectionable. I have travelled on several of these engines with full regulator and 10 per cent cut-off for miles without experiencing knocking: I think it is the exceptionally felicitous arrangement of motion and valves that makes them such admirable engines.

In 1938 a second five streamlined Pacifics were built and also a further five to the improved design but not streamlined: one of these, No. 6234, *Duchess of Abercorn*, was fitted with double blastpipe and double chimney. This was highly successful and became the standard and was later incorporated in the re-built " Royal Scots." Stanier took a particular interest in smokebox detail: he had seen from the Running Shed angle

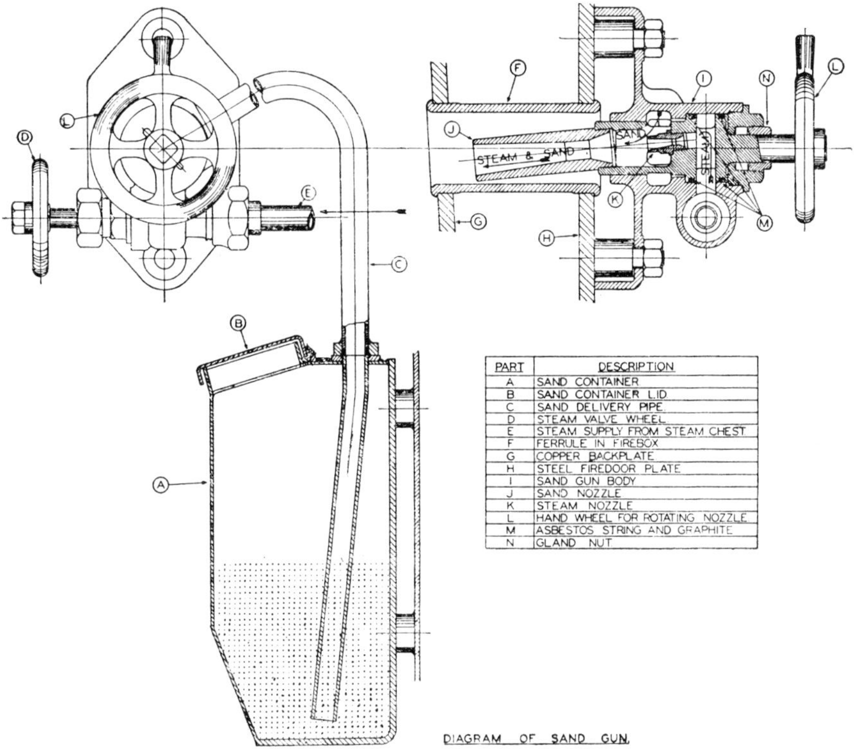

PART	DESCRIPTION
A	SAND CONTAINER
B	SAND CONTAINER LID
C	SAND DELIVERY PIPE
D	STEAM VALVE WHEEL
E	STEAM SUPPLY FROM STEAM CHEST
F	FERRULE IN FIREBOX
G	COPPER BACKPLATE
H	STEEL FIREDOOR PLATE
I	SAND GUN BODY
J	SAND NOZZLE
K	STEAM NOZZLE
L	HAND WHEEL FOR ROTATING NOZZLE
M	ASBESTOS STRING AND GRAPHITE
N	GLAND NUT

DIAGRAM OF SAND GUN

the ill-effects of excessive blast when engines have to work exceptionally hard and slowly, and like all engineers he disliked the pulsating, excessive smokebox vacuum and the attendant excessive back-pressure in the cylinders. So he did not like the suggestions for smaller blast-pipe orifices on the "Jubilee" 4-6-0s and the "Royal Scots," even though the smaller orifice fitted by Riddles had been the major step in making the "Jubilee" steam well, back in 1934. He took his time looking around the subject, and compared notes with Bulleid about the Lemaitre multiple-jets on the S.R. Pacifics. Moreover it took time to obtain sanction for re-builds and for sizeable modifications—there was the Stamp economy regime in operation, and rumours of Wars were about. Hence the double blastpipe and chimney did not appear on the re-built "Scots" and on two "Jubilee" class engines till 1942. These re-built "Jubilees" and "Scots" were classified "6P" and both had the same boiler; it steamed excellently and finally vindicated the Stanier application of Churchward boiler principles permitting the "Scots" to perform better than with their original parallel boilers which had 220 sq. ft. more heating surface.

Brisk progress was made with Automatic Train Control. Every one of the 30 years since he had been involved in the first A.T.C. experiments had conformed his belief in the principle; and when the L.M.S. decided they needed A.T.C. and would the C.M.E. and the Signals Engineer please get together, Stanier and Bounds worked hard in collaboration with Hudd and success was reached in a set-up on the Southend line. It was not practicable to use the G.W.R. system because hard frosts for example at Shap would prevent adequate electrical contact on the ramps: accordingly the Hudd system with a magnetic proximity detector was developed. Fog men were dispensed with by late 1938.

Stanier was President of the A.R.L.E. from 1938 till the War suspended its meetings, and he was again President of the Institution of Locomotive Engineers 1938–9. His second Presidential Address, on 22nd January 1939, was far more down-to-earth than the first one: he showed a film on the Crewe loco repair system as organized by Beames, and he took as his text the four main criteria of a good loco—Safety, Reliability, Availability, and Efficiency. I think in the second and third of these criteria one detects the presence of H. G. Ivatt, who had joined him at Euston as Principal Assistant late in 1937.

Another preoccupation in 1938 was a second trip to India, this time on Col. Sir Alan Mount's " Pacific " Committee. Stanier found himself short of time for his own work, particularly on the carriage side where he was working with J. Purves of Derby on a new standard 60 ft. passenger coach to weigh less than 30 tons. A paper on this subject was in fact arranged to be given at an A.S.M.E. Symposium in New York in September 1939. Stanier did not want to go, on account of the international situation; but Lord Stamp said that the war clouds would " blow over in a few weeks." In the event Stanier and his wife made an abortive return trip to New York—there and back on the same ship, the return journey being uncomfortably hazardous.

And so once again Stanier saw a railway bent to the War effort. He lost Ivatt, who took over a full-time tank design job for the War Office. Demands on his time further increased, and he could seldom settle down to his favourite authors, Kipling and Nevil Shute, nor relax in his workshop, where though no great craftsman he always enjoyed doing the odd domestic jobs. He became President of the Institution of Mechanical Engineers in April 1941, and duly settled down with E. S. Cox to write his Presidential address, given on 24th October 1941. This was entitled " The Position of the Locomotive in Mechanical Engineering." It was indeed a summary of the Stanier results, and included a section on Operating Efficiency. Table 3, giving some closely-compared Dynamometer Car test results, is reproduced below: Stanier called particular attention to the effects of mileage, cols. B and C; the *Coronation* with light and heavy loads, cols. F and H; and low versus high superheat, cols. J and K. I would nostalgically add that the " Claughton " comes off better if you compare cols. A and J.

TABLE 3. DYNAMOMETER CAR TEST RESULTS WITH VARIOUS L.M. & S. RAILWAY LOCOMOTIVES

Route, miles	Euston–Carlisle and return; 300, each way			Euston–Glasgow 402			Euston–Glasgow and return; 402, each way	Crewe–Glasgow and return; 244, each way	St. Pancras–Leeds and return; 196 each way	
Col.	A	B	C	D	E	F	G	H	J	K
Engine No.	5917	6158	6158	6210	6202	6225	6220	6234	5067	5079
Class	4-cylinder 4-6-0 *Claughton;* principal express type 1913–27	3-cylinder 4-6-0 *Royal Scot;* principal express type 1927–33		4-cylinder 4-6-2 *Princess Royal;* introduced 1933	4-6-2 "Turbo-motive"; built 1935	4-cylinder 4-6-2 *Coronation*			2-cylinder 4-6-0 mixed traffic	
		Low mileage	High mileage			Light load	Normal *Coronation Scot* load and timing	Maximum load	14-element superheater; approx. steam temp. 500 deg. F.	21-element superheater; approx. steam temp. 580 deg. F.
Miles since last piston and valve examination ..	12,506	6,480	22,770	1,718	—	3,502	220	20,733	20,600	4,622
Miles since last heavy repair	12,506	6,480	92,270	98,977	102,915	3,502	29,788	50,107	20,600	4,622
Average weight of train, tons	347	440	440	522	485	232	331	604	292	292
Average running speed, mph	51·2	52·1	52·1	52·0	55·0	59·2	60·4	55·2	51·9	50·9
Coal consumption,										
lb. per mile	46·6	37·1	39·3	45·0	41·6	28·2	39·2	68·7	49·5	43·7
lb. per ton-mile (including engine)	0·101	0·066	0·069	0·068	0·067	0·073	0·080	0·091	0·098	0·085
lb. per drawbar h.p.-hr.	5·03	3·25	3·50	2·98	2·78	3·32	3·03	3·12	3·97	3·23
lb. per sq. ft. grate per hr.	79·2	62·4	65·1	62·2	50·7	33·4	47·3	75·7	74·1	63·6
Water consumption,										
gal. per mile	32·1	30·3	33·1	37·3	37·1	26·7	32·3	52·1	38·2	32·8
lb. per drawbar h.p.-hr.	34·5	26·5	29·5	24·7	24·8	31·6	25·0	24·1	30·6	24·3
Evaporation, lb. water per lb. coal	6·9	8·15	8·41	8·30	8·93	9·51	8·24	7·74	7·72	7·49

Stanier was seconded full time to the Ministry of Production as Scientific Adviser in October 1942 and resigned from the L.M.S. in 1944. And so from late 1942 he largely faded from the Railway scene, though he was called upon for advice more than is generally realized. He had more than "just a word" in the succession when Fairburn died late in 1945; and he was called upon for a report on the conjugate valve gear soon after Sir Nigel Gresley's death in April 1941. He had the linkage set out, estimated likely wear at relevant points, and showed the consequent extent of lost motion, thus voting against this arrangement and supporting E. Thompson's case for spending money on the third set of valve gear.

Stanier studiously followed the principle of getting to know the best current techniques and applying them wholeheartedly, with pauses for modification to incorporate later improvements. He never claimed to invent, and no patent rests against his name. After 1937, criticisms against the 1500 engines he built whilst with the L.M.S. were negligible: for he was ready to drop even a cherished conviction when evidence proved him wrong. The Award of his Knighthood came on New Year's Day, 1943.

Lots more Stanier engines were built after his resignation in 1944 at age 68, and since the 2-8-0s had been adopted as the standard W.D. type they were built at Doncaster and Darlington; Eastleigh, Ashford, and Brighton; and Swindon. But as the War approached its end Sir William, a brisk 70, was embarking on an industrial career, and had but little time to keep up Railway interests. If he felt any pangs of regret about his L.M.S. achievements it was because Collett failed to show a friendly interest in them. But he had numerous pleasant Railway recollections, when he wished to dream . . . his successful efforts with Ivatt to extend locomotive availability and mileages between repairs: his pleasure at the Crewe loco repair layout, engineered by Beames and Riddles: and above all a decidedly paternal affection for the "Black Staniers" "You see them all over the place, and the drivers like them because they're such a deuce of a good engine!"

Newburn, the C.M.E.'s house at Swindon built for Joseph Armstrong by the G.W.R. in 1868 was so named by him after Newburn-on-Tyne where his boyhood days had been spent. Churchward was its last occupier, and when it was eventually demolished Sir William christened his current and subsequent house Newburn. This is his own private salute to the G.W.R. There he learned locomotive design, and elsewhere he achieved fame by applying it.

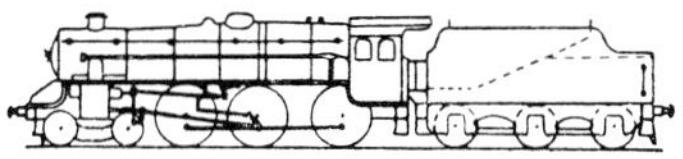

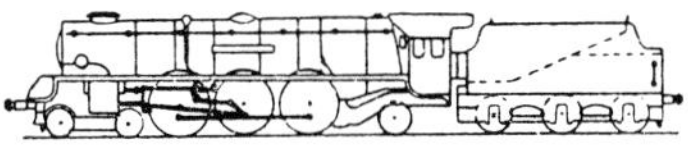

CHAPTER 6

The last C.M.E.—H. G. Ivatt; North Staffordshire to British Railways

" Come on chaps, the thirds are all full—we'll have to go first "—and three youths dashed on to the just moving train past a suspicious station-master who at once telegraphed the next station. Duly challenged, the three innocents presented their first class tickets. Thus H. G. Ivatt and his friends, returning home from Uppingham for their holidays, during which they would shatter the peace of the H. A. Ivatt household in Regent Square, Doncaster.

Asked later if he had ever passed a formal examination, George Ivatt replied " I never even sat one."

Summer holidays in the 1900–4 period were quite colourful and included many bicycle outings. When H. A. Ivatt was at Crewe North Shed he became friendly with two Brown brothers—one a driver and one an inspector—whose third brother later started up a bicycle business at Doncaster: therefore all Ivatt bicycle demands were met by him as of right. The Ivatt daughters and their girl friends all had bicycles, even though some of them were such incompetent riders that they had to be placed on the bicycle and someone had to be ready at the other end to catch them because they could not get off without help. Sometimes the boys went out on their own, and it is said that the price of the " Eat As Much As You Like " teas at Ye Olde Bell, Barnby Moor, was increased from 6d. to 1s. after a particularly voracious visit by George and two of his friends. H. A. Ivatt's youngest brother, Col. George Ivatt, thought nothing of cycling over from Lincoln for the week-end.

Fortunately, George Ivatt had inherited from his father both an exceptionally pleasant disposition and a quite remarkable flair for engineering in general and for craft work in particular. He always intended to go in for railway engineering and, naturally, his father started him as an apprentice at Crewe. By some mysterious agency, his starting date is entered in the Visitors Book at Crewe—3.10.1904, aged 18 years and 5 months.

During the first week of young Ivatt's apprenticeship, his father combined the pleasure of revisiting Crewe with the duty of seeing his son safely settled in. On this visit, H. A. Ivatt stayed with the Whales, and George was asked up to the house to dinner on the last evening. Webb's retirement and Whale's succession were still talking points, notably with the immediate success of the " Precursors," and George Ivatt listened with interest as his father and Whale talked about the last days of Webb. Whale said that what precipitated the expected end was when Webb was shown a new drawing, to which he took an immediate dislike. He scribbled over it with a pencil held in his fist, tore it up, flung the pieces on to the floor and stamped on them. Too many of the staff witnessed this unfortunate scene. Whale, with the support of Trevithick and Bowen Cooke, went to Euston and reported to the Board that things could go on no longer in this way. Accordingly, Webb's retirement, already announced, was fixed definitely; and Whale took over on 1st May 1903. *Precursor* appeared in March 1904, and when George arrived Crewe was turning out an order for 100 " Precursors " at the rate of five per month. Mrs. Whale not only arranged his digs at Crewe—with Mrs. Parry at 17, Heathfield Avenue—but picked such good ones that he stayed there until his marriage 11 years later. In addition to their admirable and patient landlady, these digs had the geographical advantage of being near the centre of gravity of Crewe Works: the 6 a.m. start and short breakfast break made this situation invaluable because the Works were so large that many apprentices changed their digs when posted from one end to the other.

On average, George liked his apprenticeship, and even found time to work up his hobby of clock repairing, which gradually brought additional fame to 17, Heathfield Avenue. He did not much like his time spent tapping 2000 as-forged hexagon nuts per day on a 2-spindle machine in the nut and bolt shop, but on the other hand he particularly enjoyed his time in the pattern shop, although here he became involved in the only minor fracas which ruffled his apprenticeship. A pattern was required for a new standard chair for a diamond crossing to accommodate the latest standard rail section. George decided he could do this himself, even though it was a particularly tricky job requiring double shrinkage allowances because it was the original for a cast iron pattern. He duly did the work to everyone's satisfaction, and the pattern was accepted as O.K. However, on account of the importance of the new standard rail set-up, the cost office were collecting data on all related work, and George was asked how long he had taken to make this pattern. He had, in fact, done it in nine days, but after consulting his mates he put down the accepted standard time for a job of that size, namely two weeks. The cost office people recorded the labour as " apprentice." Someone spotted that an apprentice had taken the same amount of time to do a good class job as was normally booked by a skilled pattern maker. George " got in bad " with the foreman and others on account of the usual type of rumour that the information had reached the Works Manager by the wrong channels. Fortunately, however, George's personality was proof against these minor buffetings and soon after, in 1907, he started his spell in the Drawing Office.

"All machine shops are being converted to electric drives and it is a disadvantage to be ignorant of them," wrote H. A. Ivatt about this time. He probably also foresaw a great future for electric traction on the railways. So George was fixed up for one year as an apprentice to B.T.H.

Rugby, to work on the assembly and test sections. He found this experience interesting and valuable but " the digs were nowhere near as good as Mrs. Parry's."

He returned to take up an appointment as Assistant Foreman at Crewe North Shed on 21st January 1909. This was, and is, the passenger shed for Crewe, and George was immediately impressed by the routine for a quick wash out on a *Precursor* during a shortage of engines. When such an engine, due—or overdue—for wash out, arrived on the shed, they would immediately open everything to blow off steam and, as soon as possible, take out one bottom plug and one of the plugs over the boiler backplate. Through this a hose would be inserted and cold water run through for one hour. The boiler would then be cold enough for wash out, which would take a further hour. As the washing out was completed and the bottom plugs put back, 12 scoops of red hot coals were taken from the sand drying furnace in a specially made scoop which fitted the firehole door. Steam was raised in almost exactly three hours. With this drill, it was common to send the engine back off the shed in a shade under six hours. George recalled this procedure years later when W. A. Stanier issued his special instructions about minimum cooling down and washing out times for the L.M.S. Pacifics.

Typically, it happened while George was Assistant Foreman at Crewe North Shed that three " foreign " engines came in for exchange trials in July 1909. When George Whale retired, C. J. Bowen Cooke took over as C.M.E., in March 1909, and since it was immediately obvious that work would have to be put in hand to improve the " Precursors " and " Experiments " or to build larger types, he arranged to borrow on an interchange basis *Cardean* from the Caledonian, a superheated 4-4-2 tank from the London, Brighton and South Coast, and an Ivatt Atlantic from the G.N.R. Naturally, the last of these was the most interesting to George Ivatt and, in fact, the Ivatt Atlantic put up a better performance than the " Precursor." On the last day of the interchange Bowen Cooke arranged for young Ivatt to ride on the footplate of his father's engine, and a dynamometer car was added to the train, the 10 o'clock from Euston. So when the G.N.R. Atlantic No. 1449 backed on to the train they found a load of 400 tons behind the tender. Sticking on Camden Bank was a traditional fear on the London and North Western ever since the old winding gear to Camden had been discontinued; and as the G.N.R. driver and his fireman, together with George Ivatt and the L.N.W.R. pilotman stood on the footplate waiting for the right away, the pilotman remarked " If you stick on Camden Bank you won't be the first." In fact, 1449 steamed nobly up the bank, and though she lost a minute or two to Tring and passed Nuneaton about two minutes late, they arrived on time at Crewe.

One year later Ivatt was able to take further interest from the sidelines when the 4-cylinder 4-6-0 Great Western " Star " Class loco was running on L.N.W.R. metals and performing considerably better than the

" Experiment " Class sent in exchange. In the light of this exchange and those of 1909, a memorandum was written by Bowen Cooke and Sir Robert Turnbull, the Superintendent of the line, which laid down design features for a large 4-cylinder 4-6-0 express loco to be designed for the L.N.W.R. Ivatt searched Crewe in vain for this report when he was C.M.E., but recalls that the only detail insisted upon from G.N.R. practice was a large smokebox since it was thought (quite wrongly) that this feature reduced the build up of smokebox char. Ivatt held that the worst feature of the early " Claughtons " was shortage of steam due to the false economy of the boiler being designed down to use the largest existing flange blocks. Moreover, Bowen Cooke got little help from the Crewe Drawing Office under J. N. Jackson, as they positively resisted anything outside traditional Crewe designs.

At Crewe North also George found out some of those things which have to be done in a shed on account of poor communications with the Works. There had been a fairly recent change from copper to steel boiler tubes and, of course, the copper tubes had internal ferrules at the firebox end. Though not necessary with steel tubes, these ferrules were still being fitted by the Works, and they gave the disadvantage of a restriction, so they were always immediately knocked out when an engine first came to the shed from the Works. Some of the L.N.W.R. engines were fitted with so-called balanced slide valves, incorporating a rectangular frame held by springs against a rubbing plate in the top of the steam chest. The back of the valve was normally drilled with a $\frac{3}{8}$ in. hole to relieve any pressure that might build up inside the frame, although of course if functioning correctly there could be a hole of unlimited size through the back of the valve as on the Great Northern Atlantics which actually exhausted through them. Some draughtsman increased this hole to $\frac{3}{4}$ in. dia., and at once a blow of steam showed at the chimney indicating a leak at the rubbing plate. The unfortunate draughtsman was rebuked and the hole diameter changed back to $\frac{3}{8}$ in., the whole principle of the job never coming into question.

Then there were the tender axlebox brasses—those for the middle wheels invariably ran hot and it became standard practice at Crewe North to remove them and chip off about a quarter of an inch each side to give the centre wheels plenty of lateral play. Ivatt took this particular problem back with him into the Works a few months later when, in the autumn of 1909, he was appointed Assistant to the Works Manager, Trevithick, but he quite failed to put the point over—it was felt that more lateral play would be desirable in all the wheels and the job got generally bogged down.

Ivatt did a lot of odd jobs for Trevithick but, in particular, he did some experimental work on a Spark Arrester because at that time there was one of the periodical alarms about engines throwing out excessive sparks. This was hardly surprising with the " Precursor " class which was notorious, when hard driven, for putting a sizeable proportion of the fire straight through to the chimney. George set about his experimental

Spark Arrester with considerable drive. He fitted a 6 in. dia. glass window in a porthole at the side of an " Experiment " smokebox and had a wooden front end shelter (as for taking indicator diagrams) erected on this engine, and then followed it on various runs. Inside the smokebox he had various arrangements of plates fitted to baffle the direct exit of sparks through the chimney. Sufficient light came down the chimney to permit a good view of the blast pipe, and he noted with some surprise the comparatively small cone of exhaust which appeared to emerge from the centre of the blast pipe and only occupied the middle part of the chimney petticoat. Another phenomenon he particularly noticed was that at normal cruising speeds around 50 mph he could stand looking through his porthole with his head a couple of feet above the wooden shelter and the air was still enough for him to light his pipe; this very much impressed on him that the air striking the rather flat front end of an L.N.W.R. smokebox swept away almost at right angles, leaving a dead zone immediately behind. It also convinced him that a Capuchon on a chimney is mere ornament.

On account of a succession of moves, the job of Assistant Outdoor Machinery Superintendent at Crewe became vacant and, possibly with some slight advantage from his name, Ivatt was promoted to this job on 1st May 1910, his boss being G. C. Bickersteth (" Old Bick ").

The gimmicks worked by these (and modern) bosses conceal considerable wisdom. Bickersteth's gimmick was to ask his assistants to explain the reasons for their choice of technical and layout details. " See me," he wrote on mail as he distributed it: duly, what became known as the " see mes " were brought back to him by his assistants with suggested schemes which he then asked them to explain. Ivatt was once faced with a poser when a new water column was required and there were two equally good positions for it. So he drew the new tank in one of these positions and Bick. asked, " Why have you put it there? " " It could equally well have been in either position," replied Ivatt. " Then why did you choose *that* position? " Bick. demanded, and in the ensuing impasse muttered that he wished people knew why they did things. Only retrospectively does one value the mental discipline of accounting for all conscious decisions.

It is worth recalling that the L.N.W.R. at this period, 1910, was decidedly go-ahead and had a fine reputation. It was already using films in its publicity methods to project the L.N.W.R. " image," and it offered such modern features as a shorthand-typist service on the London–Birmingham two-hour expresses.

Partly because he had the time and partly just because he so much liked engines and riding on them, Ivatt frequently went on footplate trips. Harry Mason, a Crewe North top link driver, was a close friend of his, and Ivatt's procedure was to accompany Mason and his fireman on one of their normal turns, *viz.* the 6.18 p.m. Crewe to London, returning with the 11.50 p.m. Euston to Crewe. He got back to his digs between 3 and 3.30 a.m., and Mrs. Parry, taking this routine in her stride, always got him back to work on time the following morning. Ivatt thoroughly enjoyed this trip, which he did quite often, driving the engine from Crewe as far as Willesden whilst Harry Mason kept a fatherly eye on proceedings from the other side of the cab where, incidentally, he could reach both the regulator and the brake because the steam and vacuum brakes were inter-connected and could be operated from either side. The engine in use was normally a " George V," but occasionally a " Precursor." Both these engines were remarkable in that they could blow off steam with both injectors on. Ivatt found out by sheer experience on these runs that individual engines " liked " particular settings of the cut-off. They all had wheel-operated reversing gears, with 4½ turns from full gear to mid-gear, and the wheel had six spokes with two notches per spoke. In the stock parlance of the drivers, the gear setting was described as, for example, " three turns, one spoke and one notch." The percentage cut-off was not marked. Ivatt found that most " Precursors " and " George Vs " preferred 3½ to 3¾ turns; and that it was far better to close the regulator slightly at the preferred setting than to notch up any further—in spite of the official instruction always to drive with the regulator fully open.

All the L.N.W.R. top link drivers of the period were dedicated to arriving *on time*, and it was the fashion to run with five minutes in hand where possible; they liked to acquire this time up their sleeve in the early part of the journey—and they were rather less liable to signal checks than is current experience. A much discussed performance was the time taken to pass Rugeley from a standing start at Stafford: the 9½ mile stretch is mainly level and could be covered in 10 minutes with a good engine and a train within the permitted loading. Ivatt determined to have a go, so one evening when they set off from Stafford he left the engine in full forward gear until 25 mph was attained. He then only eased the gear back in stages so he still had another spoke or two to go when they were travelling at 60 mph. The lineside noise must have been quite invigorating. They passed Rugeley comfortably within the 10 minutes. Asked to comment, Harry Mason merely remarked " You made a good start." Then, as now, drivers were curiously loath to attain a respectable speed before notching up.

Miss Dorothy Harrison had known the Ivatt sisters for years and was a particular crony of Dorothy Ivatt, so much so that the Ivatts rather ruthlessly changed her name to Sukey. She and George Ivatt were married in London on 23rd January 1913, and George's main regret was leaving his Heathfield Avenue digs and the faithful Mrs. Parry. His secondary regret was missing his footplate trips with Harry Mason. Little more than a year later came rumours of wars, and these were reflected in the unusually meagre attendance at the Crewe Dinner on 11th June 1914, when George and his friend, John Shearman, were among those present, and H. A. Ivatt took the chair. Then came the day in September when Ivatt and Shearman went to volunteer for the Public Schools Battalion. They lined up in the queue of enthusiasts and were indignant when they were sent away, only three short from being signed on, because the recruiting sergeant had run out of attestation papers. They both later enrolled in the Mechanical Transport Division of the Army Service Corps, in February 1915; and on the whole fortune smiled on George Ivatt during the war. He took over to France, and remained in charge of, a mobile Workshop, and later joined the Inspection Branch of Mechanical Transport with the rank of Captain. Moreover, his wife, who spoke fluent French, worked in a hospital at Chaumont, for which, incidentally, she received the usual medals. He took his leaves with her in Paris.

The railways kept in fairly close touch with members of their staff on active service during the war, and in the autumn of 1918 Capt. Ivatt received a message from C. J. Bowen Cooke suggesting he applied for the post of Deputy Locomotive and Carriage and Wagon Superintendent to J. A. Hookham of the North Staffordshire Railway. Just at this time, Ivatt was transferred to Col. Davidson's G.H.Q. staff with the rank of Major, which had the incidental effect of incorporating his allowances into his pay leading to a better gratuity. He obtained special leave and called on Hookham at Stoke where they had a good chat. George wanted to see round the Works but Hookham kept putting him off. In fact, George's main interest was to see where the Works could be in such a closely built locality as Stoke, but of course his mind was running on the vastly greater area of Crewe Works. In due course he received a letter stating that he had been appointed to the job at a salary of £350. This was a considerable disappointment and so, always being a keen believer in facing and stating the facts, he wrote back and said so. He next received a brisk letter from Bowen Cooke which opened "Dear Ivatt, what have you done?", at which George decided a personal discussion was again necessary, and he obtained further special leave, turned up at Euston Station, found Bowen Cooke occupied with the Board, and sent in a note "When could I see you?—Ivatt." This was passed back with a laconic "2 o'clock" scribbled on it; at which time Bowen Cooke pointed out that Hookham had already obtained sanction from his Board for the appointment at the salary offered and was rather tetchy at the Ivatt reaction. "But," added Bowen Cooke, "If Hookham won't have you, you can come back to Crewe." But Hookham did have him, and within six months obtained for him two salary increases, both back-dated to his date of joining—8th September, 1919.

Aged 33¼, armed with good early training and with subsequent experience enhanced by his war service, Ivatt settled in excellently at Stoke.

From the very outset he enjoyed his work on the North Staffordshire Railway; he got on extremely well with the Potteries people, and he liked being with a small company where details of procedures in other departments were readily explained on demand. He also enjoyed exceptional opportunities of deputizing for Hookham whose natural will to bring on his new young deputy was undoubtedly helped by the facts that the North Staffordshire Railway was likely to lose its identity in two or three years and that he himself was due to retire within six.

Hookham was a very good C.M.E. on the Works side and was ahead of his time in such operations as machining piston rods and packings to a range of definite standard sizes to avoid the costly process of mating individual components. He was also a leader in using cast iron gland packing rings, and he supplied Gresley with information leading to their use on the G.N.R. and, later, L.N.E.R.

At the Railway amalgamation on 1st January 1923 Hughes of the Lancashire and Yorkshire was appointed C.M.E. of the London, Midland and Scottish Railway. Within a month he appointed a committee consisting of all the pre-grouping L.M.S. Chief Mechanical Engineers in order to discuss the design of a proposed new mixed traffic engine and to incorporate, as Hughes frequently urged, all the best points of previous design work in the constituent design offices. These meetings were attended by Fowler from Derby, Beames from Crewe, Urie from Scotland, and H. G. Ivatt deputizing for Hookham from Stoke. Billington, the Chief Draughtsman from Horwich, also attended to collate the information and Hughes took the chair. Of course the committee was doomed to failure from the start, simply because from such assemblies of opinion one could never hope to obtain an integrated design. How indeed does one combine the advantages of the wide firebox and the narrow firebox? Ivatt recollects that the committee turned into a Tower of Babel, and on leaving one meeting after a particularly large display of irreconcilable design suggestions, he said to the Chief Draughtsman " What do you propose to do now? " Billington replied, " I am going back to Horwich to design the engine." This in fact he did with considerable success, and the resulting " Land Crab " achieved deserved popularity at both Derby and Crewe in spite of its predominantly Horwich origins.

June 1926 found Stoke Works temporarily closed down by the General Strike and Ivatt, with a local bricklayer as fireman, driving an ex North Staffordshire 0-6-0 side tank engine on emergency services between Stoke and Crewe. One of the main trials of this type of driving was at Level Crossings where the volunteer train crew had to get off the footplate, open the gates for the railway, drive through, and then walk back the train length to re-open the gates for the road, the whole manoeuvre commonly being accompanied by uncomplimentary remarks from pickets. However, the pickets in the Potteries were quite amiably disposed to the occasional Staff driver, although they were likely to take a dim view of such drivers being assisted by craftsmen and, accordingly, Ivatt chatted with the pickets whilst his bricklayer fireman kept out of sight.

Handling engines under any conditions, strike or otherwise, is extremely valuable for all design staff, and it was one of the tragedies of the railway amalgamation that this type of management detail rather became forgotten in the remote headquarters links between design and operating departments. For example, one of Ivatt's North Staffordshire engines had a Giffard injector which was unbelievably temperamental and had to be copiously cooled with buckets of water. Operating it was quite beyond the capability of his fireman, even though he was an admirable bricklayer.

Sir Henry Fowler took over as C.M.E. of the L.M.S. when Hughes retired in 1926, and about the middle of 1927, with the closing down of Stoke Works complete, Ivatt was appointed Special Assistant to Fowler at Derby. A major reason for this attachment was to enable a joint enquiry to be made from the C.M.E. and the Motive Power sides on the designation of locomotive repairs, and so much importance was attached to this liaison that in fact Anderson, the Motive Power Superintendent, interviewed Ivatt to approve his suitability.

At that time all locomotive repairs were designated " heavy " or " light " according to a schedule for railway accounting drawn up to Government requirements. This had the aim of protecting shareholders, but the accountancy bridle quite easily turns into a strait jacket. The designation was causing various anomalies and, for example, the Motive Power people had no idea how much life they could still expect from an engine returned to them after a " light " repair. Ivatt and Foster, his opposite number on Anderson's staff, therefore introduced " general " and " service " repairs. General repairs were a complete overhaul, after which the engine would have the same performance (and life to next repair) as a new engine. Service repairs were defined as attention to wheels, boxes, and such other details as would allow the engine to give at least six months further service. Allied with this, Ivatt started work which he was to return to and improve from time to time during his career, namely rationalization of general repairs. It was the fashion at that time for most worn components and fittings to be renewed at a general repair, but Ivatt introduced examiners, and the concept that these examiners, who had great experience and competence, should call for the re-use of all fittings and components which could be expected to perform satisfactorily for a further 80,000 miles, i.e. till the *next* general repair.

This liaison work by Ivatt and Foster also attempted to rationalize the shop system throughout the L.M.S. Railway. At Derby, it was the practice for the Motive Power Department to propose engines for general repair, after which the C.M.E.'s examiner inspected their boilers and, depending on the expected boiler life, either accepted the engine or put it back for proposal again in as many months as the boiler had life. This system resulted both in general repairs being allocated to the most deserving engines and in the shops having a few months' warning of coming general repairs, so that availability of components and balancing of workload on the shops could be arranged. In contrast, the practice at Crewe, which I think has a decidedly Webb flavour about it, was simply to demand a certain quantity of engines for repair at a certain date in order that the repair shop should not be short of work. In 1927, paperwork sent to Crewe, based on the Derby system, was often filled in and returned quite aimiably but no notice whatever was taken by the shops who continued as before.

In parallel with this work, Ivatt proceeded with a comprehensive list of all L.M.S. locos, detailing power classification, quantity of the particular type, general availability, etc.; and upon this information, after discussions with the Motive Power Department, fairly long-term decisions were taken as to the programme of scrapping and replacing the least satisfactory engine types.

In September 1927, there happened one of those interesting coincidences when Shawcross, the new boss at Horwich, was on leave and his Works Manager was away ill, and Ivatt was lent for one month to take charge at Horwich. In this short period he undoubtedly benefited from his North Staffordshire experience, where familiarity with the other small departments removed any fear of paperwork and accounting methods and, incidentally, gave him a good idea of such ratios as engines under repair to total stock. He found 6 per cent of all the loco stock awaiting material from the shops, and the main reason for this emerged as a swamping of the Stores Department with paperwork. For example, if the Stores placed an order for 12 castings and one turned out to be scrapped, the order was kept open in the vain hope that the Works would make one off by itself as replacement. There were hundreds of such orders, and Ivatt cancelled the lot, pointing out how difficult it is to make one replacement and how easy it is simply to add one to the next batch ordered. Several people were fairly pleased by the results of this and other simple exercises in commonsense by Ivatt: shortly after, he went to Sir Henry Fowler and pointed out that he had been " with " him six months and would like to have his job properly defined. It seems than that Fowler asked R. W. Reid, the Engineering Vice-President, whether he should take Ivatt as a Principal Assistant; but the decision was to give this job to Symes, and Ivatt instead replaced Symes as Works Superintendent, Derby, in 1928, R. A. Riddles being appointed at the same time as his Assistant.

Fowler paid Ivatt less than Symes had been getting on the grounds that Symes was available at Derby for advice in case of difficulty. When, about two years later, Symes was promoted away from the district, Ivatt still got the reduced salary. The facts that even after protest from Ivatt, Riddles' salary remained low and, incidentally, that the Chief Draughtsman was also receiving a meagre salary, throw some light on the Fowler mentality. He undoubtedly thought such economies were in the best interests of the L.M.S., and indeed there was an economy drive on a level that would hardly be realized to-day; but of course one can take restrictions in salary and responsibility to a point where fear and uncertainty reduce competence and lead to an industry going downhill, as staff who can earn more go elsewhere to do so.

The new Works Superintendent at Derby may not have been particularly brilliant academically, but he had two outstanding attributes: he was a first class practical engineer, and he had the ability to grasp the essentials of work flow and put them over to his subordinates with exceptional clarity. Both these illuminated the boiler shop reorganization. Here the problem was that boilers took about twice as long as the rest of an engine for general repair. Ivatt saw that the only way to synchronize these times was to have a float of repaired boilers and to get so organized that the tubing and mounting of any type of boiler could be carried out during the time taken to repair the rest of the engine. This he succeeded in doing, mainly by improving the tooling of each operation and by progressing each boiler step by step along the repair line. It involved some detail invention—for example, he invented the screwed collet chuck for driving firebox stays, so arranged that when the chuck struck the boiler shell it was pushed back and after about two further revolutions it released the collet and thereby freed the pneumatic tool from the stay. This device worked admirably and so delighted Ivatt that he went into the Works one day during the annual holiday and personally drove more than half the stays on a boiler under repair. " Don't do any more," said the foreman, " or there will be nothing to do on Monday." The machine shop head foreman, who was responsible for the tool room at that time, also came down to watch the operation and see the chuck release mechanism working. Ivatt persuaded him to drive a stay, but about half-way through he let go of the pneumatic tool which then rotated alarmingly round the stationary stay until it switched itself off, having fractured the pneumatic hose. This incident did not prevent them discussing the possibility of patenting the quick release collet, but they found they had been anticipated.

R. A. Riddles was, in Ivatt's words, " a wonderfully good Assistant," and the two of them set about loco repair work at Derby so effectively that they reduced the average number of engines under or awaiting repair from about 150 to 60—i.e. to less than 3½ per cent of the total loco strength concerned. " You do it by decluttering the place," said Ivatt, unconsciously echoing his father's advice to Gresley. They always had a drink together on Saturdays at noon, and if the figure was under 3½ per cent Ivatt paid . . . He usually had to pay. They both thoroughly enjoyed planning each improvement and then exploiting it to the full, and their layout alterations caused Fowler to remark during one of his trips round the Works " This place alters while I go through it."

Most engineers suffer some indignation from accounting procedures: about a year after Sir Josiah Stamp took command he had all spare boilers, which had already been charged to engine repairs, credited to Stores Stock. This had the effect of putting the asset value of the Stores up by about £2m. The understandable annoyance to the Works people was that subsequent engine repair costs were considerably increased because they had to indent for the boilers and were duly debited for them by the Stores.

One day in April 1929, Ivatt and Riddles decided they would nip up to London to see "Journey's End," which had recently started its phenomenally successful stage run. When they were half-way across the bridge from the Works to the station they met Sir Henry Fowler, who asked them where they were both going. They said they were going to see "Journey's End." "But what will happen to the Works with you both away?" Sir Henry asked. Ivatt replied, "The Works are so well organized that if we were away for a month, nobody would notice." Characteristically, Sir Henry laughed heartily and hoped they would enjoy their evening out. Fowler could be wonderfully nonchalant at times, as on the occasion when Ivatt got him involved with some modifications they were making to the Walschaert's valve gear on the 2-6-4 tanks, and Sir Henry remarked "Quite honestly, I don't understand the thing."

Ivatt's technical improvements included details borrowed from Stoke, of which an interesting example was the cast iron piston rod packing to replace white metal which was not adequate for superheated steam. Difficulties were experienced with cast iron at first, because the packings were individually sand-cast by the foundry at Derby and all had a hard skin, murderous to machine. Then they tried annealing, which made them malleable—easily machined but useless as packings. And so for a time the L.M.S. purchased the necessary cast iron in the correct tubular form from the foundry at Stoke, which had supplied this metal ever since Hookham introduced it to the North Staffordshire Railway, whose Works had no foundry.

Ivatt also introduced a range of definite standard sizes for piston rods and packings to obviate the costly existing Midland Railway method of individually machining packings to suit rods, after which they had to be kept together until erection. He then made corresponding improvements to the gauging procedures, replacing the normal plug gauges with slices which also indicated ovality. Later he furnished the examiners with "Christmas trees"—a series of stepped slice gauges which speeded and simplified gauging, particularly in the case of components stripped from engines coming into the shops for general repair.

The first 50 "Royal Scots" had cost about £7,000 each but when a further 20 were needed, the North British Loco Co. quoted £10,000. Fowler and the accountants, reckoning the cost-per-ton of a "Scot" would about equal that of a "Compound," did a calculation which showed that Derby could build the 20 at £7,350. When he got the sanction and work had started, Sir Henry realized that in the "per-ton" comparison the tender weight had been included by mistake, which meant that the price for the "Scot" was badly underestimated. Characteristically he explained his horrid predicament to Ivatt, and promised him the best lunch he could think of, if the engines came out close to the estimate. So Ivatt resolved on a high-speed exercise and, nobly supported with the boilers from Crewe, succeeded. Ivatt had an equally characteristic comment on this exercise: " Sir Henry forgot all about the lunch and I never got the opportunity to remind him."

But the price-conscious attention and hurry had one throw-back to Crewe. Back in 1904 all the " Precursors," also built in a hurry, had interchangeable cylinders and frames—they were jig-drilled using the same jig for both, a piece of considerable initiative on the part of chargehand Teddy Battams, which duly impressed apprentice Ivatt. The gimmick used by Battams to sell the idea was a demonstration of the sag at the centre of a conventional setting line. Years later, in the face of a dampening but unoriginal remark from the erecting shop foreman that " fools rush in where angels fear to tread," Ivatt successfully introduced similar jigs at Stoke. Now he brought the method to Derby on the 20 " Royal Scots," adding the precaution of checking from a centre-line specially scribed round the cylinder castings, before rose-bitting out the holes for the fitted bolts. After sorting out the inevitable teething troubles and misunderstandings between machine and erecting shops, Ivatt was able to extend the principle to the motion plates.

Whereas Fowler was inclined to be casual and amiable when he got his Works Superintendents to take him round the Works, a different technique was adopted by E. J. H. Lemon, Engineering Vice-President, whilst he was Chief Mechanical Engineer during the year 1931. He was decidedly more critical and quick to make positive but rather superficial proposals for improvements. These were not always well received, and on one occasion at Derby after Lemon had told Ivatt and the foreman how a job could be done faster and better the foreman, on recovering his breath, ran after his two bosses and insisted on explaining in embarrassing detail why the proposal was entirely impracticable.

Works Superintendents develop techniques for taking " top brass " round Works, and Ivatt certainly obtained practice. When W. A. Stanier appeared on the scene in 1932, he was essentially a one-Works man and found it extremely difficult to grasp that a technical instruction could not be given to Derby or to Crewe in isolation; a formal instruction with drawing had to be sent out by the Drawing Office. The Swindon ideal of one Works was quite impracticable at L.M.S. scale but a great deal of patient inter-Works co-operation went on, despite the various buffetings of fate and displays of temperament, throughout the L.M.S. period.

In fact, Ivatt was rather deflated on the first occasion he took Stanier round Derby Works quite early in 1932: he was still very pleased with the boiler shop, in particular with the step-by-step repair line which had halved the number of boilers held in the Works under repair. He explained the layout enthusiastically and successfully demonstrated the few details Stanier asked to be shown, such as the fit, in a tube-plate being drilled, of a tube taken at random. As they emerged—" What do you think of it? " Ivatt asked, fishing for some small compliment. " I don't think very much of it," said Stanier rather non-committally. There was a pause, and he added, " I don't like the floor." Apart from the trucking gangways economically laid in flattened scrap firebox wrapper plates, it was a simple " dirt " floor—sympathetic to the feet and miles cheaper than wood blocks. Ivatt had a sudden mental picture of the Countess being shown carefully over the new Rolls and not liking it—" I don't like the colour." No more was said at the time, but it is rather characteristic of both men concerned that a day or two later Stanier sent, and Ivatt was very happy to receive, a brief personal note saying that in fact he had been properly impressed by the good work he had seen in the Derby boiler shop.

It so happened that Stanier was chatting to Ivatt, on Derby station one day in the late summer of 1932, awaiting the London train, when J. E. Anderson joined them and said that D. C. Urie was to succeed him as Chief Motive Power Superintendent. Without a moment's hesitation Stanier said to Ivatt, " That means you'll be going to Scotland." They parted on a distinctly gloomy note because Stanier foresaw the loss of the co-operation he was receiving from Jimmy Anderson, and Ivatt hated the idea of moving his home from Melbourne. Besides, his two cats might not like Scotland. But he duly took over on 1st November 1932 as Mechanical Engineer, Scotland; stationed at St. Rollox, Glasgow, and living at Fairlie. He was elected to the Association of Railway Locomotive Engineers in October 1933, proposed by Stanier.

An interesting detail of the Scottish job was that the incumbent also attended the Scottish Directors' meetings. There was a certain healthy independence north of the border; for example an instruction from the Chief Mechanical Engineer, London, to have all new boilers built at Crewe was withdrawn after a polite note that the Scottish Directors wished them to be made locally.

The healthy independence was also, on occasion, extremely practical. For example, all the batteries on electric vehicles were filled directly with Loch Katrine water straight from the tap—much to the horror of Derby, who complained vigorously when they heard that their instructions to use nothing but distilled water were being studiously ignored. But people the other end ignoring your instructions and doing something wrong is worse than people your end receiving wrong instructions and by ignoring them doing things right.

" No stripping until everything is available for the re-building " was an instruction which Ivatt found so hard to put over at St. Rollox that he took the action, rare for him, of instituting paperwork. Before stripping of any engine could start, the head foreman had to send up a formal note, " I propose to strip engine No. . . . I have all necessary spares ready." Ivatt would endorse this " I agree." This little incident contains the valuable lesson of making absolutely certain that essential instructions are obeyed.

Ivatt also found McIntosh's instruction still in force, that the centre line of the blast pipe should be $\frac{1}{16}$ in. forward of the chimney centre line, in order to allow for the effect of the engine moving forward! His mind boggled.

The method of running boiler stays at St. Rollox was probably as effective and certainly cheaper than the Derby automatic chuck: they simply held the stay by means of the last three threads only, and when the holder struck the boiler side these three threads stripped, thereby providing the release. Ivatt liked the sheer simplicity of this, but he did not like the local custom of two men operating the pneumatic stay-driving machine: he reduced this to one without any argument just by a simple personal demonstration—recalling that day in Derby a few years before.

And then, quite suddenly, with effect from 1st October 1937, a cross-posting inspired by Sir Harold Hartley placed Riddles at St. Rollox and Ivatt as Chief Assistant to W. A. Stanier at Euston. Both parties received salary increases at which Ivatt laughed loud and long

Stanier and Ivatt got on famously. Stanier liked Ivatt's approach of *telling* people when it was merely information and *asking* them when it was an instruction. He also rather liked the Ivatt philosophy that if an experiment works too well first time, watch it. Moreover, he appreciated the sheer quantity of cool engineering knowledge concealed behind a disarmingly nonchalant manner. It was to Stanier that people hinted Ivatt was lazy or casual. "Don't be misled," Stanier would retort, secure in the knowledge that the job in Scotland had never been done better, and growing to appreciate, more and more, the value of Ivatt as an Assistant at Euston.

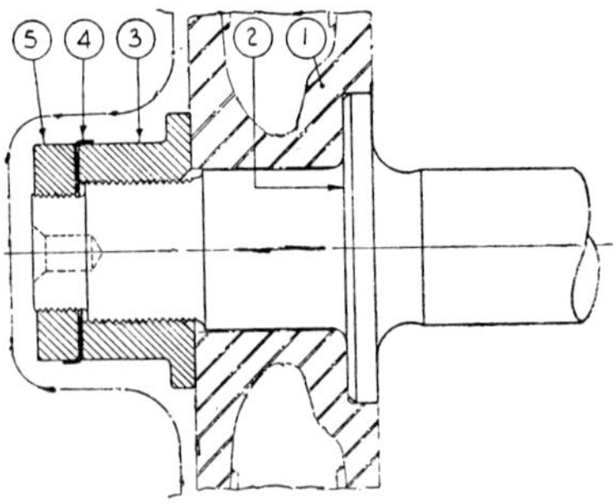

Fig. 39. Ivatt located the piston head 1 on flange 2 and secured it by right-hand nut 3, locking washer 4, and left-hand nut 5.

Not that they always agreed. Stanier had a rooted conviction that difficult machining jobs successfully managed over the years by Swindon were generally a good thing. Ivatt, on the other hand, strongly disapproved of any design which placed an unnecessary demand on workshop quality. "The draughtsmen will ask the Works if they can do it and, of course, the Works always agree," Ivatt would comment, with a rare show of irritation, when some unnecessarily demanding design appeared: for example, three bearings accurately in line, or the accurate placing of a collar on a taper.

A notable example of the latter was the piston head. It was a persistent trouble to the machine shops so to maintain the accuracy and the position of the taper on the piston rod and the piston head that they would mate together with the head in its correct position. Ivatt won over a reluctant Stanier to a simple arrangement in which the head located on a collar integral with the rod and was secured by a large nut which, in turn, was prevented from working loose by a second nut, with left hand thread. He also added the finesse of a couple of holes in the piston head to enable a tool to be inserted to drag the head off the rod when it needed replacement. The advantage of the Ivatt piston mounting was that piston heads and piston rods became interchangeable, and in the event of damage or wear a head could be replaced by a spare held at the Sheds. But rather typically Ivatt had to wage a considerable battle to stop Derby Works persisting in individually mating piston heads and rods. Usually such insistence was not due so much to a misplaced love of craftsmanship as to the love of an operation, real or imaginary, to which time could be booked on a bonus card. It was at this stage, incidentally, that a dimensional error was uncovered on the 3-cylinder 4-6-0s which made it impossible to drag the piston head clear of the cylinder for fitting new rings without breaking the crosshead.

In 1938, in the shadow of war, Ivatt found himself working again for General Davidson, when he built up a design team to satisfy War Office requirements for tanks. Ultimately 5,000 were built, including a couple of hundred at Crewe. Ivatt's team did quite a variety of war work and at peak had over a thousand manufacturing orders running.

C. E. Fairburn took over from Stanier as C.M.E. in 1945, Ivatt remaining as Principal Assistant. This was not an easy period: strength was only slowly regained after the worst years of the war, and Fairburn though an excellent organizer had the triple disadvantages of a mainly electrical professional outlook, a purely mathematical upbringing, and being dogged by illness to an extent which made him a "difficult" colleague. During 1945 there was an epidemic of the first few rebuilt "Royal Scots" bending their side rods. Fairburn became unnaturally worried about this and had neither the knowledge nor the competence to accept Ivatt's accurate explanation that it was due entirely to bad driving—the rebuilt engines had that extra punch which made them slightly more prone to slipping, and a driver who recklessly applied sand before shutting off steam was simply asking for a bent coupling rod, particularly when, as was not uncommon, the flow of sand served one wheel ahead of the others.

It must have been uncertainties of this type which prompted Fairburn to build, in the Carriage Shops at Derby, a full-size model of an engine in wood; the purpose of this extraordinary venture was never made clear, but Ivatt remarked that it was as good a way of spending money as the piece of chain which had been fashioned, link by link, from wood as part of a full-scale model of his wartime tank made at the ordnance factory.

Another of those problems of succession, which were a feature of L.M.S. history, came with Fairburn's unexpected death late in 1945. The President, Sir William Wood, sent Ivatt a telegram the same day, asking him to take over in an acting capacity, and sought the advice of the recently-retired Sir William Stanier. Stanier had no hesitation whatever in recommending Ivatt, and his recommendation was accepted; and in due course Ivatt was formally appointed as from 1st February 1946. The Board had already decided at that time that R. A. Riddles, who on return from the war became Chief Stores Superintendent, would be made a Vice-President as from 1st March 1946. It was thought by some of the staff that Fairburn and Sir Harold Hartley had not considered Ivatt a suitable successor, and this prompted R. G. Jarvis to write to Sir William (whom he knew well from the 1944 trip to India) urging his influence to ensure that Ivatt was appointed: at a casual meeting in 1946 Sir William remarked to Jarvis " You nearly didn't get him."

" Congratulations, I can think of only one person more suitable for the job," Riddles wrote jocularly to the new Chief Mechanical and Electrical Engineer. " Well done," said Shearman, loud enough to be overheard—" I think you will reach 60 before being found out." Aged 59½, and feeling 50, Ivatt was of course exceptionally well placed to settle, apparently effortlessly, into the job. He " toured the perimeter," as it were, and checked that everything was in reasonably good trim. In particular, he kept up and encouraged the locomotive inspectors belonging to the C.M.E. Department, as inaugurated by Stanier. He lost no time in having the embarrassing wooden engine at Derby torn apart and burnt. Well aware that there were still difficulties on account of the split allegiance of the running sheds between the C.M.E. and the Chief Operating Manager he turned up the Board Minute with its definition that the Chief Motive Power Superintendent was responsible to the Chief Operating Manager for operating and to the C.M.E. for maintenance. At the first sign of a clash, he confronted Col. Rudgard with this Minute and insisted upon it being honoured; and with such effect that a marked improvement in relations between the departments developed, which persisted so well that soon after nationalization Abraham once said at a meeting " As long as Ivatt is the Chief Mechanical Engineer I shall respect him as my technical chief."

Touring the L.M.S. perimeter took a bit of time—it stretched from Thurso to Bournemouth with seven main Works and a pay roll of nearly 45,000. The old Lancashire and Yorkshire Railway was completely engulfed somewhere near its middle. It was commonly believed to be far too big, but it was a great deal smaller than British Railways.

Every new C.M.E. is faced with three categories of jobs: those thrust upon him by circumstances, those which " at last he is in a position to carry out," and those involving the inevitable new locomotive designs.

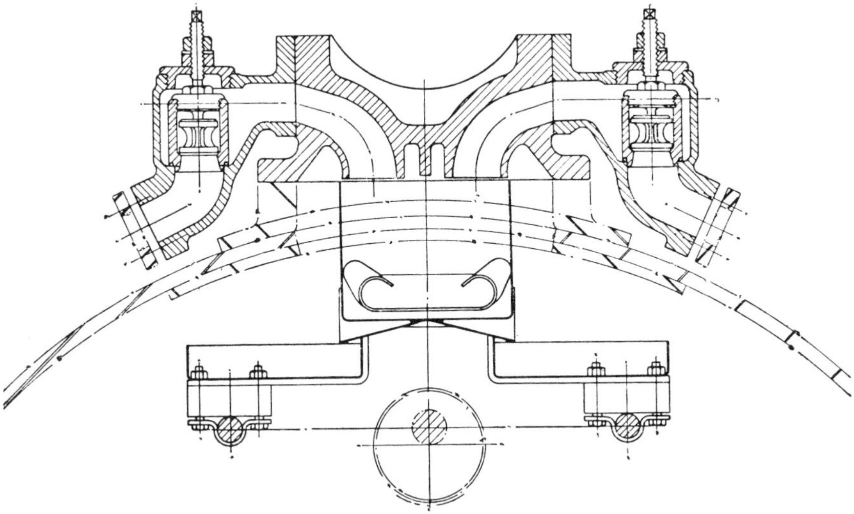

Fig. 40. Stanier's top feed arrangement, showing the distributing trays which slope towards the front end.

A good example of the first category which faced Ivatt was persistent trouble with the top feed arrangement on the Stanier boilers. It proved exceptionally difficult to prevent unsightly external leakage where the feed pipes met the top feed casting and, more seriously, the internal trays rapidly filled with sludge so that raw feed water was discharged straight on to the tubes causing serious local sludge deposits. Ivatt remedied the first by an improved arrangement which, incidentally, was placed nearer to the smokebox end of the boiler, and the second by simply removing the trays

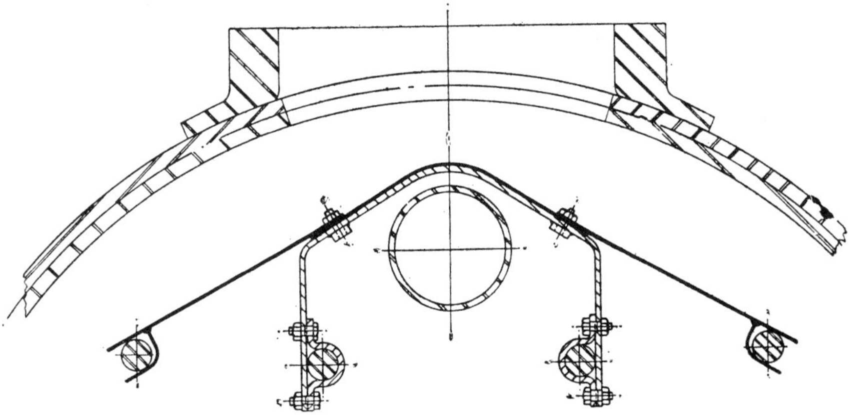

Fig. 41. Ivatt's top feed arrangement—at the front end of the boiler and trays replaced by a simple plate shielding the tubes.

and, instead, fixing a saddle plate over the tube nest. The feed water dropped on to this and made its way down the sides of the boiler, carrying all sludge straight to the bottom.

An excellent example of the second category was the fitting of 20 "Black Staniers" with Caprotti valve gear. Stanier disliked these "fancy" valve gears, partly because he thought they introduced more complications than their potential advantage could warrant, and partly because they had been tried elsewhere in England by Gresley and others and failed to prove themselves. Ivatt, on the other hand, considered the improved exhaust port openings an advantage well worth going for, and he also felt that their comparative lack of success in previous applications in England had been largely due to the application being approached with insufficient enthusiasm. Ivatt's desire for the very best possible valve events stemmed from his range of experience, from "Precursors" to "Coronations." The boilers of these engines had about the same efficiency, and since a "Precursor" would cheerfully consume about 70 lb. per mile on a job which a "Coronation" could do at 50 lb. per mile, one can see how comparatively wastefully the "Precursor" used its steam. A large share of the blame for this inefficiency must be laid at the valve gear and the limited exhaust port openings.

One previous source of trouble in fitting Caprotti gear had been the driving box mounted on the return crank; Ivatt gave particular attention to this and a decidedly superior design was produced. He also arranged for the operating handwheel to have the same range of movement as normal practice; this was in contrast to the Caprotti gear fitted by Beames to one of the larger-boilered "Claughtons," where one turn of the wheel moved the gear from full forward to full backward. Mid-gear was reached after a mere half turn, and Ivatt recalled a minor accident which he attributed to a driver inadvertently winding past mid-gear.

Quite soon the 20 4-6-0s duly emerged fitted with the Caprotti gear and went into general service. Reports began to come back that they were not as powerful as those fitted with the normal Walschaert's gear. Ivatt of course knew perfectly well this was not so; and since the rather vague estimate of one engine being "as powerful" as another depends mainly on the setting of the valve gear, he carried out the very simple modification of falsifying the scale so that at the 30 mark the gear was actually set at 40 per cent cut-off. Complaints ceased and the engines ran satisfactorily ever after.

Meantime, Ivatt was making very fair progress with the design for a new small engine, and this appeared in two forms from Crewe before the end of 1946. One was a 2-6-0 Class "2F" engine replacing some of the old Class "2" 0-6-0s, a useful type which had not been built since Midland Railway days. The tenders were fitted with cabs and the coal space was arranged to allow clear vision when running tender first. The other was a 2-6-2 Class "2P" tank engine which again was a modern version of the old standard L.M.S., ex Midland, 0-6-0 tank. Principal dimensions common to both these engines are as follows:

Cylinders	16 in. dia. × 24 in. stroke
Coupled wheels	5 ft. dia.
Boiler pressure	200 lb. per sq. in.
Grate area	17.5 sq. ft.
Heating surface:	
Tubes	924.5 sq. ft.
Firebox	101.0 sq. ft.
Superheater	134.0 sq. ft.
Total	1,159.5 sq. ft.

One's first impression on seeing these engines was that accumulated modern design knowledge and features giving easy maintenance had been incorporated in a *modern* small engine of business-like appearance. The three features which gave most satisfaction to Ivatt were the self-cleaning smokebox, the rocking grates, and the self-emptying ash pans.

Fig. 42. Ivatt's self-cleaning smokebox, showing baffle plate 1, deflector 2, and ¼ inch mesh screen 3. Arrows show the path of the flue gases: the self-cleaning action by scouring depends on the setting of deflector 2.

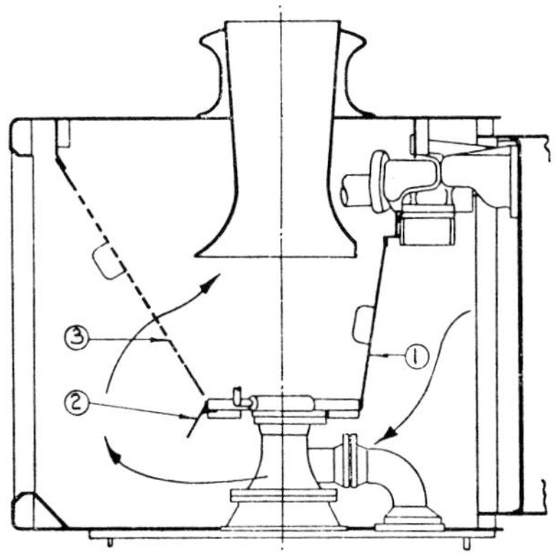

Ivatt had taken an interest in the possibilities of a self-cleaning smokebox ever since L.N.W.R. days. He remembered the smokebox flaps fitted by Webb; they opened under the weight of accumulated ash, which then discharged on to the track; but the incurable trouble was that sometimes they failed to re-close completely, after which it was common for a fire to start in the smokebox. Besides being dangerous, this burned off the paint and the resulting large rusty patch gave the engine a rather debauched appearance. Then Whale had two perforated steam pipes fitted at the bottom of " Precursor " smokeboxes: about every mile the fireman was expected to open the steam supply valve momentarily and the stirred the char, most of which was ejected through the chimney.

When the " Coronation " Pacific went to America it had to be fitted with baffle plates in the smokebox to comply with American railroad regulations; a plate between the blast pipe and the tube plate minimized the risk of live sparks being emitted through the chimney, and a further plate reaching from the blast pipe towards the smokebox door produced a sweeping motion which cleared the spent ash through the chimney, making the smokebox self-cleaning and, incidentally, keeping the bottom rows of tubes effective. Ivatt got the Civil Engineer's O.K. to discharge smokebox char along the line (as Webb may have done in 1870), and fitted the self-cleaning device progressively to more and more engines: they carried the code " SC " on the smokebox door because it need no longer be opened except for a check at wash out time—in sharp contrast to some engines, including the " Land Crabs," which sometimes covered their three bottom rows of tubes with ash after a few hours' running.

What finally made Ivatt determined to fit rocking grates was the procedure for dropping the fire on a 2-8-0. The first two firebars and the remains of the fire had to be lifted out and dropped through, and it was particularly difficult for the man below to pull these from the ash pan because the front damper was obscured by the third coupled axle. With the rocking grate a simple lever in the cab permitted the firebars to be rocked for normal cleaning or, on releasing a catch, to be turned completely on end to drop the fire.

For self-emptying, it had always been thought necessary to have a hopper type ash pan, and Ivatt was struggling to find a solution to this problem for engines such as the 2-8-0 whose design left no room for the hopper shape. Then R. G. Jarvis came across the very thing that was wanted on a German engine, whilst on a trip to Turkey, namely, making the bottom of the ash pan from a series of centrally-pivoted slats. These,

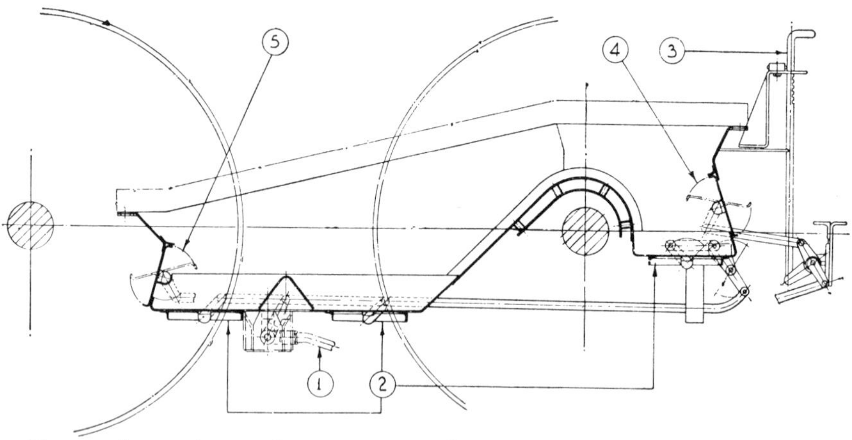

Fig. 43. Ivatt ash pan. Lever 1 operates the three ash pan doors 2. The damper control lever 3 in the cab operates back damper 4 and front damper 5 (part of the linkage is omitted for clarity).

linked together and turned through 90° by a simple lever, discharged all the ash.

The time for dropping a fire and emptying the ash pan was reduced to five minutes, compared with 35 minutes (and an exchange of derogatory language) on the 2-8-0s as built. It was a source of lasting regret to Ivatt that the consequent saving in shed labour seemed very difficult to exploit.

C.M.Es. have various crosses to bear, and one of Ivatt's, when he first took office, was his inability to secure the undivided attention of his Vice-President. He would go into Sir Harold Hartley's office by appointment with an agenda, only to encounter a string of interruptions, most of which appeared more palatable than the actual business in hand. Once, Hartley expressed a wish to take the chair at the C.M.Es. periodical meeting of Works Superintendents, at which Crewe, Derby, Horwich, St. Rollox, Wolverton, and Earlstown were represented: his chairmanship of this meeting was wholly admirable in every way, and, as Ivatt remarked afterwards, " he had set his mind to it."

When Riddles became Vice-President he was at first much occupied with committee work, but of course time was found for Works visits, and then he and Ivatt would be seen setting off together, as of old, Ivatt wearing his inseparable mackintosh and mellow trilby. On one such occasion, at Horwich, there was a demonstration of a pneumatic spanner, guaranteed to loosen the most obstinate nut. The demonstration was set up with the spanner ready to loosen the securing nut on a piston head: the air was turned on and the percussion tool hammered away noisily but the nut would not budge. Ivatt and Riddles walked away—with sympathy born of experience—but the demonstrators ran after them and brought them back, having realized that they had omitted to cut through the welding which was always used at Horwich to tack piston head nuts! After this, the pneumatic spanner proceeded successfully although, later, it met its match with firebox crown stay nuts. The Horwich wisdom of tack-welding piston head nuts was corroborated when pistons secured by Ivatt's twin-nut arrangement were found to have worked loose, and he agreed to a welding modification, " Though how in the name of Fortune they manage to work loose I have no idea."

Unfortunately, Ivatt had no more success than Stanier in obtaining a real measure of fruitful work from the Research Department at Derby. They started making one of the classic mistakes which are probably an occupational hazard of engineering research work, i.e. extending their work into day-to-day design features at which they were naturally far less competent than the Loco Drawing Offices. Engineers who have " rested " too long in research or academic circles fail to realize the value of the large body of " know-how " in a design office. The Research Department at Derby brought out an impracticable axlebox design but, on the other hand, they did some admirable work for Ivatt on stress propagation in the corners of the horn gaps in frame plates. This established the principle that the horn stays below the axlebox should always be in tension.

The next request for more engines was the perennial, classic, 100-year-old operating request—" another batch of 0-6-0s, please." This time the Fowler Class " 4 " 0-6-0s were wanted, and Ivatt could have pressed the button and added to the several hundreds already contentedly working on the L.M.S. These, and earlier 0-6-0s were once described by Stanier as " simple, reliable, cheap to maintain, and beloved of the operating departments." But some of this love was simply custom, and the " devil-you-know " slant, and putting up with shed tasks which repetition made easy but no less costly. These 0-6-0s offered much scope for improvements in the 20 years since they were designed; and having inside cylinders they were very heavy on driving axleboxes. Ivatt insisted that a large 0-6-0 was obsolete and that the new Class " 4 " freight standard type must be a 2-6-0, with the advantages successfully demonstrated in his class " 2 " 2-6-0.

Feature		*Ivatt Class " 4 " 2-6-0*	*Fowler Class " 4 " 0-6-0*
Boiler pressure	psi	225	175
Combined heating surface	sq. ft.	1233	1158
Superheater area	sq. ft.	246	253
Grate area	sq. ft.	23	21
Wheel diameter	feet	5¼	5¼
Cylinders	in.	17½ × 26	20 × 26
Total weight in working order, tons	engine	58½	48¾
	tender	41¼	41¼
Tractive effort at 85 per cent b. pressure	lb.	24,172	24,555

In the campaign to increase the periods of engine availability between shop repairs Ivatt decided to try roller-bearing axleboxes with manganese steel rubbing-surfaces on boxes and horn cheeks. These were applied to all engine and tender axles except the bogies, on 20 " Black Staniers " and on two Pacifics built in 1947, which also had a number of design improvements at the back end of the frame, trailing truck and reversing gear. Only one name, *City of Salford* had been chosen for the last two Pacifics, and Ivatt, Riddles and Bond were thinking about the other when suddenly Bond suggested *Stanier.* " That's a damn good idea," said Riddles, " I wish I'd thought of it myself." No. 6256, *Sir William A. Stanier, F.R.S.*, proved as robust as its namesake. It duly achieved 100,000 miles between attentions to wheels and axleboxes, and 200,000 between general repairs.

In June 1947 appeared Ivatt's sole contribution to the Proceedings of a Learned Society. Asked for by Bulleid, and compiled by E. S. Cox, it was presented as one of a set of four short papers by the four C.M.Es. of the main line railways, describing their current and future proposals for motive power. Ivatt took the opportunity for a policy announcement:

> It is believed that the conventional reciprocating steam-locomotive is still capable of considerable advance and that the ceiling of operating availability and maintenance cost per mile has not yet been reached. If, for the sake of higher thermal efficiency, or still higher availability, any departure from the simple, inexpensive, rugged steam locomotive of normal aspect is envisaged, the L.M.S.R. authorities hold that a complete breakaway from steam towards the internal combustion engine is the logical step to take.

Ivatt also stated that he had two types of main-line diesel-electric locomotives under construction—

(1) One 800 h.p. loco on two four-wheel bogies, comparable with a class "2" 2-6-2 tank engine.

(2) Two 1,600 h.p. locos either (a) comparable alone with a class "4" 2-6-4 tank engine or (b) comparable, when coupled together, to a class "7" 4-6-2 engine.

He added that these two types would enable the whole traffic field to be surveyed so as to settle where diesel-electric traction was most likely to justify itself.

Thoughts of a diesel-electric express passenger engine had first stirred in Ivatt's mind early in 1945. Others were doing it: it would be good fun; steam engines admittedly had room for improvement but not much room for any more power under English track and loading gauge conditions; the diesel was developing fast and had clearly a great deal of further development potential; and the electric traction motors were available and comparatively trouble-free. But was it remotely practical, Ivatt wondered, because the diesel cost about the same per mile to run and about the same to maintain as a steam engine, yet the first cost was four or five times more. Moreover, they *had* the steam engines and the repair facilities for them. So when he broached the subject with Fairburn he was not surprised at getting, in effect, a cool brush-off.

After he became Acting C.M.E., however, Ivatt perceived another factor in the project: it would permit something hitherto impossible, namely, an English manufacturer to offer such a locomotive to world markets with practical demonstrations and performance data on English railways. Meantime, he had got the project clear in his mind: it would be an engine of about 1500 h.p., mounted on two 6-wheel bogies, each with two traction motors. Top speed would be rather above the current track limit of 75 mph, and the tractive effort would be about the same as the Pacifics, namely, 40,000 lb. Weight at about 22 tons per axle would come out at 132 tons compared with 160 tons for a Pacific with tender. Ivatt visualized making one contractor responsible for the diesel engine, generator, control gear, traction motors, and all directly related auxiliaries, whilst the L.M.S. would design and build the bogies, frame, and all the other equipment.

And then one day an opportunity arose to put the project before the President, Sir William Wood. He was on a visit to Derby, whither Ivatt had restored the C.M.E.'s headquarters, and he saw at once the force of the Ivatt proposal. More, he saw an excellent prestige and pioneering slant which would be good L.M.S. publicity. So he immediately authorized Ivatt to approach the manufacturers, and to come back to the Board in due time with a definite proposal and a request for the necessary capital for two such main line diesel express locomotives. That forgotten day in December 1945 was really the historic instant of conception for diesel locomotives in this country.

The upshot of Ivatt's speedy discussions with several manufacturers was an arrangement with English Electric that they would supply two sets of all the necessary equipment, to be paid for when and if satisfactory; and June 1946 found Ivatt and E. S. Cox visiting Stafford to make the initial decisions and the arrangements for controlling and progressing the design work. A new standard 1,600 h.p. diesel engine and generator was chosen, as then being offered for the Egyptian Railways; and to match this power with existing designs of traction motors there would have to be one on each axle—to Ivatt's regret as this complicated the bogie design. Design schemes proceeded well at Derby under Langridge, who ran the small scheming office for Coleman. As schemes were approved, they went

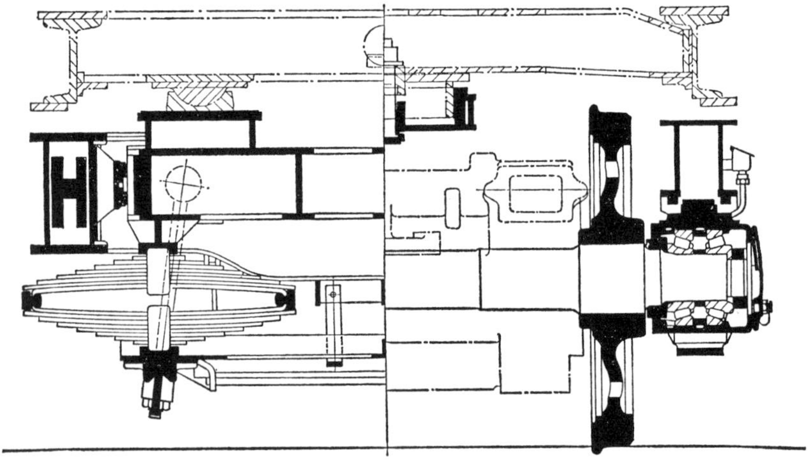

Fig. 44. Part sections of Ivatt's power bogie for No. 10,000

to the main loco Drawing Office for completion of design and detailing. English Electric designers stayed at hand throughout. Ivatt took a great deal of direct interest, and his arrangement of four bearing pads on each bogie to carry the frame, leaving the centre bearing solely for traction, was later patented in his name in the U.S.A. by the Commonwealth Steel Corporation. Equally, Ivatt got English Electric to incorporate numerous improvements, for example in the driver's control which was originally planned as a tram-style wheel. The proposed driving cab was mocked-up full size in the Carriage shops at Derby to inspire further improvements, and there was access from the engine to its train (and from engine to engine when worked together).

In addition to about £45,000 per loco for the bought-out equipment. Ivatt estimated £7,500 each for the bogies, frames, and other parts of L.M.S. supply. He arrived at this figure, shades of Fowler, by guessing that it was generally similar in cost-per-ton to a loco tender. As design proceeded and the cab and vacuum brake-gear became more complicated, he had to go back and ask for the sanction to be increased to £15,000 per loco. The main frame grew in complication, and since it would deflect when carrying the diesel engine they went to the trouble of securing the side sheeting independently. Numerous other extras caused Ivatt gloomily to curse himself for being so foolish as to compare this job in any way with a loco tender, as he went back, cap in hand, to ask for £30,000 each. Even this was slightly overspent. It has been said that good engineers and bad engineers have one thing in common—they are hopeless estimators. Meanwhile, manufacture proceeded at a canter: not only was there exceptional enthusiasm, and the rather dedicated support Ivatt seemed effortlessly to inspire, but his staff included the powerful trio of Bond, Pugson, and Harper all keeping up the pace. They were, respectively, *Mechanical Engineer, Loco Works; Mechanical Engineer, Carriage and Wagon;* and, delightful title, *Mechanical Engineer* (*Electrical*). "Why in the name of Fortune they chose that title I cannot imagine," remarked Ivatt. From October 1946 Bond was also deputy C.M.E.

R. A. Riddles, considerably interested in these goings-on as the responsible Vice-President, then moved in and proposed that an 800 h.p. diesel loco should also be designed, using a Paxman engine and to be built by North British: this would widen the L.M.S. diesel experience and permit matching class "2" steam engine duties. A few months ahead of their mention in the Ivatt paper to the Institution of Mechanical Engineers, both these projects leaked out, and caused fairly loud buzzings from the other railways. The Southern and the Great Western took some brisk diesel action, but the L.M.S. sauntered home with the others unplaced when, in the late afternoon of 8th December 1947, Ivatt drove No. 10,000 out of the Diesel Shop, Derby. He duly recorded the event and prognosticated the future in his Christmas card for 1947.

Only three weeks later, on 1st January 1948, the L.M.S. lost its identity and Ivatt lost Scotland and became Chief Mechanical and Electrical Engineer, London Midland Region, British Railways. But 10,000 did not worry about all this, as it took the traditional Derby Works trip "round Trent" and then set off, with saloon and brake, to Euston for a high-level inspection trip to Willesden. In mid-January there was an impressive and well-reported Press trip, St. Pancras to Manchester. Then there was a moment of alarm when marks were found on the leading wheel flanges suggesting the engine had been close to derailment. Patiently Ivatt had the engine run slowly over the exact route around St. Pancras which it had travelled the day before and, sure enough, a faulty crossing was found to be the culprit. Then followed a number of successful trips and impressive performances, interspersed with teething troubles: but in spite of these Ivatt was paid the best compliment an engineer can enjoy—everyone queued up to stake their claim either to have thought of, or inspired, or just helped with, the 10,000 project. It was not until mid-1949, after 10,000 and 10,001, coupled together as planned, had worked the return Euston–Glasgow express trip six times a week for six months, that Ivatt released the purchase money to the manufacturers.

Ivatt was a bit too independent to take really kindly to the Railway Executive Design policies. He thought they were wasting effort and money designing a new 2-cylinder 4-6-0, for example, when the various regions were well stocked with proved types such as the " Hall " class, the " B 1s " and the " Black Staniers." He saw the new standard engines as odd men out in sheds accustomed to and holding spares for the existing engines. Thinking back to the Hughes design committee of 1923, he felt the Regions were so large that they should retain their distinctive types of engines. He strongly disapproved of the Carriage and Wagon side being separated from the Loco. He also got a bit tetchy when he sent up suggestions from Derby and they were not accepted by London! Nor did he like Riddles disbanding the A.R.L.E. It was a good thing he had plenty of work on the diesels to interest him, and in particular he was engrossed with the Fell engine which was completed early in 1951. And when he retired at the end of June 1951 no one was surprised when he coolly started a new career in the manufacture of diesel locomotives which were, and are, popular with British Railways.

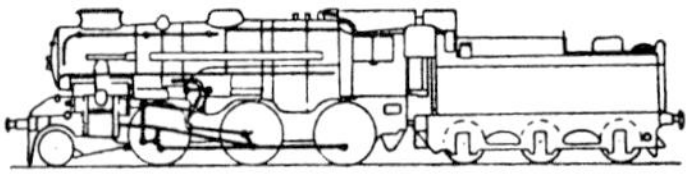

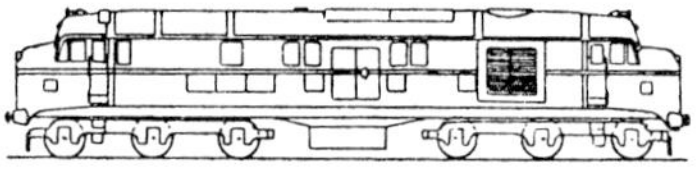

INDEX